D1570543

Missouri Brothers
in Gray

William J. Bull, shown in his Camp Jackson Engineer Corps uniform
(Courtesy of the Missouri Historical Society)

UNWRITTEN CHAPTERS OF
THE CIVIL WAR
WEST OF THE RIVER

VOLUME I

Missouri Brothers in Gray

THE REMINISCENCES AND LETTERS OF
WILLIAM J. BULL AND JOHN P. BULL

Author/Editor: Michael E. Banasik

Camp Pope Bookshop
1998

Library of Congress Catalog Card Number 97-77924

ISBN 0-9628936-8-4

Printed and Bound in the United States of America

Press of the Camp Pope Bookshop
P.O. Box 2232
Iowa City, Iowa 52244

Series Dedication:

Dedicated to the forgotten soldiers of both North and South, who fought in the American Civil War west of the Mississippi River; their deeds of perseverance and valor shall not be lost through the ravages of time, but rather recorded for all to remember.

Volume I Dedication:

To my parents Eva and Orville Banasik
on their fiftieth wedding anniversary.

Special Dedication:

To my dearest love Brenda;
always the patient and supportive wife.

Acknowledgement: I would like to thank the Missouri Historical Society, St. Louis, Missouri for their permission to publish the Bull Family Papers contained in this book.

Michael E. Banasik

CONTENTS

Appendices

Photographs

Maps

Introduction

Long overlooked by historians, the Civil War in the Trans-Mississippi region provides a fascinating study of war under the most severe conditions. Unlike the eastern region of the country, the states west of the Mississippi River were faced with an almost complete lack of a railroad system, a decrepit road net, and terrain that varied from the arid deserts of New Mexico, to the rugged Ozarks of Arkansas and Missouri. Breaking up this varied region were rivers and streams which seemed to focus the antagonists' attention on such key points as Lexington and Jefferson City on the Missouri River; St Louis and Helena on the Mississippi River; Little Rock and Fort Smith on the Arkansas River; and Shreveport on the Red River in Louisiana.

For the years following the Civil War most historical attention has focused on the great battlefields east of the Mississippi River. Numerous soldier diaries, letters, and other first-hand accounts were published on the Army of the Potomac, Army of Northern Virginia, Army of the Cumberland, and other Civil War armies east of the Mississippi River. Primary accounts of the conflict in the Trans-Mississippi region go begging for but a mention in this fascinating war and have been largely ignored by publishers. This series of books is an attempt to bring to Civil War enthusiasts' attention the war west of the river as seen by the participants. At the same time, it will offer the serious student of the war source material to expand the study of this lost conflict.

The first offering in this series brings to light the service of a Confederate artilleryman (William Jeffery Bull) and his brother (John Payne Bull) who served most of their military careers west of the Mississippi River. William and John served in Gorham's/Tilden's/Lesueur's/Third Field Battery Missouri Artillery, until John transferred to the cavalry service in late 1862. John then served in MacDonald's Missouri Cavalry and Newton's/Fifth Arkansas Cavalry until the end of the war.

William Bull was born in Augusta, Kentucky on March 5, 1843, while John was born on December 4, 1840 at Vicksburg, Mississippi. Their parents were staunch Southerners, the mother being the daughter of Revolutionary War General John Payne of Kentucky. In 1848 the Bulls relocated to St. Louis, Missouri, where the family became prominent in the mercantile trade of the city. Both brothers were educated in St. Louis and attended St. Charles College. In 1857 John Bull became a founding member of the Second National Guard Company, St. Louis, Missouri Volunteer Militia. William joined the same unit in 1861.[*]

The story of the Bull brothers begins prior to the firing on Fort Sumter and presents the reader with some fascinating information on ante-bellum military

---

[*] John Moore, "Missouri," *Confederate Military History Extended Edition* (19 vols., Clement A. Evans and Robert S. Bridgers, eds.; Atlanta, 1899; reprinted Wilmington, NC, 1987), vol. 12, 251-254

preparations for the upcoming war. From Camp Jackson in May 1861, William takes the reader through four years of military service, covering the battles of Pea Ridge, Corinth, Prairie Grove, Helena, the Red River and Camden campaigns, and a few smaller engagements.

In Part I William mixes his personal reminiscence with his diary entries to give the reader a sergeant's view of the war west of the Mississippi. The war is one against the elements of hunger and disease, with the fatal military conflict at times being almost a sideshow. Interwoven with these subject areas, William gives the reader a look at wartime St. Louis, camp life, and smuggling from the abundant north to the beleaguered Confederate Army.

Part II contains the war-time letters of the two brothers, including an important account of the Battle of Helena, written by John as a cavalryman. I hope that you as a reader will find the contents of this book as interesting as I found in preparing it for your enjoyment.

Future books of this series will alternate between Confederate and Union participants. They will be a mix of unpublished diaries, letters, or reminiscences. In most cases rosters, like the one in this volume, will be provided as well as biographies and photos of selected Civil War personalities who fought west of the river.

Any thoughts, comments, or recommended subject matter you have regarding this series may be addressed to the publisher. Remember, this series will only survive with your support.

Note: The material presented in parts I and II constitute the original work of William and John Bull. I have corrected some spelling errors, reconstructed a few sentences and as needed I have added some words for readability. All added words or changes are noted by [   ].

Part I

Reminiscence and Diary of
William Jeffery Bull

Reminiscence and Diary
of
William Bull
[Third Field Battery Missouri Artillery—Confederate]

Why I wrote:

Thinking one day how interesting it would be to me to read the personal experiences of my ancestors in the war in which they were engaged, written with their own hands, I concluded to write my experiences in the War Between the States—Not expecting to add anything of interest to history but believing that the writing of them would give me pleasant employment for my leisure hours and the reading of them in after years would be of interest to me if not to others.

I undertook the task and have found it very appreciated. I soon realized, however, that too great elaboration would render the work wearisome in the preparation and more so to the reading as, except in rare cases, the experience of common soldiers are so uneventful and so much alike as to render them uninteresting, except to those interested in the individual.

I am not an exception to the rule and can only hope to interest such as feel a special interest in me.

W'm Bull

St. Louis April, 1906

Chapter 1
First Military Adventure

Previous to 1860 there had existed in St. Louis a strong antipathy, I might say hatred, on the part of the American, French, and Irish population for the Germans, who even then were here in large numbers and inhabited the lower part of the city which was known as Dutch Town. Why this condition of affairs existed I am unable to say unless, it was due to the fact that the French and Irish assimilated more readily with the Americans, and the Germans were inclined to keep aloof and more to themselves and seemed fonder of their homeland than of their adopted country. They also exhibited an over fondness for their native language and frequently used it when policy and good taste would have suggested the use of English.

There may have been other reasons for the bad feelings towards the Germans other than those mentioned, but I am sure they contributed to it.[1] This bad feeling was intensified during the Presidential Campaign of 1860, when the Germans constituted almost all of the Republican, or as it was known then, the Abolition Party of the city.[2] They were active and offensive to the greatest

---

[1] Between 1840 and 1850 about 201,000 immigrants poured into Missouri from other parts of the United States.

Kentucky	70,000
Tennessee	45,000
North Carolina	17,000
Other Southern States	15,000
Total From South	147,000
Ohio, Indiana, Illinois	40,000
New York, Pennsylvania	13,000
New England	1,100
Total From North	54,100

Additionally, during the same period, 15,000 immigrants came from Ireland and 50,000 from Germany, boosting Missouri's 1850 population to 682,044. The Irish settled along the rivers of Missouri and disliked Germans, whom they called Dutch. The Germans scattered about the state. The antipathy of the Irish for Germans dated back to the days of William the Orange and his persecutions against Ireland in 1689. Beginning in the late 1840's Missouri received 150,000 German immigrants who had fled their homes following the 1848 revolution. St. Louis received about one half the number. The Germans brought with them their many customs, but more importantly, their dislike of slavery and Irishmen. The Southerners, Irish, and old resident French were supporters of the "Sacred Institution of Slavery," thus ensuring unending conflict with the Germans of Missouri. John McElroy, *The Struggle For Missouri* (Washington, DC, 1909), 14-17, 38; James Neal Primm, *Lion of the Valley St. Louis, Missouri* (Boulder, Colorado, 1981), 149, 173.

[2] During the Missouri Presidential Election of 1860, the Republican Party represented the radical Northern faction, which came mostly from St. Louis. The Southern Rights Democrats, which represented the radical Southern faction, received their heaviest support from along the Missouri River. The Constitutional Unionists and Regular Democrats represented those Missourians who wished to remain neutral in the slavery debate. Vote Totals of 1860:

degree, frequently parading the streets at night in torchlight processions. They had their military uniforms, a military organization, and were thoroughly drilled in military tactics. It developed afterwards that this was for the purpose of easily converting them into soldiers which, as it will be seen, was done. They were known as "Wide-a-Wakes."[3] They always turned out several thousand strong and with their black glazed caps and capes and flaring torches which made really a very impressive and I might say diabolical appearance.

The excitement and bad feeling engendered during the campaign was still further increased by the important events which quickly followed each other, including the election of a President by a party pledged to emancipation of the slaves, the seceding of Southern States, and the preparations of the Federal Government to coerce them.[4]

The question of coercion caused an immediate realignment of parties and any of the [John] Bell and [Edward] Everett Party and the Democratic Party, who had earnestly desired the preservation of the Union, when it came into question of coercion, aligned themselves on the side of the South. A very large majority of the best people of St. Louis were for the South. Many of them owned slaves and all had relatives or dear friends in the South and it was natural independence of their ideas of right and wrong, that their sympathies should have been with the South.

War between the sections seeming inevitable, I determined to join a military company and receive the instruction which would fit me to fight for the South. I had just attained the military age of 18 years, and in April 1861 made application for membership in the company known as "The National Guard" or "Engineer Corps of Missouri," whose armory was on the top floor of a building on the South West corner of Pine and 3d Streets. William Hazeltine was the captain, W'm Finney 1st lieutenant, and John Gilkerson 2nd lieutenant. The membership consisted of young men and boys belonging to the prominent families of the city.[5]

Abraham Lincoln—Republican Party	17,028
John C. Breckinridge—Southern Rights Democrats	31,317
John Bell—Constitutional Unionists	58,372
Stephen A. Douglas—Regular Democrats	58,801

As the election results show, Missourians overwhelmingly wanted neutrality. McElroy, *Struggle For Missouri*, 18.

[3] The St. Louis Wide-Awakes organized in the summer of 1860 following the Missouri Republican Convention, which was held in Chicago, Illinois. They were armed with clubs to drive hecklers away from political rallies. In December 1860, the Wide-Awakes disbanded, forming "Union Clubs," which took on the military aspects described by William Bull. The Union clubs added muskets and rifles in February 1861. James Peckham, *Gen. Nathaniel Lyon, Missouri In 1861. A Monograph of the Great Rebellion* (New York, 1866), xi-xiv, 33-37.

[4] Dates of the initial Southern states secession: South Carolina, December 20, 1860; and in 1861 Mississippi, January 9; Florida, January 10; Alabama, January 11; Georgia, January 19; Louisiana, January 26; and Texas, February 1. Virginia, North Carolina, Arkansas, and Tennessee seceded following Lincoln's call for troops to put down the rebellion in their sister states. McElroy, *Struggle For Missouri*, 23.

[5] The "National Guard Company" or "Engineer Corps" represented one of many volunteer

I felt greatly elated when I received a notice of my election as a member of the company dated April 30, 1861, and also a copy of Company Orders No. 36 ordering me to appear for drill on the evenings of May 1st and 3d (Wednesday and Friday). These two orders I still have among my papers.

I reported promptly Wednesday evening and was, of course, assigned to the awkward squad. The squad was being put through the rudiments of the drill in the gun room by Sergeant [Edward F.] Chappel[6] when an order came from the captain to the sergeant to report with his squad to him in the main drill hall. We were marched in and forward on the left of the company which we found in line.

The captain then stated he had received an order to make a detail from his company to go on a search mission. He said he preferred to have volunteers rather than make a detail and requested those willing to volunteer to step two paces to the front. I was anxious to be of the detail but feared I would not be accepted being a new member and unfamiliar with the drill. But the old members were a little slower in stepping forward I concluded I would risk being rejected and stepped to the front and very much to my delight no objection was made to me. The balance of the company was dismissed.

We were supplied with ammunition and put through the loading and firing drill for a short time and then marched from the armory. I had no uniform but as we passed out members of the company brought me different parts of uniform including cap, jacket, and finally a pair of baggy red trousers which belonged to the Zouave Uniform which the company sometimes wore. All of these I put on and must have cut a ludicrous figure as none of the articles fit me and the baggy trousers were not confined at the ankles by garters as they should have been.

The impression prevailed among the men that we were going to attack the arsenal[7] and secure the large amount of arms the Government had stored there, but when we reached 5th Street and took a north, instead of a south bound car, we were entirely in the dark as to our destination.

We left the car at the northern terminal which was then Brennen Avenue. The officer in command drew us up in line in front of a beer saloon and sent in

---

militia companies that existed in ante-bellum St. Louis. The company was first organized in August 1852 with Robert M. Renick as captain, J. N. Pritchard as first lieutenant, and E. S. Wheaton as second lieutenant. "Military Matters," St. Louis, Missouri Volunteer Militia scrapbook, page 5 of unnumbered pages, Missouri Historical Society.

[6] Edward F. Chappell was a founding member of the Second National Guard Company, St. Louis, Missouri. Volunteer Militia. He was captured at Camp Jackson, exchanged in October 1861, and went south aboard the steamship *Iatan* in December 1861. He joined the same artillery company as the Bull's, the Third Field Battery Missouri Artillery. See Appendix A for service record. "Military Companies of St. Louis—No. 4 National Guard Company—2nd Company," Missouri Militia scrapbook, page 6 of unnumbered pages.

[7] In 1861 the St. Louis Arsenal was the focal point of conflict as both Northern and Southern supporters wanted access to the 60,000 muskets stored there. On April 24, 1861, well before Camp Jackson, Captain Nathaniel Lyon evacuated the arms to Illinois, thus securing them for the Union. McElroy, *Struggle For Missouri*, 36; Christopher Phillips, *Damned Yankee: The Life of General Nathaniel Lyon* (Columbia, MO, 1990), 166-167; Peckham, *Missouri in 1861*, 119.

for beer which was brought out in buckets. Before we had finished drinking we saw a large body of men approaching from the south. We supposed they were "Home Guard" and they were after us. The German Wide-a-Wakes of the political campaign had been organized by the Government into a military body and were called the "Home Guards."[8]

Our commander, although greatly outnumbered, prepared for a fight by facing us about so as to face, what we supposed to be, an approaching enemy. To our surprise they passed without apparently noticing us. We finished our beer and then our officer declared he would overtake that body of men and learn who they were. We went at a double quick.

As we approached them we saw them stooping and picking up stones. When they passed us we saw they had no guns but thought they had side arms. We now saw they were preparing to fight us with stones. When we reached the head of their column our officer halted them and then learned they were details from companies recently organized. We also learned that they were friends and that their destination was the same as ours, which soon proved to be the powder magazine on the bank of the Mississippi River above the water works. They had mistaken us for "Home Guards" and as we suspected, were going to fight us with stones.

Upon reaching the magazine, details were made; one for guard duty and another a working party to remove the powder from the magazine to the two boats which were lying at the wharf. The State of Missouri had bought the powder from the private parties owning it and it was the intention to remove it to Jefferson City for future use.

Great secrecy and haste was used for fear that the United States Authorities would interfere. The Government had a very fast boat in service, the *City of Alton*[9], with artillery and soldiers aboard. She was up the river somewhere but it was feared she might intercept us before we could get into the Missouri River.

I was detailed for guard duty, went on post about midnight and through some mistake was not relieved until after daylight the next morning. It rained during the night and I was thoroughly wet and had a slight chill but after getting some hot coffee and breakfast felt all right. Later, when volunteers were called for to go on the second boat, the first having already gone, I volunteered for the duty. (The first boat was the *Isabella* commanded by Captain Jno. P. Kaiser. The guard was Capt. [Joseph] Kelly's Company[10] under his command. The second

---

[8] The Home Guards supported the Federal Government in Missouri and numbered 3,506 officers and men at the time of the surrender of Camp Jackson. United States War Department, *The War of the Rebellion: A Compilation of the Official Records of the Union and Confederate Armies* (70 vols. in 128, Washington, DC, 1880-1901), Series 1, vol. 3, 4 (Hereafter cited as *O.R.*; all citations of *O.R.* refer to Series 1 unless indicated otherwise).

[9] This is the same boat that Captain Lyon used to evacuate the arms from the St. Louis Arsenal on the evening of April 24, 1861. Phillips, *Damned Yankee*, 167.

[10] Kelly's Company was known as the "Washington Blues." It was part of the First Regiment, First Brigade, Missouri Volunteer Militia and organized in the late 1850's. The company was not

boat was the *Augustus McDowell.*)

Captain Martin Burke[11] was in command of the military escort, on the second boat, which was made up of details from different military companies. I did not know a soul on the boat but a common danger causes soldiers to fraternize and we were soon on the most intimate and friendly terms.

As we approached the mouth of the Missouri River we saw a boat coming down the Mississippi River which we soon learned to be the dreaded *City of Alton.* She followed us into the Missouri River. We had not any too much the start of her as she was much faster than our boat. To our dismay the captain of our boat announced he would have to land and take on wood. We had very few roust-abouts on board so all of the soldiers had to turn out and carry wood aboard. With the many hands to help the task was soon accomplished and with a good head of steam we soon passed a place in the river which was too shallow for the *City of Alton* to follow and she had to abandon the chase.

Our next fear was that an effort would be made to stop us at St. Charles, Union, or Herman, where the German population predominated, but we passed those places at night with all lights shaded, and if we were seen no movement was made to stop us.

We finally reached Jefferson City, where we were received with great enthusiasm. Great quantities of powder in cases and kegs were loaded on the lower deck, merely covered with tarpaulins, and it is a great wonder we were not all blown up as the sparks from the basket torches, which were in use at night, flew all over the boat. This powder was of great benefit to the Confederates.

At the approach of the Federal troops it was scattered through the country and hidden in hay stacks and other safe places. Gen'l [Sterling] Price[12] got quantities of it at the time of his attack on Lexington and no doubt it greatly assisted him in the capture of that place.

We joined the detail which arrived on the first boat and with them were reviewed by Governor [Claiborne F.] Jackson,[13] who praised us for the service

---

captured at Camp Jackson on May 10, 1861, having departed camp on May 7 to guard arms and ammunition destined for Jefferson City. Thomas L. Snead, *The Fight For Missouri From the Election of Lincoln to the Death of Lyon* (New York, 1886), 163-164; J. Thomas Scharf, *History of Saint Louis City and County, From the Earliest Periods to the Present Day; Including Biographical Sketches of Representative Men* (Philadelphia, 1883), vol. 2, 1860.

[11] Burke commanded the St. Louis Grays, the oldest volunteer militia unit in St. Louis. The company was organized in 1832, served in the Mexican War, the Southwest Expedition of 1860 and quelled numerous city riots during the fifties. "St. Louis Grays—Company A," Missouri Militia scrapbook, page 18 of unnumbered pages; Scharf, *History of Saint Louis,* vol. 2, 1860.

[12] See biography in Appendix B.

[13] Claiborne F. Jackson was born in Kentucky in 1806, immigrated to Missouri in 1822, and served in the Black Hawk War as a captain. In 1836 he was elected to the Missouri Legislature and served in the legislature, on and off, until 1861 when he attainted the post of Governor of Missouri. He was pro-slavery and considered a Southern Rights Democrat, though he supported Stephen Douglas for President. Snead, *Fight For Missouri,* 17-18; McElroy, *Struggle For Missouri,* 20.

we had performed. When the line was formed for review, my red Zouave trousers, being the only pair in the line, must have marred its beauty as I received an order from the commanding officer to remove them. This I did quickly and stepped back into the line. Fortunately I had another pair of trousers on underneath them.

After a short stay in Jefferson City, we returned to St. Louis by the Missouri Pacific Rail Road. At some point on the road a lot of recruits for the Federal Army boarded our train for St. Louis. When their identity became known it was difficult to prevent our men from attacking them and driving them from the train, but fortunately they were in another car and our officers posted guards to prevent our men leaving the car they were in.

At Herman a delegation of prominent men from St. Louis met us, treated us to the native wine and congratulated us upon the success of our expedition.

I have never seen an account of this affair published and, as it was one of the important events in the early part of the war in this state, I think it unfortunate that it should have been lost to history.

Chapter 2
War Comes to Missouri

There was an organization in St. Louis at about this time what was known as the "Minute Men."[14] It was organized in opposition to the "Home Guards" and to assist in the capture of the arsenal. It was several hundred strong. I joined Captain O. W. Barett's Company.[15] When they were afterwards mustered into the state guard,[16] I withdrew from the organization as I was already a member in the state guard.

The Minute Men had their headquarters in the "Burthold Mansion"[17] on the northwest corner of 5th and Pine Streets. Some of the members found a flag of "strange devise," which afterwards proved to be the flag of the "Sons of Malta"—a secret, humorous, fun-making order which existed before the war. The Minute Men in a spirit of deviltry hung the flag out from their headquarters.

The "Home Guards" hearing it was a "secesh" flag threatened to tear it down. While it was originally hung out as a matter of fun the Minute Men, learning of the threat to tear it down, announced in very emphatic language it should stay there and immediately prepared to defend it. They got an old cannon, after putting into it a big charge of powder, they loaded it to the muzzle with iron slugs and nails and planted it just inside the front door, fully determined to fire it into any mob which might attempt to molest the flag. Fortunately for all concerned the attempt was not made, but excitement ran high until the State troops were ordered into camp.

A few days after our return from Jefferson City, the entire militia of the city was ordered into a camp of instruction.[18]

---

[14] On January 1, 1861 the German Turner Societies pledged unconditional support for the Union. In response, those supporting Southern aims organized "Minutemen" units on January 8, 1861; they numbered between 300-500 men. Next, the German Turners and Wide-Awakes transitioned into the Union Clubs, producing the Union Home Guard of St. Louis in February 1861. The Minutemen joined the St. Louis, Missouri Volunteer Militia and were assigned to the Second Regiment, setting the stage for their capture at Camp Jackson on May 10, 1861. Phillips, *Damned Yankee*, 137-138; Snead, *Fight For Missouri*, 110.

[15] O. W. Barett commanded Company B, Second Regiment, First Brigade, Missouri Volunteer Militia. The unit was also known as the "Missouri Videttes." It was captured at Camp Jackson on May 10, 1861. Peckham, *Missouri in 1861*, 134.

[16] Name given to the Missouri Militia after Camp Jackson. The State Guard supported the Southern cause.

[17] Primary location where the Minutemen gathered and drilled. The mansion was under constant surveillance by Union sympathizers, seeking to learn the Southerners' plans. Phillips, *Damned Yankee*, 138.

[18] Governor Claiborne F. Jackson issued General Order No. 7 on April 22, 1861, which ordered the Missouri Volunteer Militia to be assembled. Brigade commanders were required to specify the point of assembly by May 3, 1861. In St. Louis, General Daniel M. Frost ordered his brigade to assemble on May 6, 1861 at Lindell Grove on Olive Street Road. "Governor's Proclamation—General Order No. 7," *Missouri Republican* (St. Louis, Missouri), May 2, 1861; "Military—General Order No. 23," *Missouri Republican*, May 5, 1861.

The Minute Men were mustered into the State Militia and constituted the Second Regiment[19] under command of Col. Jno. S. Bowen.[20] The National Guard or Engineer Corp was attached to that regiment. The 1st Regiment was commanded by Col. Jno. Knapp[21]—the brigade by Gen'l D. M. Frost,[22] which in addition to the command named contained a battery of artillery commanded by Capt. Henry Guibor[23] and a troop of cavalry commanded by Capt. Emmett MacDonald.[24]

The camp was established on May 6, 1861 in Lindell Grove, situated on the south side of Olive Street, east of Grand Avenue and was named Camp Jackson[25] in honor of the Governor of the State.

During the day the camp was constantly filled with visitors, mostly those with Southern sympathies, which as I have stated, included nearly all of the best people of the city. On May 8, I got a pass to the city signed by John Gilkerson,[26] Lieut. Comd'g National Guard and J. R. Shaler,[27] Maj. Comd'g 2nd Reg. M. V.

---

[19] The St. Louis, Missouri Volunteer Militia consisted of a brigade with two regiments. Each regiment contained ten companies. See Appendix C for a complete list of companies assembled at Camp Jackson.

[20] See biography in Appendix B.

[21] Despite long held belief by many authors that the St. Louis Militia was made up of Southern sympathizers, such was not true. John Knapp, editor and publisher of the St. Louis *Missouri Republican* was the colonel of the First Regiment of Missouri Volunteer Militia. After his capture at Camp Jackson he was exchanged in late 1861 prior to the general exchange of the Camp Jackson prisoners and does not appear on the October 1861 Camp Jackson exchange list. Knapp joined the Union cause, commanding the Eight and Eleventh regiments of Enrolled Missouri Militia Cavalry. He also served as volunteer aid to the governor during Price's 1864 Missouri Raid. *O.R.*, vol. 34, pt. 4, 87; *O.R.*, vol. 41, pt. 1, 464; *O.R.*, Series 2, vol. 1, 132, 553-557.

[22] See biography in Appendix B.

[23] Henry Guibor—A St. Louisian, Mexican War veteran, and member of Missouri Volunteer Militia, he commanded an artillery company at Camp Jackson. After his parole, which he considered illegal, Guibor joined Sterling Price's army, where he commanded a four gun battery. He participated in the Missouri battles of Carthage (July 5, 1861), Wilson's Creek (August 10, 1861), Lexington (September 20, 1861), and Pea Ridge, Arkansas (March 6-8, 1862). Guibor finished his military service on the east side of the Mississippi, serving in the Army of Tennessee. Snead, *Fight For Missouri*, 217; *O.R.*, vol. 3, 32, 101, 186; *O.R.*, vols. 17, 24, 32, 38, 39; *O.R.*, Series 2, vol. 1, 556; William L. Shea and Earl J. Hess, *Pea Ridge Civil War Campaign In the West* (Chapel Hill, NC, 1992), 162-164.

[24] See biography in Appendix B.

[25] The camp the previous summer had been named Camp Lewis after the explorer Meriwether Lewis. It opened on June 30 and closed on July 6, 1860. "'Volunteer' Reviews History of First Missouri Regiment," News Clippings, 2-4, Camp Jackson Papers, Missouri Historical Society.

[26] Though captured at Camp Jackson and exchanged in October 1861, John Gilkerson's (or Gilkison) name never appeared on any Confederate, Union, or Missouri State Guard roster. According to the 1860 Missouri census he would have been twenty-six years old when Camp Jackson was captured.

[27] James R. Shaler was captured at Camp Jackson and exchanged in November 1861. He fought at Pea Ridge, where he earned the praise of General Frost. When Thomas C. Hindman rebuilt the Trans-Mississippi Army in the summer of 1862, he appointed Shaler to command the Twenty-seventh Arkansas Infantry Regiment. Shaler's Arkansas command considered him a "tyrant" and openly questioned why Hindman appointed a Missourian to command an Arkansas

[Regiment Missouri Volunteers]. This pass is still among my papers.

The General's orderly was selected each day from the guard detail. He was supposed to be the best drilled and neatest appearing man on the detail. It was considered a compliment not only to be the man selected but also to the company to which he belonged so there was considerable rivalry between the companies in the matter. I had the honor to be selected on Thursday, May 9.

Captain, afterwards General Nathaniel Lyon,[28] was in command of the Federal troops. They were stationed in and about the arsenal and numbered about 10,000, mostly Home Guard, but there were some regulars.[29] Rumors were rife that Gen'l Lyon had decided to capture Camp Jackson. Many thought the rumors ridiculous and that he would not dare attack State troops, but Gen'l Frost was sufficiently impressed by them to have scouts out on Thursday [May 9] to watch the movements of the Federal troops.

When at retreat on Thursday I asked the general, as was usual, if I should go to my quarters. He told me to remain at Head Quarters until he told me to leave as he would need my services. He would send me for officers he wished to confer with and I heard the scouts make their reports to him. They first reported that the Federal troops were assembling and that the impression provided among them that a night attack was to be made on Camp Jackson. Finally it commenced raining very hard and then the scouts reported that the Federal troops had been ordered to their quarters and that they believed the movement had been abandoned or postponed.

The next morning [May 10] it became known that they were again assembling and that they were moving in our direction by several different routes. At about noon we found our camp completely surrounded by infantry and artillery to the number of six thousand. Our commanding officer was compelled, under protest, to yield to the demand for the surrender of his camp of State troops numbering 620, principally young boys of about my age.[30]

Our force had been reduced by the detailing of Capt. Kelly's Company of the 1st Regiment to guard the bridge across the Gasconade River on the Missouri Pacific Rail Road near Jefferson City. That company escaped capture and was afterwards mustered into the Southern Army going south from Jefferson City

---

regiment. In the latter part of 1863, Shaler was voted out as colonel of the Twenty-seventh Arkansas. Sterling Price subsequently appointed him major and inspector general of his command. Silas C. Turnbo, unpublished manuscript, *History of the Twenty-Seventh Arkansas Confederate Regiment*, Turnbo Collection, University of Arkansas (Little Rock), 81-82, 306; *O.R.*, vol. 41, pt. 1, 719.

[28] Lyon was one of the first heroes of the Union, having been killed at the Battle of Wilson's Creek. He played an instrumental role in the early months of the war in Missouri, first as a captain when he captured Camp Jackson and later as a brigadier general when he secured Missouri to the Union by his rapid advance across the state. *O.R.*, vol. 3, 4-5, 54.

[29] The volunteers numbered 3,506 and another 484 men came from the regular army. Ibid., 4; McElroy, *Struggle For Missouri*, 54.

[30] In his official report, Captain Lyon listed 79 officers and 590 men as captured at Camp Jackson. *O.R.*, Series 2, vol. 1, 116.

with the Governor of the State.

After surrendering our arms, we were marched from our camp and formed in Olive Street between files of Federal soldiers. Almost immediately, for some reason, which has never been explained, the "Home Guards" commenced firing. This was taken up very generally by them and resulted in the killing and wounding of some twenty-five or more people, mostly citizens who were innocent spectators. Some of the Federal troops were victims, but strange as it may seem none of our men were injured.[31]

When the firing commenced many of the "Home Guards," thinking an engagement was on, threw away their guns and ran from the field. This was the great victory of Camp Jackson which some of our German fellow citizens still celebrate on the 10th of May each year.

Just before starting on our march as prisoners word was secretly passed down our column that the citizens would make an attack on the "Home Guards" as we passed the Planters House on 4th Street and the order was for us to fall flat on our faces in the street when the firing commenced. This attack was avoided by taking us by a different route. We were marched east on Olive Street to 14th Street, south to Chouteau Avenue, east to 7th Street and thence to the arsenal. This took us through the German part of the city where the population turned out *en mass,* and men, women, and children cursed and abused us for everything they could think of. They would have massacred us, I have no doubt, but for the fact that we were guarded by regular troops of the Federal Army.

When we arrived at the arsenal, we were crowded into one large room where we could not sit down much less lie down. Fortunately for the members of our company, Captain [William A.] Hequembourg,[32] who formerly belonged to our company, was an officer in the Federal Army and had us moved to another building where we were less uncomfortable.

We did not know at first the object of our removal. We were taken out in small squads. As the squad I was in reached the door we heard volley firing out in the grounds and the report was spread that we were being marched out to be shot. With this report in mind I thought I was justifiable in deviating from the truth when asked by Federal officers before leaving the building, if I had any weapon concealed about my person. I answered I had not, although I had a pistol in my inside jacket pocket and was determined to use it if the rumor that we were to be shot was true. Fortunately it was not true and we were marched to another building. We afterwards learned that the firing was in obedience to an order

---

[31] Bull is mistaken. Three members of Frost's command were killed along with twenty-five civilians, including two women and one child; ten were wounded. The Federal forces lost two dead and several wounded. See Appendix E for list of St. Louisians killed or wounded in days surrounding the capture of Camp Jackson. McElroy, *Struggle For Missouri*, 155-156.

[32] Captain William Hequembourg commanded Company E, Third Regiment, United States Reserve Corps. In Price's 1864 Missouri raid Hequembourg served as a lieutenant colonel of St. Louis City Guards and later commanded Schofield Barracks in St. Louis. *O.R.*, vol. 41, 3, 611; *O.R.*, vol. 48, 872; Peckham, *Missouri in 1861*, 127.

requiring the "Home Guards" to discharge their loaded guns to prevent them being used on us.

The following day we were paroled, the terms of which required that we remain within the limits of the city until exchanged.[33]

Our officers adhered to the opinion that being State troops, the Federal troops had no legal right to capture us and Captain Emmett MacDonald was selected to remain a prisoner and list the matter in the courts. The case was afterwards tried in a Federal Court in Illinois and the position of our officers sustained.

The Federal authorities not wishing to take the risk of again sending us through the German population of the town, sent us by boat to the city. This was very fortunate as, at about the time we left the arsenal a Federal regiment was passing through the city and as they were marching from 5th Street west on Walnut Street, a pistol was fired into their ranks from the steps of a church which stood on the corner of those streets. The soldiers became panic stricken, turned, and fired into the crowd filling the streets and then ran west on Walnut Street. Fortunately their aim was defective, the balls passed over the heads of the people and were imbedded into the walls of the buildings lining the street. The people infuriated at this outrage pursued the soldiers, picked up guns they had thrown away, fired into their ranks and killed and wounded many.

Fortunately, as I have said, we had left the arsenal on the boat for the city when the news of this street fight reached the arsenal. Otherwise the Federal authorities, even if they had tried, which is doubtful, would I have no doubt, been unable to have prevented the "Home Guards" from killing us all.

The following day was know as "Black Sunday" from the fact that a report became current that the "Home Guards" and their German friends were going to sack the city. So generally believed was this rumor that thousands of citizens left the city on steam boats and such other conveyances as could be obtained, and General [William S.] Harney,[34] who was still chief in command, and

---

[33] Each enlisted man took the following oath: "You do solemnly swear that you will not serve in any capacity against the Government of the United States during the civil war now existing."

The officer parole read, "We, the undersigned, do pledge our words as gentlemen that we will not take up arms or serve in any military capacity against the United States during the present civil war. This parole to be returned upon our surrendering ourselves at any time as prisoners of war. While we sign this parole with a full intention of observing it, we nevertheless protest against the justice of its exactions." *O.R.*, Series 2, vol. 1, 112.

[34] William S. Harney was born in Tennessee, served in the Mexican War as a colonel. On June 14, 1858 he received a promotion to brigadier general in the regular army. Harney assumed command of the Department of the West, in St. Louis, on November 17, 1860. By the Civil War, Harney was one of only four general officers in the U. S. Army and expected to support the South. The local secessionists expected Harney to support their cause, but he never did. St. Louis Unionists did not trust Harney and successfully had him removed from command following the Camp Jackson affair. Frederick H. Dyer, *A Compendium of the War of the Rebellion* (Des Moines, 1908; reprinted Dayton, OH, 1978), 254; Ezra J. Warner, *Generals in Blue: Lives of the Union Commanders* (Baton Rouge, LA, 1964), 208-209; McElroy, *Struggle For Missouri*, 30-31.

conservative, had a battery of artillery planted in 4th Street and announced he would open fire on any body of troops or mob that would attempt to enter the American portion of the city. His firmness, no doubt, prevented serious trouble and in a few days restored order and confidence.

When those who had left returned to the city, General Lyon and his supporters had Gen'l Harney removed after which, until the close of the war, the city was constantly under the most radical rule. All sorts of outrages frequently occurred thereafter.

After the decision was rendered as to the illegality of our capture at Camp Jackson, many felt at liberty to go south and did so. Others of us remained in the city until exchanged.

On the tenth of August 1861, just three months after the capture of Camp Jackson, the Battle of Oak Hills[35] was fought near Springfield, Mo. It was one of the most desperate and bloody battles of the war—the numbers engaged being considerable.[36]

Generals Price and [Ben] McCulloch[37] commanded the Confederates and Gen'ls Lyon and Franz Sigel[38] the Federals. The Confederates, notwithstanding their inferior numbers and inadequate equipment gained a most glorious victory. The Federals retreating in great disorder from the field, left the dead body of Lyon and many of the Germans who had participated with him in the capture of Camp Jackson in the hands of the victorious Confederates.[39]

The Federals continued their retreat to Rolla, and Gen'l Price occupied Springfield. A month latter, having reorganized his army, he moved with 4,500

---

[35] Called Wilson's Creek by the Federal forces.

[36] Lyon's command numbered 5,400 troops while the Confederate forces consisted of 10,175. Snead, *Fight For Missouri*, 310, 312.

[37] Born in Tennessee in 1811, Ben McCulloch fought at the Battle of San Jacinto, searched for gold in California in 1849, and was a U. S. Marshal in Texas. He received the surrender of the Federal forces in San Antonio in February 1861, and was commissioned a brigadier general in the Confederate army on May 11, 1861. He commanded the troops in Arkansas and won the Battle of Wilson's Creek. On March 7, 1862 he was killed at the Battle of Pea Ridge, while directing the attack of the Confederate right wing. Ezra J. Warner, *Generals in Gray: Lives of the Confederate Commanders* (Baton Rouge, 1959), 200-202.

[38] Franz Sigel was born in Germany in 1824, and immigrated to the United States in 1852 following the 1848 revolution in Germany, where he acted as Minister of War for the revolutionary forces. He settled in New York and moved to St. Louis to teach school. With the approaching civil war, Sigel organized the German community in St. Louis, forming the Third Regiment Missouri Volunteers (three months). He was elected colonel of the regiment and participated in the capture of Camp Jackson. On August 7, 1861, Sigel became a brigadier general and fought in the Battle of Wilson's Creek, where he commanded a wing of Lyon's army. Sigel was at Pea Ridge in 1862, after which his career west of the Mississippi ended. Warner, *Generals in Blue*, 447-448; Peckham, *Missouri in 1861*, 121; Mark M. Boatner, *The Civil War Dictionary* (New York, 1959), 761.

[39] Federal forces lost 258 killed, 873 wounded, and 186 missing for a total loss of 1,317. Among the dead was General Nathaniel Lyon. Confederate forces lost 279 killed and 951 wounded for a total of 1,230. Snead, *Fight For Missouri*, 310, 312.

men and seven pieces of artillery to the Missouri River and attacked Col. [James A.] Mulligan[40] and his command of regulars in an entrenched position at Lexington. After a few days fighting he captured Mulligan and his entire force of 3,500 men, also quantities of stores and supplies of every kind. In addition to these he recovered the great seal of the State, the public records, and nearly a million dollars in money which had been taken from the Lexington Bank by order of Gen'l Frémont[41]. The money he returned to the bank.[42]

---

[40] James Mulligan was born in Utica, New York in 1830. He was the colonel of the Twenty-third Illinois Infantry Regiment, and by virtue of seniority commanded the Lexington Garrison. Exchanged in November 1861 for General Daniel M. Frost, Mulligan served the rest of the Civil War years on the east side of the Mississippi River. He was subsequently wounded (mortally) and captured at Kernstown, Virginia, on July 24, 1864. McElroy, *Struggle For Missouri*, 206; *O.R.*, Series 2, vol. 1, 554; *O.R.*, vol. 37, pt. 2, 601.

[41] See biography in Appendix B.

[42] Lexington surrendered on September 20, 1861. The Confederates lost 25 killed and 72 wounded. In addition to his troops, Mulligan surrendered 5 pieces of artillery, 2 mortars, 3,000 stands of arms, 750 horses, $100,000 worth of commissary supplies, the great seal of Missouri, the state's public records, and about $900,000 in specie or cash. General Price returned the money to the local banks from which the Federal forces had removed it for the "banks' protection."

Mulligan's Command:

23rd Ill. Inf. (James Mulligan)	800
Home Guards (Robert White)	500
13th Mo. Inf. (Everett Peabody)	840
1st Ill. Cav. (Thomas A. Marshall)	500
	2,640

O.R., vol. 3, 188; McElroy, *Struggle For Missouri*, 206.

Chapter 3
Going South To Join Price

It was Mulligan's command for which the Camp Jackson prisoners were exchanged, and we were sent south on December 2, 1861.[43] It was at first the intention of the Federal authorities to send us to Gen'l Price, who was then at Springfield, Mo. by the Missouri Pacific Rail Road and we were marched for that purpose to the depot on 7th Street. I suppose it was decided to make it more difficult to get to Gen'l Price as we were later marched to the levee and sent south by boat—the *Iatan*.

This was a great disappointment to us as we were fearful Gen'l Price would have captured St. Louis before we could reach him and we would not be of the triumphal army when it entered the city. We were also greatly disturbed by a rumor that we were being sent to Cairo to work on the Federal fortifications about that city.

We numbered about one hundred men[44] under the command of Gen'l Frost. Our Federal guard was under command of Captain Hequembourg, who befriended us while prisoners at the arsenal.

Our parting of friends would have been sadder could they and we have foreseen the years that would intervene before meeting again and the dangers and hardships that would fill those years. But could all this be known, I do not think it would have deterred one from doing what I considered my patriotic duty. We were in high spirits, particularly when we left Cairo, where we stopped only a short time, for Columbus, Kentucky—the Confederate outpost.

It was a warm bright day as we approached Columbus with a flag of truce flying from our flag staff. When we got within a few miles of the city we saw from the hurricane deck of the boat, where we were all congregated, a puff of smoke from a high point above and over looking the city. We then heard the report of a gun which was the signal for the Federal boat to halt, which immediately and hurriedly obeyed the command by casting her anchor.

In a very short time we saw approaching us from Columbus one of the finest of the floating palaces for which the lower Mississippi River was famous at that time. From her flag staff floated the Confederate flag. Every deck was crowded with officers in the beautiful and gorgeous uniforms of the Confederate Army and a fine band of music discoursing Southern airs. What could have been more inspiring to the young boys who had come so far to get into the Southern Army.

---

[43] Of the 79 officers and 590 enlisted men captured at Camp Jackson, all the officers and 399 of the enlisted men accepted exchange; 191 enlisted men cast their lot with the Union. *O.R.*, Series 2, vol. 1, 123.

[44] The *Iatan* records sixty-three names of former Camp Jackson captives. See Appendix D for complete list. "The Camp Jackson Prisoners," *Missouri Republican*, December 3, 1861.

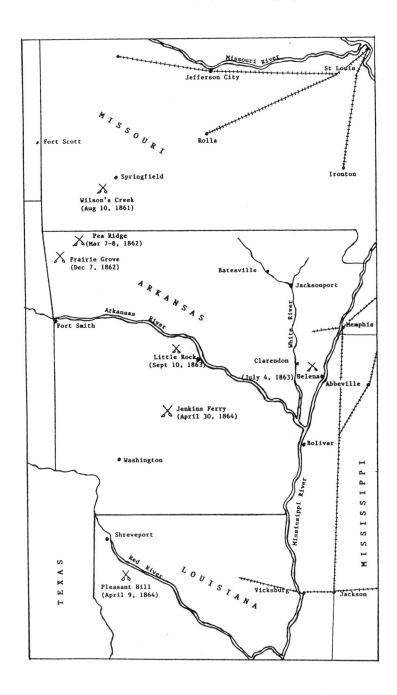

Trans-Mississippi Area of Operations
(1861-1865)

After much mutual cheering and embracing, we were soon transferred to the Confederate steam boat and after a short delay, which was caused by an ineffectual effort to find some of the crew of the Federal boat who, wishing to unite their fortunes with the South, had hidden on the Confederate boat. We were headed for Columbus. This is our reception into Dixie.

At Columbus we met many St. Louis friends, members of Bowen's First Missouri Regiment[45] which was on duty there. We found the Confederates greatly elated over a victory they had recently gained in an engagement known as the Battle of Belmont.[46]

A small Confederate force had been camped at Belmont, Mo., directly across the Mississippi River from Columbus, Ky. General, then Colonel U.S. Grant, who was in command at Cairo, concluded he would capture them. He placed 3,000 men[47] on transports and escorted by gunboats, moved down the river. Landing a short distance above Belmont, he attacked the Confederates who, being greatly outnumbered, were unable to with stand the assault, fell back and were in danger of being captured.[48]

The commander at Columbus, learning of the situation, hurried reinforcements across the river in any kind of craft that could be had. The

---

[45] The First Regiment, Missouri Infantry, Confederate, was organized on June 22, 1861 at Camp Calhoun near Memphis, Tennessee.
Command Staff:

John S. Bowen	Colonel
L. L. Rich	Lieutenant Colonel
C. C. Campbell	Major
L. H. Kennerly	First Lieutenant and Assistant Adjutant
F. H. Haines	Captain and Assistant Quartermaster
James M. Quintain	Captain and Assistant Commissary
C. N. Hawes	Major and Surgeon
J. S. Leonard	Captain and Assistant Surgeon
F. Haley	Sergeant Major
C. Corin	Second Master Sergeant
James Kennerly	Drum-Major
Frank Shaw	Hospital Steward

Janet B. Hewett, ed., *Supplement to the Official Records of the Union and Confederate Armies* (approx. 100 vols., Wilmington, NC, 1994-ongoing; cited hereafter as *O.R.S.*), pt.2, vol. 38, 378-379.

[46] The Battle of Belmont, Missouri was fought on November 7, 1861. *O.R.*, vol. 3, 266.

[47] Grant's command consisted of two infantry brigades with some cavalry and a six gun battery. John A. McClernand and Henry Dougherty commanded brigades. Grant lost 85 killed, 301 wounded and 99 missing out of 3,114 engaged. Of the wounded, 125 were left as prisoners of war. Ibid., 269, 271.

[48] The Confederate command, though initially outnumbered moved additional regiments from Columbus, Kentucky to Belmont to boost their strength to about 4,000 effective men. Generals Gideon Pillow and Benjamin F. Cheatham commanded the Confederates until Leoniadas Polk took command late in the contest. Polk lost 105 killed, 419 wounded and 117 missing. Ibid., 308, 310; Boatner, *Civil War Dictionary*, 57-58.

reinforced Confederates drove the Federals, in great confusion, back to their transports and in their hurry to get away came near leaving their commander on the shore—he had to ride his horse aboard on a strap plank, which was hurriedly shoved out to him.

This engagement having been so completely overshadowed by the greater subsequent events, has almost been lost sight of. Its importance consists principally in the fact that it was Gen'l Grant's first engagement and defeat and also furnishes food for speculation as to what might have been the result to him and to the country had he been captured.

After a short stay in Columbus, we were taken to Memphis and quartered in the Gayoso Block. Finding there was a six gun battery at Memphis to go to Gen'l Price, we organized a provisional artillery company with the understanding that we were permitted to join any command we preferred when we got to Gen'l Price. Captain Henry Guibor was given command of the battery. Those who had been officers at Camp Jackson were made cannoneers and those who were enlisted men were made drivers. Gen'l Frost also organized a cavalry bodyguard under Captain John Rock Champion.[49]

The entire command was transported to Jacksonport, Arkansas on the White River, where we went into a camp of instruction and where our real soldiering commenced.

Champion's company consisted of but fifteen men but they were as desperate a lot of fighters, as was afterwards developed, as I ever saw together—but they were a green lot. One of them, Jack Murphy, was a most original character. He had a great fondness for horse flesh, indeed this passion, so it was reported had gotten him into trouble before the war.

Jack had a little horse he brought from Missouri he called "The John Horse." It was small, with a coat of long, badly kept hair which looked as though it had never made the acquaintance of curry comb and brush. It had a despondent look and walked with such an unsteady gait as to cause the impression it was so weak it could hardly stand. Jack said it was a race horse, at which everybody laughed, regarding the statement as a good joke or as evidence that Jack was crazy.

Some of the natives were very much amused at Jack's boasting as to what his horse could do and finally arranged a race with him with a horse they would produce. They expected to pick up some very easy money. The money was put up and all preliminaries agreed upon for a certain day. They appeared at the appointed time with their horse, which was a beauty, and had beaten everything in that part of the country. In the side-betting they offered large odds on their horse, which Jack promptly accepted until all the money they could raise was up

---

[49] A Missouri Minuteman, John Rock Champion helped to organize St. Louis, Missouri Volunteer Militia companies in early 1861. Champion was absent from his unit when it was captured at Camp Jackson in May 1861. He later fought at Wilson's Creek, Lexington, and Pea Ridge. He was a daring and reckless cavalryman and died August 30, 1862, while leading a charge into Bolivar, Tennessee. Snead, *Fight For Missouri*, 110; *O.R.*, vol. 17, pt. 1, 120.

on the race.

It was a matter of surprise where Jack got so much money to put up, but as one of his comrades was the stakeholder it was expected they were in "cahoots" and that he would pass the stakes back to Jack who would bet them over and over again until all of the native money was exhausted. The natives were so sure of winning, they were not very vigilant.

A straight away course was measured in the road and the horses brought to the stake. At the word go the John horse, which seemed to have taken little interest in the proceedings up to this time, shot forward like he had been shot out of a gun. He took the lead and held it to the finish, coming in an easy winner, very much to the surprise of everybody except Jack.

The discomfiture of the natives was painful to see. They thought something must be wrong with their horse but could not be induced to arrange for another race.

We remained at Jacksonport a month or six weeks and during that time were drilled daily in the manual of arms and the manual of the piece and the marching by competent officers. In the mounted drill we were instructed by Gen'l Frost who, I think, was the best drill officer and disciplinarian I have ever known. When we broke camp at Jacksonport the last part of January '62 and entered upon the long and difficult march to Springfield, Mo., we were a thoroughly drilled and disciplined company.

My brother John, Dave Holliday[50] and I drove on the same gun—John in the lead, I in the swing and Dave the wheeler. We had not only to drive our two horses each, but fed and groomed them. The weather was intensely cold, being mid winter, particularly in the Boston Mountains which we crossed. It was probably the hardest experience we had during the war being, as we were, in that transition step from the easy and comfortable life of the civilian to the life of the soldier which is full of hardships and privations.

Reveille was sounded before daylight when we had to rise, dress in the cold, attend roll call, feed and curry our horses. Then got our soldier breakfast of bacon, hardtack and black coffee, which while it would have been considered most sumptuous later in our experience, seemed poor indeed to us so recently from our good eating at home. After breakfast "boots and saddles" would be sounded when we would have to put the heavy artillery harness, which had become frozen during the night, on the horses and prepare for the march which was resumed at daylight. Many of us had hands and feet frost bitten but we were cheerful under it all feeling that no sacrifice, even to the loss of life, was too great for the cause.

---

[50] Dave Holliday was the fourth corporal of the Second National Guard Company of the St. Louis, Missouri Volunteer Militia. He was not captured at Camp Jackson, but made his way south and joined Guibor's Battery. "The Grand Encamping and Encampment of the First Missouri Brigade, at Fort Lewis," Missouri Militia scrapbook, page 20 of unnumbered pages; List of exchanged prisoners captured at Camp Jackson, Camp Jackson Papers, Missouri Historical Society.

But our life was not all hardship. There were the jokes, the stories and the songs around the camp fire at night and the constant association of friends whom common hardships and dangers drew us very close together.

During the march from Yellville, Ark. to Springfield, Mo.[51] frequent rumors came to us of a Federal force in our vicinity, which was liable to intercept us and we were delighted at the prospect of a brush with the enemy. We were disappointed in this and reached Springfield, our destination, on Feb'y 11, 1862. We were delighted to be at last under the command of Gen'l Price and to meet our many friends in the army.

---

[51] Guibor's Battery took a northern route across Arkansas and into southwest Missouri.

Chapter 4
Pea Ridge and Crossing the Mississippi

We were greatly disappointed and chagrinned to learn the following day that Price's Army had been ordered to fall back into Arkansas to form a junction with the Confederate commands of Generals [Ben] McCulloch and [James M.] McIntosh.[52] These commands not being allowed to come to us, as it was the policy of the Confederate Government, at that time, not to invade a state not a member of the Confederacy.[53] The retrograde movement commenced on Feb'y 12th.

Price's army consisted of about 8000 men. We were closely followed by a Federal Army commanded by Gen'l [Samuel R.]Curtis,[54] of about 17,000 men.[55]

Our first halt for the night was on Cane Creek. Just as our supper was about ready to be eaten a cannon shot from a hill immediately in front of the position of our battery, landed near us without doing any damage, but served to cause the greatest surprise and excitement as we had no idea the enemy was so

---

[52] James McQueen McIntosh was born in Tampa Bay, Florida in 1828. Upon graduation from West Point in 1849 (last in his class), he was assigned duty on the frontier, where he rose to the rank of captain. When the Civil War began he was elected colonel of the Second Arkansas Mounted Rifles. He participated in the Battle of Wilson's Creek, where General N. B. Pearce recorded that the "brave" McIntosh was "always in the midst of the fight cheering and leading his men forward to victory, his name and conduct, were a host in our behalf." In the latter part of 1861, he helped drive the Federal Indians out of Indian Territory, winning the Battle of Chustenahlah (December 26, 1861). On January 24, 1862 he was commissioned a Confederate brigadier general. He was killed at the Battle of Pea Ridge a short time after Ben McCulloch died. Warner, *Generals in Gray*, 202-203; *O.R*, vol. 3, 121; *O.R.*, vol. 8, 22-24; Anne Bailey, "James McQueen McIntosh," *The Confederate General* (6 vols., William C. Davis, ed.; National Historical Society, 1991), vol. 4, 124-125.

[53] McCulloch and Price hated each other. Price wanted to secure Missouri, while McCulloch had orders to protect Arkansas and Indian Territory. McCulloch failed to see that the best way to complete his mission was to assist Price in securing his. To unify the Arkansas and Missouri commands General Earl Van Dorn was given command of the army. Shea and Hess, *Pea Ridge*, 19.

[54] Samuel R. Curtis was born on February 3, 1805 in Clinton County, New York. He attended West Point, graduated in 1831, and served one year at Fort Gibson, Indian Territory before resigning. Curtis practiced engineering in Ohio until the Mexican War when the governor made him colonel of the Second Ohio Infantry. Serving with distinction under Zachary Taylor, he returned to Ohio and moved to Keokuk, Iowa. Curtis practiced engineering and law, was elected mayor of Keokuk, and served three terms as a representative in the United States Congress. When the Civil War began Curtis became colonel of the Second Iowa Infantry and brigadier general on May 17, 1861. He commanded the Army of the Southwest, won the Battle of Pea Ridge, and was promoted to major general for his efforts. In September 1862 Lincoln appointed him Department of the Missouri commander, a post he held until May 1863. Curtis finished the war serving as commander of the Department of Kansas and then of the Northwest. Warner, *Generals in Blue*, 107-108.

[55] On February 12, 1862 Curtis's army contained 12,095 effective men and fifty pieces of artillery. *O.R.*, vol. 8, 554.

near us.[56]

We were ordered to hitch up and take position to resist an attack. The engagement which ensued was of small consequence, consisting of a skirmish between a small force sent out by Gen'l Price and a small scouting party of the enemy which was quickly driven back. Our men took some prisoners and the importance of the affair consisted merely in its being our first taste of real war.

Gen'l Price concluded that it would be better to put a greater distance between his command and the superior force of the enemy, so he ordered a night march which we immediately took up. We did not get back to our camp, where our untouched supper was awaiting us and not only lost our supper but many of our cooking utensils which later was a very serious loss to us. Our only consolation was that both supper and utensils fell into the hands of some other command of our army.

We continued the retreat, marching almost continually day and night until we reached Cross Hollows, Arkansas[57] on the 17th of Feb'y. Up to this time our rear guard had fights daily with the enemy, which were more or less severe. Our battery was frequently ordered to take position to resist attack should our rear guard be overpowered but this emergency never arrived and to our great disappointment we did not get to fire a shot.

The most serious skirmish of all occurred at Cross Hollows, after which the enemy seemed inclined to let us alone—due no doubt to the close proximity of our reinforcements.[58]

We remained at Cross Hollows a day to rest men & animals and then marched to Cove Creek, in the depths of the Boston Mountains, where we found a force of about 8000 Confederate soldiers, consisting of troops from Louisiana,

---

[56] The engagement, known as the skirmish at Crane Creek, began about 6:30 P.M. February 14, 1862, and was an attempt by Curtis to see if the Confederates would stand and fight. Ibid., 59.

[57] Cross Hollows is about ten miles north of Fayetteville, Arkansas on the Telegraph or Wire road. It was known for its natural defenses and expected by Curtis to be where the Confederates would make a stand. Instead, the rebels retreated. Ibid, 559, 561-562.

[58] Beginning with the retreat from Springfield the two armies fought many small skirmishes over the next eleven days. The engagement referred to by Bull did not occur at Cross Hollow but at Little Sugar Creek. The Federals lost 13 killed and 15-20 wounded and reported rebel losses as 26 dead.

Skirmishes February 12-23, 1862:

Springfield, Mo.	February 12
Cane Creek, Mo.	February 14
Flat Creek, Mo.	February 15
Potts' Hill, Ark.	February 16
Little Sugar Creek, Ark.	February 17
Bentonville, Ark.	February 18
Fayetteville, Ark.	February 23

Ibid., 59-64, 68; Shea and Hess, *Pea Ridge*, 43.

Arkansas, and Texas under Gen'l Ben McCulloch and Gen'l McIntosh and Indians from the Indian Nation under Gen'l Albert Pike.[59]

A controversy arose between Gen'l Price, who was a Major General in the Missouri State Guard and Gen'l McCulloch, who was a Brigadier General in the Confederate service as to who should have supreme command. As they could not agree, Gen'l Price wrote to Gen'l Earl Van Dorn, who commanded the Trans-Mississippi Department, with headquarters at Pocahontas, Arkansas, explaining the situation and suggesting that he come and take command in person.[60] This he did and on March 4 moved the entire command, consisting of about 17,000 men,[61] to find the enemy and give him battle.

General Curtis's (Federal) command consisted of about 18,000 men with Headquarters in the Elk Horn Tavern.[62] Gen'l Van Dorn decided to divide his command and attack from two sides; McCulloch from the south and Price from the north, General Van Dorn going with Price's command, which delivered its attack on the morning of March 5th (My birthday).[63] It was a most furious attack—McCulloch hearing Price's guns attacked from the south.

The battle raged desperately all day and when night came we had driven the enemy at every point and our command occupied Elk Horn Tavern. The following morning, soon after the battle resumed, Gen'l McCulloch was killed and Gen'l McIntosh, in an effort to recover his body, was also killed.[64] The death

---

[59] Albert Pike was born in Boston, Massachusetts on December 29, 1809. Educated at Harvard, he went west in 1831 and taught school in western Arkansas near Fort Smith. He became a lawyer in 1835 and continued in the profession until the Mexican War. Pike raised a company of volunteers and was at the Battle of Buena Vista. Returning to Arkansas, Pike practiced law, becoming the attorney for the Creek Indians. Pike was adamantly against secession, but joined the Confederacy to protect his property interests in Arkansas. His principle contribution to the Confederate war effort was convincing the five civilized tribes of the Indian Territory to sign treaties with the Confederacy. Pike was made brigadier general on August 15, 1861, fought at Pea Ridge, and resigned his commission on July 12, 1862 following a bitter disagreement with General Hindman over the extent of Pike's command. John M. Harrell, "Arkansas," *Confederate Military History,* 13 vols., (Clement A. Evans, ed., Atlanta, 1899; reprinted Secaucus, NJ, 1974), 408-410; Warner, *Generals in Gray,* 240-241; Michael E. Banasik, *Embattled Arkansas: The Prairie Grove Campaign* (Wilmington, NC, 1996), 102-103.

[60] The Confederate War Department assigned Van Dorn to command the Trans-Mississippi District on January 12, 1862. Van Dorn assumed command in Little Rock on January 29, 1862 and immediately established his headquarters in northeast Arkansas at Pocahontas in early February 1862. See biography in Appendix B. *O.R.,* vol. 8, 734, 745; Letter and order book, Daniel M. Frost's command, December 1861-April 1862, 36-37, Mesker Papers, Missouri Historical Society.

[61] The Confederates began the march with about 16,500 men, but had fewer than 13,000 for the Battle of Pea Ridge that followed. Shea and Hess, *Pea Ridge,* 270-271; *O.R.,* vol. 8, 283.

[62] Depending on source cited, Curtis had about 10,500 men engaged at Pea Ridge with 49 cannon. *O.R.,* vol. 8, 196; Shea and Hess, *Pea Ridge,* 270.

[63] The battle began on March 6 with only some minor skirmishing and continued in full fury on March 7 and 8, 1862.

[64] Both McCulloch and McIntosh died on March 7, while fighting on the right of the Confederate line. General Pike assumed command after the fall of McIntosh and broke off the

of these two leaders so demoralized their troops they fell back and left Price's command to bear the brunt of a united attack of the entire Federal force. This proved too much for the command to withstand and it was withdrawn in good order from the field.

The battle resulted to the Federals in 300 killed, 600 wounded, 300 prisoners and four pieces of artillery captured and to the Confederates in 200 killed and 500 wounded and missing.[65] The advantage was with the latter although they had to abandon the field.

When the battle opened our battery was ordered to take a position on a high hill. We took but 4 of our 6 guns into the fight as we had only men enough to properly serve the four guns. I considered it very fortunate that my gun was left with the wagon train and that I was permitted to go into the fight as a cannoneer. My brother John had been promoted to sergeant and Dave Holliday and I were assigned to his piece. Ben Von Phul[66] was the gunner on this piece. I was No. 6, my duties being to issue the ammunition from the limber chest.[67]

We had a fine position. Sigel's battery occupied a position about 200 yards from us and our fire was directed principally at it. We succeeded in exploding several of their ammunition chests, killing and wounding many of their men and horses and finally in driving them from their position.[68]

Gen'l Price was wounded in the arm, early in the engagement, immediately behind our battery, but he refused to leave the field. In the evening we were ordered to a position immediately in front of the Elk Horn Tavern, while two of our pieces, which were in a narrow road, were firing rapidly at a regiment of infantry which was charging.[69]

---

engagement on the rebel right. *O.R.*, vol. 8, 284.

[65] Curtis reported 203 killed, 980 wounded and 201 captured or missing. There is no exact accounting of Confederate losses at the battle. Van Dorn places his losses at 800-1,000 killed and wounded with 2-300 prisoners. Shea and Hess in their book on Pea Ridge stated that the losses amounted to about 2,000 of all types. *O.R.*, vol. 8, 206, 282; Shea and Hess, *Pea Ridge*, 271.

[66] Ben Von Phul was captured at Camp Jackson and upon exchange joined Guibor's Missouri Battery. He later commanded a temporary battery in the Trans-Mississippi known as "Von Phul's Missouri Battery." The unit was assigned to Thomas F. Drayton's Brigade. *O.R.*, vol. 22, pt. 2, 1,086; National Archives, Record Group M322, roll no. 90, Service Record, Von Phul's Battery.

[67] A typical gun crew consisted of eight or nine men: the commander of the piece sighted the gun; four cannoneers (Nos. 1-4), sponged the tube, loaded the piece, vented the gun, and shifted the gun's tail; three or four auxiliaries (Nos. 5-8), issued the rounds or passed it to the piece. As a No. 6, Bull was part of the auxiliary. Jack Coggins, *Arms and Equipment of the Civil War* (Garden City, NY, 1962; reprinted Wilmington, NC, 1987), 63, 70; James Street, Jr., *The Civil War: The Struggle for Tennessee, Tupelo to Stones River* (Alexandria, VA, 1985), 137.

[68] Bull is probably referring to Martin Welfley's Missouri Battery, which was one of four batteries used by Franz Sigel during the battle on the eighth. Of his other three batteries, the First Flying was held in reserve until late in the day, only two guns of the Second Ohio were present, and Hoffman's Fourth Ohio had only one man wounded with no losses of guns, horses, or caissons reported. *O.R.*, vol. 8, 204-205, 236-238, 242-243.

[69] Guibor's Battery proved instrumental in halting the Union pursuit on the final day of battle. Shea and Hess, *Pea Ridge*, 255.

Louie Gilespie, acting as No. 1 on one of the guns, thinking his gun had been fired, stepped in to sponge out just as the lanyard was pulled to fire his gun. His arm and part of his skull was blown off but he was still alive when we left the field the following day. We left him with great regrets in the Elk Horn Tavern where he was moved soon after the unfortunate accident. Strange to say, his was the only casualty we had among the battery boys, but we had several horses killed and wounded.

Rock Champion with his fifteen men charged the regiment of infantry which was attacking our battery, when the accident occurred and drove them back. Champion delivered his attack on the flank of the infantry regiment. It was so bold they thought them to be the field officers of a regiment as they carried sabers which our cavalry generally did not do.[70]

When we left the battle field the enemy was too crippled to follow us and we marched unmolested to Van Buren, Arkansas. Gen'l Van Dorn paid the following tribute to the Missouri troops in his report of the battle to the Government at Richmond.

> During the whole of this engagement I was with the
> Missourians under Price and I have never seen better
> fighters than these Missouri troops or more gallant
> leaders than Gen'l Price and his officers. From the
> first to the last shot they continually rushed on
> and never yielded an inch they had won and when at
> last they received orders to fall back, they retired
> steadily and with cheers. Gen'l Price received a
> severe wound in the action but would neither retire
> from the field nor cease to expose his life to danger.[71]

We called the engagement the Battle of Elk Horn, the Federals called it the Battle of Pea Ridge.

We remained at Van Buren about ten days. While there our army received orders to go to the east side of the Mississippi River.[72] After the most difficult and disagreeable march through constant rain and almost impassable mud we

---

[70] Champion lost two men wounded while inflicting a loss of six or eight upon the enemy. *O.R.*, vol. 8, 324.

[71] Ibid., 285.

[72] Initially General P.G.T. Beauregard "urged" Van Dorn to unite with his army in Tennessee. Van Dorn intended to move east, not to unite with Beauregard, but to attack St. Louis or relive the pressure on New Madrid and Island No. 10. General Albert S. Johnston settled the matter and issued instructions on March 23, 1862 for Van Dorn to move his army to the Memphis, Tennessee. Van Dorn received his orders on March 29. Ibid., 785, 790-791, 804; *O.R.*, vol. 10, pt. 2, 354.

finally reached Des Arc on the White River.[73] We had slept in wet blankets every night on the march and were greatly rejoiced when it was finished. Bob Tandy and other St. Louisians came to us at Des Arc and we were delighted with comparatively late news from home. Bob Tandy burst into tears when he saw my dilapidated condition. I had been driving and my right trouser leg which had been between the horses was worn off up to the knee and on account of the rain and mud I was altogether a most disreputable looking citizen.

After a few days our army took steam boats for Memphis, Tenn. We had been so constantly on the go since we left Memphis in December '61 that we could not exercise the right we received when we joined Guibor's Battery to join any other command we might prefer when we got with Price. On our return to Memphis John and I and several others decided to transfer to James C. Gorham's Battery[74] as there were many old St. Louis friends in that company including Charles Buck Tilden,[75] Alex Lesueur,[76] Ed Bridell,[77] John Tatum,[78] and others.

---

[73] The lead elements of Van Dorn's army arrived at Des Arc on April 7, 1862. Bull's battery, now part of Daniel M. Frost's artillery brigade, departed Des Arc on April 15 and arrived in Memphis a few days later. *O.R.*, vol. 13, 814, 818.

[74] Gorham's battery was organized from guns captured at Lexington, Missouri on September 20, 1861. It was part of the Sixth Division, Missouri State Guard. Alexander B. "Buck" Tilden was the unit's first lieutenant and Alexander A. Lesueur the second lieutenant. Both Tilden and Lesueur eventually commanded the battery after it entered Confederate service. William Bull served his Civil War days in this unit. James C. Gorham was from Marshall, Missouri (Saline County) and remained with the battery until General Thomas C. Hindman replaced him with Tilden on November 10, 1862. Richard Peterson, James E. McGhee, Kip A. Lindberg, and Keith I. Daleen, *Sterling Price's Lieutenants: A Guide to the Officers and Organization of the Missouri State Guard 1861-1865* (Shawnee Mission, KS, 1995), 192; Bull's diary, November 10, 1862.

[75] Charles B. Tilden began his Civil War service in the "Plattin Rangers Company," First Division, Missouri State Guard, as a second lieutenant. He later was elected first lieutenant of Gorham's Battery in the Sixth Division, Missouri State Guard. After the Battle of Pea Ridge, Tilden entered the Confederate service and was appointed the first lieutenant of Gorham's reorganized battery on September 24, 1862. Thomas C. Hindman appointed Tilden commander of Gorham's Battery on November 10, 1862, and redesignated the unit "Tilden's Battery." Tilden was at the Battle of Prairie Grove, but elected not to lead his battery at the Battle of Helena (July 4, 1863). He was thrown out as unit commander in December 1863, in part, because of his lack of action at Helena. Peterson, *Sterling Price's Lieutenants*, 56, 192; *O.R.*, vol. 22, pt. 1, 421; *O.R.*, vol. 53, 461; National Archives, Record Group M322, roll no. 85, Service Record, Third Field Battery Missouri Artillery.

[76] Alexander Lesueur was born in St. Louis in 1842. He joined Joseph Kelly's St. Louis Volunteer Militia Company prior to the Civil War. Lesueur fought in the early battles in Missouri and was wounded at the Battle of Wilson's Creek. He was elected second lieutenant of Gorham's Missouri State Guard Battery in late September 1861. When the battery entered Confederate service in September 1862, Lesueur remained with the battery, being appointed first lieutenant on November 10, 1862. Lesueur was elected captain of his unit in December 1863, because he led the battery at the Battle of Helena. He also participated in the Red River and Camden campaigns of 1864. Peterson, *Sterling Price's Lieutenants*, 192; *O.R.*, vol. 22, pt. 1, 421; *O.R.*, vol. 34, pt. 1, 816; Bull diary, 93; John C. Moore, "Missouri," *Confederate Military History Extended*, 12: 338-339.

[77] Edward Bridell enlisted in the Missouri State Guard in March 1862 and transferred to

We had a little difficulty, at first, in getting transferred but finally accomplished it through the influence of Governor Trusten Polk,[79] who interested himself in the matter.

Our battery (Gorham's) left Memphis for Corinth, Miss.[80] on May 2, '62; our orders being to march the entire distance. We went alone, our infantry having gone by rail. Our march lay through a beautiful section of country, where they had seen no soldiers and it was for us a triumphant march all the way. At night our camp was filled with people, who brought us quantities of everything good to eat and frequently when passing through small settlements during the day we would find lunches set out on tables for us and in passing large farms, which were quite plentiful, buckets of butter milk would be sent out to us. We had been in the service, and suffered privations and hardships, long enough to enjoy this kindness and these good things to eat.

This all ended when we reached Corinth where we found rations poor & scarce, the water horribly bad, and the camp full of sick soldiers. We fared batter than most of them as we were on outpost duty most of the time where we could get good water. We also brought to camp with us quite a good supply of provisions given us by the good friends on our march from Memphis, and this we would replenish occasionally by sending our head quarters wagons back into the land of plenty and buying hams and other provisions.

Our battery was out one night a mile or so in front of our lines, on the road to Farmington, and masked in a clump of trees. The guns were blackened with powder and branches of trees were placed over them to conceal them from the enemy, which was expected to make an attack in force the following day. When everything was in readiness we spread our blankets on the ground and prepared to spend the few remaining hours of the night in sleep. We had not long been in our beds when we felt creepy things running over us and to our horror found they were snakes. We beat a hasty retreat to the ammunition chests where we spent the balance of the night huddled together uncomfortably but safe from the snakes.

Confederate service on June 10, 1862, when he was promoted to first lieutenant. He served on Charles W. Phifer's staff as aide-de-camp. National Archives, Record Group M322, roll no. 179, Service Records, Missouri State Guard.

[78] John Tatum was one of the organizing members of the Second National Guard Company, St. Louis, Missouri Volunteer Militia. Bull will present more on Tatum later in his narrative. See also Appendix A for service data. "Military Companies of St. Louis—No. 4 National Guards—2nd Company," Missouri Militia scrapbook, page 6 of unnumbered pages.

[79] Trusten Polk was born in Delaware and moved to Missouri in 1835. He was elected Governor of Missouri in 1856, but resigned to become a U.S. Senator, replacing Thomas Hart Benton. Polk was expelled from the Senate in 1862 and joined the Confederacy. He became the chief judge for T. H. Holmes Confederate Corps in December 1862 and later an aide to General Price with the rank of colonel. McElroy, *Struggle For Missouri*, 28; *O.R.*, Series 4, vol. 2, 248.

[80] Corinth, Mississippi was the Confederate gathering place following their loss at Shiloh and the focus of a Union siege that lasted from April 29 to May 30, 1862. General Henry W. Halleck commanded the Federals while the Confederates were led by General P.G.T. Beauregard. *O.R.*, vol. 10, pt. 1, 660.

The expected attack was not made and under the cover of darkness the next night we withdrew quietly within our lines very much to our relief and also, no doubt to the snakes', who were left in peaceful possession of their haunts.

Gen'l [Henry W.] Halleck[81] commanded a Federal force estimated at 90,000 men in front of Corinth, which place was defended by [P.G.T.] Beauregard[82] with a force slightly more than half that number.[83] But he [Beauregard] maneuvered so constantly as to create the impression, both upon the enemy and his own troops, that he was receiving large reinforcements and was on the eve of attacking the enemy. The foe with their greatly superior force, were quietly awaiting the attack behind their breastworks.

Having accomplished his purposes in holding the enemy in check, among which was the removal of his supplies, Beauregard quietly withdrew the latter part of May, without the loss of a man or a wagon. Early one morning when Price's command had spent the night in line of battle and we all thought an engagement was near at hand, we learned the balance of the army had retired and that he [Price] was ordered to follow as the rear guard. The enemy during the day opened a furious cannonading on our former position, receiving no response. To their utter astonishment and chagrin, they found Beauregard had evacuated and was a long way on his march and that the formidable artillery showing above his [Beauregard's] works were logs of wood known as "quaker guns." No attempt at pursuit was made.

Price's command, with short halts, finally reached Tupelo, Miss. and from that point what remained of the Missouri State Guard left for the Trans-Mississippi Department under the command of Gen'l Monroe M. [Mosby Monroe] Parsons.[84]

His command consisted of about 2,500 infantry and Gorham's and [James W.] Kneisley's Batteries.[85] We moved to Abbeyville, Miss., where we awaited

---

[81] Known to his men as "Old Brains," Halleck took command of a Federal Army Group following the Battle of Shiloh and began a slow and deliberate advance on Corinth. In addition to his field command, Halleck commanded the Department of the Mississippi, which included Missouri. When Halleck left his headquarters at St. Louis in April 1862, he appointed John M. Schofield the Missouri commander. Though an intelligent officer, Halleck lacked, according to John McElroy, "military instinct and soldierly intuition." McElroy, *Struggle for Missouri*, 253-255; *O.R.* vol. 13, 8, 409.

[82] P.G.T. Beauregard assumed command of the Confederate forces opposing General Halleck, following the death of General Albert. S. Johnston at the Battle of Shiloh. Beauregard commanded the Western Department, consisting of the armies of the Mississippi and the West. The Bulls were in the Army of the West. *O.R.*, vol. 10, pt. 1, 766-768.

[83] Halleck's command numbered 108,538 present for duty on May 31, 1862. Prior to the evacuation of Corinth, Beauregard's armies contained 52,706 effectives. *O.R.*, vol. 10, pt. 1, 791; *O.R.*, vol. 10, pt. 2, 235.

[84] See biography in Appendix B.

[85] Bull is misleading the reader. When Parsons's Missouri State Guard returned to the Trans-Mississippi they had about 800 troops and Gorham's five-gun battery.

James W. Kneisley commanded the Palmyra Light Battery, Second Division, Missouri State Guard. The battery formed about June 1861 and participated in the siege of Lexington, and the

the making up of a train of about 100 wagons, containing supplies for the Trans-Mississippi Department, which we were to meet at Grenada, Miss. and escort to their destination. We were delighted with this assignment as it was a move in the direction of Missouri where we preferred to serve.

---

battle of Pea Ridge. It disbanded June 29, 1862 prior to returning to the Trans-Mississippi. The remnants of the command probably accompanied the other members of the State Guard back to the west side of the Mississippi River. *O.R.*, vol. 8, 788; *O.R.*, vol. 13, 881; Peterson, *Sterling Price's Lieutenants*, 101; Shea and Hess, *Pea Ridge*, 337.

Chapter 5
Back to the Trans-Mississippi
[Diary of Events: July 18 to September 5, 1862]

In hot weather we frequently marched at night, starting at moon rise we would march until the moon set and then go into camp in the dark. One morning when my brother John and I made up our blankets we found two young rattle snakes under them. Whether they were there when we made our bed or crawled under afterwards we did not know but were very glad they were not on our side of the blanket.

From our leaving Abbeyville I kept a diary which briefly gives the movements of our battery until we reached Little Rock, Ark. on January 22, 1863 and what follows, to that time is taken from that diary.

Friday July 18, 1862:

Left Abbeyville, Miss., where we had been in camp for some time. On this date, marched to Oxford where we took the rail cars for Grenada. Our pieces went by land with the train. We reached Grenada the next morning at 2 o'clock and put up at Brown's Hotel. Our guns reached us on Monday the 21st July 1862. Had a pleasant time at Grenada. Left there the following morning July 22, 1862, marched about 18 miles and camped on the Yalobusha River. Marched about 22 miles the next day, crossed the Tallahatchie River and camped on its bank. Laid in camp the next day July 24, 1862.[86] Went to a lake about a quarter of a mile from the river and had fine fishing.

Friday July 25, 1862:

Marched to McNutt, about 20 miles.

Saturday July 26, 1862:

Marched about 21 miles, crossed the Sunflower River, a beautiful little river and camped upon its bank.

Sunday July 27, 1962:

Laid in camp. Clothing was issued.

Monday July 28, 1862:

Marched about 20 miles, camped near Bay Felia [Bogue Phalia].

Tuesday July 29, 1862:

Crossed Bay Felia and marched about 8 miles. Camped near Bolivar about one mile from the Mississippi River at about 4 o'clock. Fearing that the smoke

---

[86] The Missouri State Guard traveled across northern Mississippi, starting on July 18, 1862 and arriving at Boliver on the Mississippi River on July 29. Bull diary, 41.

from our camp fires would be seen by some Federal gun boats which were coming up the river we moved camp to Bolivar Lake about two miles from the river. The lake and surrounding are exceedingly beautiful and we have a very delightful camp.

Wednesday July 30, 1862:
Left Bolivar Lake in the afternoon. Reached the Mississippi River at about 6 o'clock, 5 miles below Bolivar. 23 Federal boats, including 5 gun boats, passed up last night.[87]

Thursday July 31, 1862:
Our battery was on the first boat that crossed the Mississippi River—Gen'l Parsons crossed with us. We made the trip without accident, although we were nearly capsized soon after starting. We landed in Cypress Creek about one mile from its mouth in Desha County, Arkansas.[88] Went into camp about three miles from the river. Remained in this camp until Aug. 6, waiting for the train to be crossed. Besides our brigade train there are about 100 wagons of supplies.

The process is necessarily slow as they have but two small flat boats, the Federals having destroyed everything they could find in the way of a boat along the river. These boats are loaded at Bolivar Landing behind an island. They are then paddled across the river and landed in Cypress Creek on the Arkansas side, about five miles below the starting point, the current of the river being as swift as to carry them that distance.

On the return trip the boats are paddled up the river some distance on the Arkansas side and make better headway across the current as they are not loaded. We were relieved of considerable anxiety when the task was finished as, added to the danger of navigation was the fear that a federal fleet would come upon us unexpectedly.

We have fine fishing—fish for supper every night. Three of our battery boys were arrested for killing a hog, which is positively against orders.

Wednesday Aug. 6, 1862:
Stuck camp at 1 o'clock A.M. and marched at 3. We passed many fine plantations and got quantities of figs, peaches, plums, and watermelons. Made about 20 miles. It rained very hard for a while just as we were coming into camp. It cleared off in about an hour and before dark we had many visitors— among the number some very pretty young ladies.

---

[87] What Bull saw was probably Flag Officer Charles H. Davis's fleet which was returning from Vicksburg, en route to Helena for rest and repair. United States War Department, *The War of the Rebellion: Official Records of the Union and Confederate Navies* (31 vols., Washington, DC, 1894-1922), Series 1, vol. 23, 270-271 (Hereafter cited as *N.O.R.;* all citations of *N.O.R.* refer to Series 1 unless indicated otherwise).

[88] The Missouri State Guard crossed about ten miles south of where the Arkansas River enters the Mississippi River.

Thursday August 7th 1862:

Marched at 3 o'clock A.M. Made about 23 miles—a long though pleasant march. Passed several fine plantations where we got all kinds of fruits and melons, also some chickens and buttermilk. Passed Lenox Lake and Silver Lake, both beautiful. Struck the Arkansas River at Desha Place. Went into camp a short distance from the river. Chappel left our mess.

Friday Aug. 8 1862:

Still in camp. Probabilities are that we will remain here some time. The Federals have landed a force at Napoleon, which is at the mouth of the Arkansas River. They will, it is reported, pursue us. Gen'l Parsons seems disposed to wait here for them. We are camped on one of the plantations of the Widow Jordon. There is a corn field on this place containing 1,000 acres.

Saturday Aug. 9 1862:

Still in camp. We have a beautiful camp, wood and water very convenient. Watermelons, figs, peaches, and other fruits in great abundance.

Sunday August 10, 1862:

Still in camp. Was on guard last night. Had a first rate breakfast this morning; fried chicken, beef hash, coffee, and corn bread. This is the anniversary of the Battle of Oak Hill [Wilson's Creek], where Lyon, who captured us at Camp Jackson, was killed.

We have just received orders for our gun and detachment to go on a scout. We are all delighted at the idea and expect to have some fun before we get back. We left camp at sundown, marched 15 miles, went into camp at about 2 o'clock near Lenox Lake. Got some of the finest watermelons I have ever seen. They grow to great size and sweetness in this country.

Monday Aug. 11, '62:

Remained in camp during the day. Marched at sun down. Kept to the telegraph road. Made about 6 miles, camped on the Arkansas River about 1 mile below the Widow Smith's plantation.

Tuesday August 12, 1862:

Moved at daylight about 2 miles down the river—laid here until sun down when we crossed the river and camped near Arkansas Post,[89] an old trading post. Mosquitoes very bad.

Wednesday August 13, 1862:

The town of Arkansas Post contains a Court House, one store and several

---

[89] Arkansas Post was located in Arkansas County, Arkansas, about ten miles above where the White and Arkansas rivers join. General Thomas C. Hindman established a fort at the Post to protect the Arkansas Valley from invasion by Federal naval vessels.

residences, all large brick houses. Geo. Roots [Rootes] and Joe Irwin[90] joined us today. We took them into our mess. One of the infantry got drowned in the evening while bathing in the river.

Thursday August 14, 1862:

Moved camp about 2 miles down the river. The rest of the battery and the train got to us in the afternoon.

Friday Aug. 15, 1862:

Had a general cleaning up of camp today. Some man, belonging to the command it is supposed, broke into a house last night and stole a number of articles. On account of this Gen'l Parsons has been very strict in regards to giving passes to town.

Saturday August 16, 1862:

Still in camp. Our colored cook Al, who had been with our mess a long time, left us this morning. We were very glad to get rid of him. Bob Young[91] and Joe Irwin are to do the cooking for the present. I today got the money on Bob Tandy's discharge $46.00, which he assigned to me. He was discharged while we were in Mississippi, having an ailment which rendered him unfit for military service and which could not be treated successfully in camp. He returned home and was compelled to take an oath of allegiance.

Sunday August 17, 1862:

In camp. Went out this morning for a review and inspection. Everything went off very well. Got two months pay in the afternoon; $27.00. Went to church in the evening.

Monday August 18, 1862:

Left camp at 3 o'clock A.M., immediate destination unknown, supposed to be either Clarendon or Des Arc on the White River or Little Rock.[92] It is generally thought we will soon have a fight. It is reported the Federals are only

---

[90] Joseph Irwin and George Rootes—See Appendix A for service record.

[91] Robert E. Young was from Jefferson City, Missouri and enlisted on May 12, 1861 in Robert "Black Bob" McCulloch's Regiment of the Missouri State Guard. Young was cited for bravery at Wilson's Creek by his regimental commander. He transferred to Gorham's Battery in June 1862 and served with the command for the remainder of the war. In the Spring of 1865, he was detailed as sergeant in charge of the Camden Arsenal. After the war he returned to Missouri and earned a medical degree. Moore, "Missouri," *Confederate Military History Extended*, vol. 12, 444-445.

[92] Both Des Arc and Clarendon attracted a great deal of attention during Curtis's advance on Little Rock during May-July 1862. In August 1862 the Confederate command still held the White River line, protecting Little Rock and, fully expected the Federals to advance on the city via the White or Arkansas rivers. Arkansas Post anchored the right of the Confederate defenses, protecting the Arkansas capital.

20 miles from us.[93] We marched 20 miles through the prairie.[94] In the evening had to go two miles off the road to get water.

Tuesday Aug. 19 '62:

Marched at 3 o'clock A.M. Some of our men got whiskey last night and got drunk. Some of them have not gotten to camp yet. Made about 17 miles. Still on the prairie.

Wednesday August 20, 1862:

Marched at 3 AM. Made about 24 miles. Still on the prairie.

Thursday August 21, 1862:

Marched at 4 A.M. Left the prairie at about 7. Struck White River at 9 o'clock. Reached camp opposite of Clarendon on White River at 10 o'clock. 3,000 Federals left here last Sunday. We are now in their camp. I just saw a tree with the following initials cut on it "L.C.D, 9th Ind. [Indiana]" I went over into the town in the afternoon. There are not over half a dozen persons in the place. The Federals destroyed or carried off everything in the place except the houses. A regiment of our cavalry crossed over this morning.[95]

Saturday Aug. 23 '62:

Got orders to move back to Pine Bluff. Cavalry recrossed the river. Marched at 10 o'clock, made about 6 miles. Camped near a beautiful spring in an old Federal camp.

Sunday August 24, 1862:

Marched at 3 A.M. Made about 15 miles, camped at Mitchell. He has a fine plantation in the middle of the prairie. We will remain here several days.

Monday August 25, 1862:

Still at Camp Mitchell. We have a great many sick. All of our mess are sick except Joe Irwin and myself. Bob Young went out foraging today and got

---

[93] The Federal troops that Bull is referring too came from Helena, Arkansas. They launched the expedition on August 16, heading for the Yazoo River in Mississippi. The first landing of the expedition was at Island No. 65, about forty miles south of Helena and then Napoleon, Arkansas at the confluence of the Arkansas and Mississippi rivers. The Federals returned to Helena on August 27. *O.R.*, vol. 13, 241-241.

[94] The prairie is known as the "Grand Prairie."

[95] Brigadier General Alvin P. Hovey led an expedition from Helena to Clarendon, which departed on August 4 and captured Clarendon on August 7. The Federals encountered only light opposition from William H. Parsons's cavalry brigade which hovered near Clarendon. Hovey's force remained in Clarendon until August 13, when they returned to Helena. The Federals reported a loss of three killed and two wounded—all by guerrilla activity. *O.R.*, vol. 13, 206-207; Telegram, August 10, 1862, Parsons to Newton, Peter W. Alexander Collection, Columbia University.

chicken, peaches, & honey.

Tuesday August 26, 1862:
Still in Camp Mitchell. This has been the happiest day I have had in a long time. I got a letter from home. I have never placed much confidence in the reports of an early peace, but I never go to sleep now without dreaming of being at home and I am superstitious enough to believe there is something in it. Tatum went to the country and got some honey.

Wednesday August 27, 1862:
Had a high fever all last night and a chill this morning; the hardest I ever had. Think the honey made me sick.

Thursday Aug. 28, '62:
Feel better today. There is a report in camp that the Southern Confederacy has been recognized by England, France, & Russia.

Monday September 1, 1862:
I have been quite sick since I last wrote, but have almost entirely recovered. My brother John, John Tatum, Bob Young, and George Roots have all recovered. We were treated to a beautiful and grand spectacle a few nights since. The prairie had been on fire for several days. This night the fire came in to full view of the camp though a long way off. We were so delighted with the sight we remained nearly all night watching it. The next morning it had disappeared.

While we were all sick Miss Mitchell, who is a beautiful young lady, sent us a plate of butter and some milk.

Quite an excitement was created in camp a few days ago by an order for every man to be sworn into the Missouri State Guard for 3 years or the war or else for them to be given their discharge, in which case they would be conscripted into the Confederate service. This was the best order, in my opinion, that ever was issued and was objected to only by a few grumblers and those who expected to go home as soon as they got into Missouri. Nearly all of the command will go in.

Friday September 5 '62:
A good many men have left our battery and joined the other artillery company during the last week.

Chapter 6
March to Hindman's Army
[Diary of Events: September 6 to November 13, 1862]

Saturday September 6, 1862:
I wrote home.

Monday September 8, 1862
To the delight of everybody we left Camp Mitchell at 8 o'clock P.M. Marched 17 miles and camped on the prairie.

Tuesday September 9, 1862:
Marched at 8 o'clock A.M. Made 17 miles. Struck White River at about 4 o'clock and went into camp. I had a high fever all night.

Wednesday September 10, 1862:
Still at Bucks Landing 7 miles below Des Arc and about the same distance above DeValls Bluff.[96] I had a very high fever in the afternoon, was very sick until 5 o'clock. Had a first rate supper; among other things, sweet potatoes and peaches and fresh milk. I could not resist the temptation to eat a very hearty supper. Commenced to rain at 8 o'clock P.M. Got orders to move as soon as it should hold up, which it did at 10 o'clock. We reached Des Arc at about 1 o'clock.

Thursday September 11, 1862:
Tatum and I being so run down in health have permission to stay in town while in Des Arc. We are staying at Mrs. Booch's. The accommodations are tolerably good. Had fever in the afternoon. Saw Memphis papers of 5th and 6th.

Friday September 12, '62:
We had a feather bad to sleep on last night. Not being used to such luxuries it was too much for us. We could not sleep and got up this morning both with head aches. Mine lasted all day and in the evening I had a chill. The Memphis papers I saw yesterday confirms a report we had received of a great battle and victory before Washington.[97]

Saturday September 13, 1862:
Had our feather bed changed for a mattress last night and had a delightful

---

[96] DeValls Bluff was the terminal point of a railroad which connected it to Little Rock. The Bluff was also a strong point in the Confederate defenses, protecting both the White River and access to Little Rock.

[97] Bull is referring to the Battle of Second Manassas or Bull Run, which was fought August 29-30, 1862. *O.R.*, vol. 12, pt. 2, 242.

sleep. Feel first rate this morning. We have a Negro woman to wait on us. She is an excellent nurse and does everything in her power to make us comfortable.

Sunday September 14, 1862:

Had another severe chill again last night. Missed my chill this morning for the first time.

Monday September 15, 1862:

Our land lady broke up house keeping this afternoon and when we came to settle we were surprised to find she only(!) charged us $2.00 per day—rather expensive for soldiers getting only $16.00 per month. We had some difficulty in finding another place but finally succeeded in getting accommodations at Mrs. Monroe's. She is a very nice lady, has a comfortable home and gave us a delightful room.

Thursday September 18, '62:

Got two months pay $32.00. News today that Lincoln has proposed peace.

Friday September 19, 1862:

Orders have been issued to march at daylight tomorrow morning. Am anxious to get on the march but it seems like leaving home to leave Mrs Monroe's. She has been so kind to us.

Saturday September 20, 1862:

The order to march was countermanded last night by Gen'l [Theophilus H.] Holmes,[98] who says we cannot move until our command is mustered into the Confederate service, which most of the men have gone in.

Monday September 22, 1862:

Still at Des Arc. Wrote home.

Tuesday September 23, 1862:

Orders have been issued to move at daylight tomorrow.

Wednesday September 24, 1862:

Got up this morning after daylight. Made breakfast on a lunch Mrs. Monroe had prepared last night. Command moved out from camp soon after daylight. Made about fourteen miles in the direction of Searcy.

Thursday September 25 '62:

Marched soon after daylight. Made about 18 miles, reached Searcy at sun down.

---

[98] See Appendix B for biography.

Friday September 26, 1862:
  Marched at sunrise. Made about 12 miles. [illegible].

Saturday September 27, 1862:
  Marched at day break. Struck the mountains soon after leaving camp. Made 18 miles.

Sunday September 28, 1862:
  Marched at day light. Made about 12 miles.

Monday September 29, 1862:
  Marched at sunrise. Made 22 miles over an awful road.

Tuesday September 30, 1862:
  Marched 6 miles. Passed through and camped 1 mile from Clinton. Had a very severe chill.

Wednesday October 1, 1862:
  Made 21 miles over the worst road I ever saw—hilly and rocky—in the first 2 miles we ascended over 13 hundred feet. It rained and I got very wet.

Thursday October 2, 1862:
  Marched at daylight. Passed through Burrville and Lebanon. Rained nearly all day—had a very severe chill. Made 20 miles. Just 11 months since I left home.

Friday October 3, 1862:
  Marched at sunrise. Made 16 miles over a miserable road. Crossed Buffalo Shoal. We caught a scorpion and a tarantula today— the first I ever saw.

Saturday October 4, '62 (Saturday):
  Marched at daylight. Made 12 miles to Yellville.[99] Had a hard chill. Am staying at the Mansion House. Met Sam Ray Burn[100] and Ned Bland today.

---

[99] Parsons's command began their march to Yellville, in north central Arkansas, on September 24, 1862. General Hindman placed Parsons in command at Yellville and envisioned a strike of some type into Missouri. Parsons recommended an attack on either Forsyth or Springfield. The movement never took place as Hindman canceled the orders in October and ordered the Missourians to join his command at Fort Smith, Arkansas. Mosby M. Parsons letters, October 15 and 29, 1862, Peter W. Alexander Collection, Columbia University.

[100] Samuel S. Rayburn, a resident of St. Louis, enlisted in Alexander Steen's Missouri Infantry Regiment on August 12, 1862. He was captured at Helena, Arkansas on July 4, 1863 and paroled in March 1865. National Archives, Record Group M322, roll no. 154, Service Records, Tenth Missouri Infantry.

Monday October 6, 1862:
   Still at Mansion House. Missed my chill today.

Tuesday October 7, 1862:
   Returned to camp today.

Friday October 10, 1862:
   It has been raining for two days. Wind quite cold today.

Wednesday October 15, 1862:
   Jeff Gilespie,[101] Geo. Chapman[102] and I went to the country today to get a food square meal. In the evening I had a chill.

Friday October 17, 1862:
   Our pickets had a fight with the Federals last night. Had a chill in the evening.[103]

Sunday October 19, 1862:
   Jno. Tatum and I went to town. In the evening I had a chill and we remained at the hotel.

Monday October 20, 1862:
   Colonel Parmley [H. A. Parmelee][104] died last night and was buried today. He was an able and popular officer.

Thursday October 23, 1862:
   [James H.] McBride's[105] command got here today. John and I are still at the

---

[101] See Appendix A for service record.

[102] See Appendix A for service record.

[103] On October 12, 1862 Major John C. Wilber led a force of about 225 men from Ozark, Missouri to Yellville, Arkansas in an attempt to destroy the Confederate base. Wilber was unaware that Yellville was occupied by about 1,100 well armed men of Parsons's command. Fortunately, the White River opposite of Yellville was unfordable, forcing Wilber to find an unguarded ferry. Meanwhile, Wilber learned that the rebels were aware of his presence and were attempting to trap him. The Federals gave up the expedition and returned to Ozark. During the return trip, Wilber encountered a seventy-five man force from Yellville, which attacked in the dark and hurried Wilber along to Ozark. The Confederates reported capturing three while having one man slightly wounded. Wilber reported only one man wounded. *O.R.*, vol. 13, 317-318; Parsons letters, October 15 and 17, 1862.

[104] H. A. Parmelee was captured at Camp Jackson and later exchanged. He became paymaster general of the Sixth Division, Missouri State Guard following his release. Peterson, *Sterling Price's Lieutenants*, 173; *O.R.*, Series 2, vol. 1., 557; William N. Hoskin diary, 19, State Historical Society of Missouri, Western Historical Manuscript Collection.

[105] James H. McBride was a Kentuckian by birth and lived in Springfield and Houston, Missouri, prior to the war. Governor Jackson appointed McBride a brigadier general of the Seventh Division, Missouri State Guard on May 18, 1861. He was captured in February 1862,

hotel. I have gotten well but John is still having chills. A good many of the old mess have been promoted. Ed Chappel to Brigade Ordnance Officer, Bill Simpson[106] Assistant Quartermaster, Joe Irwin Assistant Commissary and Geo. Roots [Rootes] Orderly Sergeant of the battery.

Saturday October 25, '62:
    Yesterday it turned very cold and last night we had quite a heavy snow. I went to a school exhibition last night, it was very entertaining.

Sunday October 26, 1862:
    A portion of the command moved in the direction of Huntsville today. The weather has moderated and is quite pleasant.[107]

Wednesday October 29, 1862:
    The balance of the command[108] left Yellville today at 4 o'clock P.M. We marched 10 miles and went into camp at 10 o'clock.[109]

Note: We had a man in our battery, a man by the name of [C.] Shiflet.[110] He was the color bearer. He was a man of powerful frame and the loudest voice I ever heard. Before the war he was a blacksmith. He was fond of singing old camp meeting hymns. While our part of the brigade was separated from the other

---

exchanged, and resigned his commission in the Guard on February 23, 1862. He remained behind in the Trans-Mississippi, when Van Dorn led the Army of the West to Tennessee, to raise troops for the defense of Arkansas and Missouri. In the summer of 1862, General Hindman temporarily appointed McBride a general in the Confederate service, subject to the approval of the Richmond government. Hindman assigned him to command the District of North Arkansas. McBride resigned in September 1862 because of disagreements with General Hindman, but more so because he did not receive a commission from the Confederate Congress. *O.R*, vol. 13, 33; Peterson, *Sterling Price's Lieutenants*, 195; Elmo Ingenthron, *Borderland Rebellion A History of the Civil War on the Missouri-Arkansas Border* (Branson, MO, 1980), 58; Special Order letter book, June-December 1862, Hindman's command, 32-33, Peter W. Alexander Collection, Columbia University; William O. Coleman letters, October 27, 1909 and November 14, 1914, W. L. Skaggs Collection, file #96, Arkansas History Commission, Little Rock, Arkansas.

[106] See Appendix A for service record.

[107] On October 26, 1862 General Hindman ordered Parsons to move his command to McQuires Store, located near Fayetteville, Arkansas. The move was part of Hindman's plans to drive the Federal Army from northwest Arkansas and eventually resulted in the Battle of Prairie Grove. Copy letter book, June-December 1862, Hindman's command, 263-264, Peter W. Alexander Collection, Columbia University.

[108] The command consisted of four regiments of infantry—Robert G. Shaver's Arkansas Regiment, James R. Shaler's Arkansas Regiment, Alexander E. Steen's Missouri Regiment, and James D. White's Missouri Regiment; in all about two thousand armed men. Parsons also commanded James C. Monroe's Arkansas Cavalry Regiment, which was stationed twenty-three miles farther west at Bellefonte, Arkansas. Parsons letters, October 23 and 25, 1862.

[109] Parsons's command travelled due west across northern Arkansas and then turned south and marched to Fort Smith, Arkansas on the Arkansas River and the border with Indian Territory.

[110] See Appendix A for service record.

portion, with which was the headquarters, we had no musical instrument at our headquarters with which to sound reveille. So the commanding officer issued an order for Shiflet to sing every morning to awaken the men. This worked like a charm as the men got up in a good humor and would join in the singing. One of Shiflet's favorite songs ran as follows:

> Yo carry the news Mary,
> Yo carry the news.
> I'm on my way to Glory
> I do believe without a doubt.
> I'm on my way to glory
> The Methodists have a right to shout
> I'm on my way to glory
> Oh Glory, Oh Glory
> Thar's room enough in paradise
> To have a home in Glory

He always wound up his singing by hollowing at the top of his voice "Wo-E-Wo" and was known throughout the command by this name. Men in the infantry would say, as the battery passed along, "There goes old Wo-E-Wo."

Thursday October 30, 1862:
Marched at day light. Made 15 miles. Camped at Bellefonte.

Friday October 31, 1862:
Marched at day light. Overtook Gen'l [Alexander Early] Steen's[111] command during the day. Camped at Carrollton at 3 o'clock. Made 18 miles. Had a chill.

Saturday November 1, 1862:
Marched at sunrise. Had a severe chill. Some prospect of a fight.

Sunday November 2 '62:
Marched at sunrise. Made 12 miles.

Monday November 3, 1862:
Marched soon after daylight. Had a long and hard march over the Boston Mountains. Made 21 miles.

Tuesday November 4, 1862:
Laid in camp all day.

---

[111] See biography in Appendix B.

Wednesday November 5, 1862:
Marched soon after daylight. Made about 12 miles. We are living well. Have plenty of fresh pork.

Thursday November 6, 1862:
Marched at day light. Made 18 miles.

Friday November 7, 1862:
Marched early. Made 15 miles. Reached Gen'l [Thomas C.] Hindman's[112] camp about 12 o'clock. We will remain here sometime most likely.

Sunday November 9, 1862:
Had an inspection.

Monday November 10, 1862:
There has been an entire reorganization of the battery.[113] Capt. Gorham has been thrown out. Buck Tilden has been appointed captain and Alex Lesueur 1st Lieutenant. No other appointments made yet. J. Duncan Holliday[114] got here today.

Tuesday November 11, 1862:
Moved camp about half a mile.

---

[112] See biography in Appendix B.

[113] On November 9, 1862 General Hindman issued Special Order No. 38, which organized his command into four divisions; the First Division contained Douglas Cooper's Indian Brigade and a brigade of Texas cavalry (dismounted); Second Division was commanded by Francis A. Shoup, and contained James Fagan's and Dandridge McRae's Arkansas brigades; Daniel M. Frost, vice M. M. Parsons, commanded the Third Division, with Parsons's and Robert G. Shaver's brigades; and the Fourth Division held Joseph O. Shelby's and Charles A. Carroll's cavalry brigades and was commanded by John S. Marmaduke. Tilden's Battery was assigned to Parsons's Missouri Brigade. Special Order letter book, 109-110.

[114] J. Duncan Holliday was an original member of the Second National Guard Company, St. Louis, Missouri Volunteer Militia. He was captured at Camp Jackson, exchanged in November 1861 and took the steamer *Iatan* south in December 1861. "Military Companies of St. Louis—No. 4 National Guards—2nd Company," Missouri Militia Scrapbook, page 6 of unnumbered pages; Exchanged prisoners of Camp Jackson, Camp Jackson Papers; "Camp Jackson Prisoners," *Missouri Republican*, December 3, 1861.

Chapter 7
The Prairie Grove Campaign
[Diary of Events: November 13 to December 25, 1862]

Thursday November 13 '62:
   Received orders to march at day light this morning. Made 18 miles. Camped on Frog Bayou.

Friday November 14, 1862:
   Marched at sunrise. Crossed Arkansas River. Made about 12 miles.

Monday November 17, 1862:
   In camp. Appointed sergeant.

Tuesday November 18, 1862:
   Moved camp about 5 miles.

Thursday November 20, 1862:
   Heard of the death of Dave Tatum, who was on his way south to join the army.

Friday November 21, 1862:
   Went to Ft. Smith to see the town. Was disappointed in the place.

Saturday November 22, 1862:
   [Entry blurred]

Wednesday November 26, 1862:
   Moved camp to a point on the Arkansas River, about 7 miles from Fort Smith and something less than that from Van Buren.[115]

Saturday November 29, 1862:
   We heard firing all yesterday in the direction of Van Buren.[116] Today while we were cleaning up and preparing for an inspection, we received orders to strike

---

[115] Hindman's First Corps, Trans-Mississippi Army gathered at Massard Prairie, a short distance from Fort Smith, in early November 1862. The various brigades, regiments and batteries came from the Arkansas towns of Little Rock, Pocahontas, Clarendon, Yellville, and the Indian Territory to join with others units already at Fort Smith.

[116] Bull is referring to the Battle of Cane Hill, Arkansas which took place about 55 miles north of Fort Smith. The day long battle occurred on November 28, being a running fight of about ten miles. The battle drove Marmaduke's cavalry division out of the Cane Hill region and set the stage for Hindman's advance to trap the exposed Federals who numbered about 5,000 men. *O.R.*, vol. 22, pt. 1, 41-42.

tents and get ready to move.[117] We left camp at about 3 o'clock P.M. Made 7 miles and camped on the river opposite Van Buren.

Sunday November 30, 1862:[118]
[Joseph O.] Shelby[119] had quite a sharp fight yesterday.[120] We could not cross the river today, had to remain in camp and await our turn to cross river.

Monday December 1, 1862:
Crossed the river. Went into camp about 6 miles from Van Buren.

Tuesday December 2, 1862:
We laid in camp. I left home just over one year ago today. Emmett McDonald has been appointed Brigadier General and he has appointed my brother John his aide, so we will hereafter be in separate commands.

Wednesday December 3, 1862:
Left camp early. Made about 10 miles.[121]

Thursday December 4, 1862:
Marched at daylight. Made 12 miles.

Friday December 5, 1862:
We got up early and made arrangements for a general engagement, our division being held in reserve.[122] At about 3 o'clock we were ordered to advance. We expected a fight but had none, except a small picket fight.[123] Marched about 6 miles, camped on Cove Creek near where we camped last spring just before the Battle of Elk Horn. In the evening the Head Quarters band played "We are Tenting to Night on the Old Camp Ground," which was appropriate and sad

---

[117] The exposed position of the Federal troops at Cane Hill encouraged Hindman to make a long anticipated movement to clear the Union Army out of northwest Arkansas. Forty rounds of ammunition were issued to each man, rations provided, and the command ordered to cross the Arkansas River, preparatory to the northern movement. Banasik, *Prairie Grove*, 291-291.

[118] Hindman held a council or war with his general officers in Van Buren, Arkansas and decided to delay the offensive for two days to allow units time to receive shoes. The army moved forward on December 3. Ibid., 294-295.

[119] See biography in Appendix B.

[120] Bull is referring to Cane Hill on November 28.

[121] Hindman wanted to march about 12-15 miles a day in order to keep his command fresh for the expected battle. His troops were in a half starving condition, which further necessitated the march pace. Banasik, *Prairie Grove*, 293

[122] Parsons's Brigade was part of Daniel M. Frost's Third Division.

[123] Hindman's cavalry advance, commanded by General John S. Marmaduke, encountered Union pickets on the Cove Creek road and quickly dispersed them. Captain Avra Russell of the Second Kansas Cavalry commanded the Union picket force and wisely withdrew, realizing he was confronting a substantial rebel force to his front. Banasik, *Prairie Grove*, 304.

considering all that had occurred since we were last here and the certainty of a battle on the morrow when many more lives would be given to the cause we love so well.[124]

Saturday December 6, '62:
Marched about 6 miles. Went into battery about 2 miles from Cane Hill—had a running fight, the battery did not get into it.[125]

Sunday December 7, 1862:
Left our position of yesterday. Marched about 9 miles in the direction of Fayetteville in order to get in the rear of the enemy at Cane Hill. Shelby had a fight this morning and took about 300 prisoners and 100 wagons.[126] While I write, I hear heavy firing on our left. We expect to be into it soon.

Friday December 12, 1862:
We did get into it. We went into battery 7 times during the day but did not get to fire a shot. We were required while under a heavy fire to reserve our ammunition for an emergency which did not arise.

We were ordered to a position on the left of our brigade when the fight was at it hottest.[127] To reach the position we had to pass in rear of and along the entire length of the brigade, which was in line and fighting most desperately with the enemy. Every shot that was fired at the infantry passed uncomfortably close to us. The cannoneers and drivers were permitted to dismount and shield themselves as much as possible behind the carriages and horses which were led, but the officers and sergeants had to remain mounted and set a good example to the men by <u>appearing</u> to be indifferent to danger. I don't know how it was with the others, but I found it very difficult to avoid <u>ducking</u> when the balls seemed to come very close to my head.

We finally reached our position and got into battery but the order came, as I

---

[124] "We Are Tenting Tonight On The Old Camp Ground" was written in 1861 by Walter Kittredge, a New Hampshire concert ballad singer who was deferred from military service for medical reasons. Being unable to find a publisher for his piece, Kittredge journeyed from Federal camp to camp, singing the song for the troops. The song eventually became a mainstay with Union troops and, it would appear, by late 1862 had found its way to Confederate camps in the Trans-Mississippi as well. Henry Steele Commager, ed., *The Blue and the Gray, Two Volumes in One: The Story of the Civil War As Told By Participants* (Indianapolis, 1950; reprinted New York, 1982), 577.

[125] On December 6, rebel cavalry had a day-long battle for Reed's Mountain, which barred the way to the Cane Hill Valley and the Union Army. Toward the end of the engagement Parsons's Brigade provided infantry and artillery support to secure the mountain. Banasik, *Prairie Grove*, 305-308; *O.R.*, vol. 22, pt. 1, 64.

[126] Bull is a bit exorbitant in his estimate of captures. Shelby captured 21 wagons and no more than 218 prisoners. Banasik, *Prairie Grove*, 346.

[127] As the battle developed Parsons's Brigade deployed to the left of the Confederate line. Ibid., map facing 432.

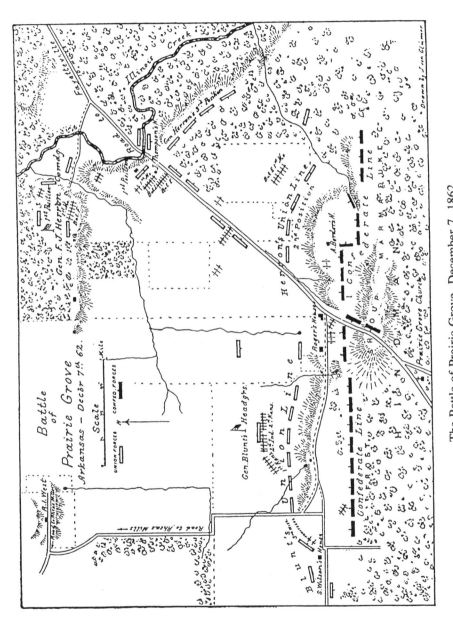

The Battle of Prairie Grove, December 7, 1862
(*Battles and Leaders of the Civil War, Vol. 3:449*)

have stated, to hold our fire for an emergency which did not come. We were particularly anxious to open fire on a Federal battery[128] that was particularly active immediately in our front and within easy range. We afterwards learned this battery was commanded by Capt. Dave Murphy and Jim Marr,[129] an old neighbor friend of ours, was the 1st lieutenant.

We remained under fire until after dark when the firing ceased and we were ordered off the field. At 8 o'clock an order came to use our blankets to muffle the wheels of our artillery. We willingly gave up our blankets for this purpose, although we knew it would be a long time before we could get others, believing it was the intention to move silently and take a position near the enemy and resume the fight in the morning. We soon learned however, that a retreat had been ordered and were not consoled for the loss of our blankets when told the enemy had received large reinforcements and our infantry was out of ammunition. We afterwards learned that the enemy started on the retreat before we did, but learning we had left came back and occupied the field.

My brother John looked me up after the battle and we were rejoiced to find that neither had been injured. We started on the retreat at 11 o'clock and reached Van Buren yesterday [December 11, 1862].

Saturday December 13, '62:

Crossed the river and returned to old camp we left on the 29th of last month.

Note: When the ladies of Fort Smith learned of the battery boys being without blankets they took the carpets from their floors and gave them to us. While these carpets, cut in strips, were fine to sleep on they were not very good for covering us. Their stiffness prevented the close adjustment to the body necessary to keep out the cold, but we were very grateful to the ladies for their kindness. We would not get blankets until we reached Little Rock and in the meantime suffered greatly from the intensely cold weather.

---

[128] The Union battery was Marcus Tenney's First Kansas, which contained six 10-pdr Parrot rifled guns. Ibid., map facing 441; *O.R.*, vol. 22, pt. 1, 75.

[129] Bull is mistaken. David Murphy's battery, Company F, First Missouri Artillery, was located on the left of the Union line, fronting the Confederate right. James Marr commanded a section of three guns of Murphy's company and operated independently from battery for part of the battle, but still fronted the Confederate right.

Company F, First Missouri Light Artillery Regiment, was organized in St. Louis in April 1861 and participated in the capture of the Bull brothers at Camp Jackson on May 10, 1861. The battery was at Wilson's Creek, Newtonia (September 30, 1862), siege of Vicksburg (June 22-July 4, 1863), and siege and capture of Spanish Fort at Mobile, Alabama (March 26-April 8, 1865).

Both Murphy and Marr served in the Union Army on the west side of the Mississippi River. Murphy resigned from the battery in 1863 and later joined the Forty-seventh Missouri Infantry and fought at the Battle of Pilot Knob. James Marr went on to command Company K, First Missouri Artillery. *O.R.*, vol. 41, pt. 1, 447; *O.R.*, vol. 34, pt. 3, 619; *O.R.*, Index, 615, 685; *S.O.R.*, vol. 48, 36-37, 40, 43, 47-48; Banasik, *Prairie Grove*, 371.

One night on the march to Little Rock we camped near a grave yard. The ground was so wet and muddy in camp a number of us went into the grave yard and slept on the flat slabs covering the graves.

Saturday December 20, '62:

Had a grand review today of [Daniel M.] Frost's and [Francis A.] Shoup's[130] Divisions. Generals Holmes and Hindman were there.

The loss of the Confederates in the Battle of Prairie Grove was 1,800 killed, wounded, & missing, that of the Federals was estimated to be greater.[131] Among the Confederate officers, killed were Gen'l [Alexander] Early Steen, Colonel [Hiram L.] Grinstead [Grinsted][132] and Lieutenant Colonel [William C.] Chappel,[133] all of the Missouri troops.

Thursday December 25, 1862 (Christmas):

Contrary to all expectations, we had a very good dinner today. Provisions are very scarce but somebody in the mess has been doing some good foraging. We had chickens, beef, pork and beans, potatoes (slightly frosted), corn bread, molasses, and Lincoln coffee.

---

[130] Francis A. Shoup was born in Indiana in 1834. He graduated from West Point in 1855 number fifteen out of thirty-four. Shoup resigned from the army in 1860, studied law in Indiana and moved to Florida in 1861. He fought at Shiloh as the chief of William J. Hardee's artillery. Shoup joined General Hindman in Arkansas in the summer of 1862, being appointed inspector general of Hindman's staff. The Confederate Congress appointed him a brigadier general on September 12, 1862. Hindman assigned Shoup to command the Second Division of his corps on October 22, 1862. After Prairie Grove, Shoup returned to the east side of the Mississippi River, where he finished his war effort. Banasik, *Prairie Grove*, 471-472; Boatner, *Civil War Dictionary*, 758; Warner, *Generals in Gray*, 275-276.

[131] Confederates lost 164 killed, 817 wounded, and 336 missing for a total of 1,317. The Federals lost 175 killed, 813 wounded and 263 missing for a total of 1,251. *O.R.*, vol. 22, pt. 1, 86, 142.

[132] Colonel Hiram L. Grinsted was born in Lexington, Kentucky in 1829. He studied law and moved to Texas in 1854 and was elected district judge. In 1859 he relocated to Camden, Arkansas, where in 1862, he organized the Thirty-third Arkansas Infantry. Thomas C. Hindman appointed Grinsted a colonel on July 11, 1862. Grinsted fought at Prairie Grove, but did not die nor was he wounded at the battle. On April 30, 1864 Colonel Grinsted died while leading a charge at the Battle of Jenkins' Ferry. Special Order letter book, Special Order No. 28, Trans-Mississippi District, July 11, 1862; Lula Grinstead Smart, "H. L. Grinstead," Confederate Scrapbook, 548-550, Camden Public Library.

[133] Lieutenant Colonel William Chappel was a private in the St. Louis Legion during the Mexican War. He joined the First Division, Missouri State Guard in July 1861 and became a aide-de-camp to General M. Jeff Thompson. He was wounded at Fredericktown, Missouri on October 21, 1861. During the summer of 1862 he helped organize Steen's Regiment (Tenth Missouri Infantry) in which he was second in command. Peterson, *Sterling Price's Lieutenants*, 43.

Chapter 8
Van Buren and the
Movement to Little Rock
[Diary of Events: December 28, 1862 to January 22, 1863]

Sunday December 28 '62:
 Received orders to pack up, strike tents and move battery out immediately as the enemy was coming down upon us.[134] We moved out and formed line in a little prairie 7 miles from Van Buren. The first section of the battery was ordered to a position to command a ford. Our section was sent to a position on the river 3 miles above the other section and 5 miles below Van Buren. During the night the enemy opened fire on the first section and slightly wounded two men.
 We were ordered back and started for Little Rock at 12 o'clock.[135] Made about 7 miles by 4 o'clock the next morning.

Monday December 29 '62:
 Marched at 7 o'clock. Made about 14 miles.

Tuesday December 30, 1862:
 Made about 8 miles. We are on the Van Buren and Little Rock Road.

Wednesday December 31, 1862:
 Got up at 4 o'clock. Weather very cold this morning. Before marching, the division was drawn up to witness a horrible sight; the shooting of two men for deserting. It is a hard punishment but the crime deserves it in most cases.
 We made 13 miles today. We left the Little Rock Road and are now on the Clarksville Road. We will march in that direction tomorrow.

Note: Food was very scarce with us at times not only with the soldiers but with the citizens also. We sometimes existed for days with nothing but horse corn to eat and even that was scarce and was issued in limited quantities to the men for food. When we had meat and bread, we had no salt—there was none to be had in the country. The citizens dug up the floors of their old smoke houses and boiled it to get the small amount of salt it contained.

---

[134] On December 28, 1862 General James G. Blunt launched a surprise attack on Van Buren, Arkansas, capturing the Confederate supply base. Prior to the attack General Hindman had dispersed much of his army, sending his cavalry to Lewisburg to recuperate, and Shoup's Division to Little Rock. Only Frost's Division and John S. Roane's brigade remained in the Fort Smith-Van Buren area to contend with the Union advance. Among the captures were three steamboats and several warehouses with supplies. The losses on both sides were minimal. Blunt reported five or six men wounded. Hindman reported no losses. *O.R.*, vol. 22, pt. 1, 167-168, 171-172.

[135] Under Hindman's original plan Frost's Division, including Parsons's Brigade, was scheduled to leave for Little Rock on December 28. Blunt's attack simply hurried the Confederates along to Little Rock. Ibid., 172.

It was also intensely cold and as we had no blankets after giving ours to muffle the artillery wheels after the battle of Prairie Grove, we spent most of the night around our camp fires. Cold hungry and homesick, we would sing songs of home such as "Do they miss me at home." We would talk of good things to eat, of the dishes our mothers excelled in making. Each in turn would tell what he would rather have to eat if he had the choice of everything in the world.

I remember after due and careful deliberation to have come to the conclusion if I could just have all the corn bread I could eat, the balance of my life would I would gladly compromise on that. Later the salt mines in Louisiana were discovered and after that we had all the salt we wanted. I have never, even in the darkest days in defeat, hardships or starvation heard a Confederate soldier say he was sorry he had joined the army.

Thursday January 1, 1863:
Marched at daylight. Made 13 miles. Camped on the river.

Friday January 2, 1863:
Remained in camp all day. Got orders at about 8 o'clock to break camp and cross the river.[136] Crossed and went into camp _ miles from the river at 12 o'clock.

Saturday January 3d, 1863:
Remained in camp all day.

Sunday January 4, 1863:
Moved at day light. Passed through Clarksville. Made about 10 miles. [Waldo P.] Johnston's[137] command joined us. Saw Jim Otey[138] and the rest of the

---

[136] The brigade camped on Cabin Creek near Clarksville, Arkansas. Copy letter book, January 2-March 14, 1863, Hindman's command, Peter W. Alexander Collection, Columbia University, entry 19.

[137] Bull is referring to Waldo P. Johnson, who was considered a strong Union man. The Missouri Legislature elected Johnson to the United States Senate from Missouri on March 12, 1861 vice James S. Green. Johnson later resigned his position and joined the Missouri State Guard and then the Confederate Army. He fought at Pea Ridge and operated the recruiting service for Missouri troops while under Holmes' and Hindman's commands. In his retreat from Fort Smith Hindman closed Johnson's camp at Horsehead Creek near Clarksville, Arkansas and added the men to his command. McElroy, *Struggle For Missouri*, 47; Snead, *Fight For Missouri*, 88-89; Copy letter book, January 2-March 14, 1863, 3; *O.R.*, vol. 8, 324, 326; *O.R.*, vol. 13, 45, 880-881, 919.

[138] James Otey was a member of the Second National Guard Company, St. Louis, Missouri Volunteer Militia. He was captured at Camp Jackson on May 10, 1861, and exchanged in November 1861. On the National Guard roster his name is spelled "Oley." On November 16, 1862 he enlisted in Richard H. Musser's Missouri Battalion (Eighth Missouri Battalion) at Horsehead Station in Arkansas. He was reduced to the ranks on March 21, 1863 for unspecified conduct. Otey's battalion combined with Charles S. Mitchell's Regiment on April 13, 1863. It appears that Otey became the sergeant major of the new regiment. National Archives, Record

boys. Jim Otey and George O'Flarity[139] took supper with us. At 10 o'clock the long roll was sounded and we got orders to break camp immediately and move back on the road. We went back 1 ½ miles beyond Clarksville. This excitement was caused by a few Jayhawkers, who made a dash into Ozark, frightened the people a little & left. Gen'l Hindman thought they might try the same on Clarksville.[140]

Monday January 5, 1863:
 Our section moved back beyond town leaving the first section on picket.[141]

Tuesday January 6, 1863:
 Went out this morning and relieved the 1st section.

Thursday January 8, 1863:
 Left on march this morning at sun rise. Crossed Piney River on a pontoon bridge and rejoined the balance of the division. Marched 17 miles.

Friday January 9, 1863:
 Marched at sunrise. Passed through Dwight and Russelville. Made 14 miles. It is the opinion not only of the soldiers but also of the citizens that there will be peace by the 1st of April.[142]

Monday January 19, 1863:
 Since making the last note we have had a very hard time. In the first place it rained for several days until the ground became so soft it was impossible for artillery or wagons to move; then it turned very cold, colder than it has been here for years. Snow fell 6 inches deep. Finally we moved to our present position[143]

Group M322, roll no. 145, Service Records, Eighth Missouri Battalion; Exchanged prisoners of Camp Jackson, Camp Jackson Papers; "Military Companies of St. Louis—No. 4 National Guards—2nd Company," Missouri Militia scrapbook, page 6 of unnumbered pages.

[139] George O'Flarity was a private in Boone's Mounted Regiment. He was captured on August 18, 1862 while on furlough in St. Louis. It appears that either he escaped or was exchanged by the time Bull met him in January 1863. National Archives, Recoup Group M322, roll no. 64, Service Record, Boone's Mounted Infantry.

[140] On January 4, 1863 a Federal scout of from 100-150 men proceeded east of Van Buren about seven miles and aroused the local population. Loyal Confederate citizens reported the Union incursion to Hindman's headquarters. Following the embarrassing loss of Van Buren, Hindman had no desire to repeat a mistake and bolstered his rear guard with Parsons's Brigade. Copy letter book, January 2-March 14, 1863, entries 11 and 19.

[141] While Tilden's Battery joined the rear guard the rest of Parsons's Brigade moved beyond Clarksville and encamped on the Big Piney River. Ibid., entry 44.

[142] The rumors of peace were a common occurrence and must have been demoralizing when the peace did not come.

[143] Parsons's Brigade was at Camp Crystal Hill and received orders to move by boat to Little Rock on January 14. On January 15 over a foot of snow fell, making it impossible for the brigade to move. Copy letter book, January 2-March 14, 1863, entries 57, 42, 45-46.

on the Arkansas River about 20 miles above Little Rock waiting for a boat to take us down the river. She has arrived at last. It is the Tallaqua [Tahlequah]. We got ready to leave by 5 o'clock.

Tuesday January 20, 1863:

Reached Little Rock at 8 o'clock last night. Met Captain Fulton this morning. He received us very kindly. Went over the city today and like it very much. Moved to camp in the evening.

Thursday January 22, '63:

Moved to our permanent camp where we will remain during the rainy season. We have a very good camp 1 mile from the city.

Here My Diary Ends

There was a great deal of sickness and many deaths among our soldiers at Little Rock, the result no doubt of our hard march from Van Buren. Among those who died was George O'Flarity a friend and neighbor at home, indeed most of the victims were those who had recently come to us and had not become inured to the hardships and privations of soldiers life.

On February 20, 1863 I received my first furlough for 30 days, which I spent near Searcy, Ark. I went hoping to see my brother John, but his command moved and I did not get to see him. I still have the furlough. At its termination I returned to the command.

Chapter 9
Battle of Helena, Arkansas
(July 4, 1863)

It was decided by the superior officers to make an attack on Helena, Arkansas, in the hope of capturing the place and relieving Vicksburg, which place was being sorely pressed. It was thought if we could get possession of Helena we could interfere with the navigation of the Mississippi River by the Federals to such an extent that they would be compelled to send a large force from in front of Vicksburg to dislodge us, thereby raising the siege of that place.

We commenced the movement from Little Rock about June 1, '63.[144] We crossed the White River at Jacksonport and marched through the bottoms from there to Helena. We found this a most difficult task. There had been heavy rains which made the roads impassable and corduroy roads had to be constructed the entire way; this with the building of bridges across all swollen streams delayed the movement so much that the enemy learned of our coming and had ample time to prepare for our reception and in order to make it as warm as possible had received heavy reinforcements.[145]

While on the march to Helena I had some trouble with some of the officers. As sergeant in command of a detachment I was entitled to a horse to ride. I had a little horse which I had taken good care of and he was in very good condition. One day another sergeant came to me and said he had orders from his Lieutenant to take my horse and hitch him to one of our teams in the place of one of his horses which was broken down. I refused to give up my horse. This was reported to the Lieutenant, who reported me to the Captain for disobedience of orders. The Captain sent for me. I explained to him that the good condition of my horse was due to the good care I had taken of him, that he was too small to work in the

---

[144] General Holmes relocated Price's Division to Jacksonport in early June 1863. Parsons's Brigade arrived in Jacksonport on June 7. On June 14, Holmes requested permission from General E. Kirby Smith, to attack Helena. On June 16 Holmes ordered his commanders at Jacksonport, Arkansas, to begin the movement on Helena. Smith subsequently approved the movement, having been encouraged by the Confederate War Department to make the attempt at relieving pressure on Vicksburg. Price's Division, including Parsons's Brigade, departed Jacksonport on June 22, 1863. Holmes's command united near Cotton Plant, Arkansas on June 26, 1863. *O.R.*, vol. 22, pt. 1, 408-409, 413; James T. Wallace diary, June 7, 1863, Collection No. 3059, Southern Historical Society Collection, University of North Carolina at Chapel Hill.

[145] General Benjamin M. Prentiss had ample warning of the impending attack on Helena. He cited rumors in the local press weeks before the rebel advance began as the initial indications that an attack was imminent. Ten days prior to the battle evidence of an impending attack multiplied; the Confederates closed their lines to citizens, residents of Helena seemed reserved, and rebel pickets were advanced and strengthened. One week prior to the battle Prentiss had the garrison up at 2:30 A.M. in preparation for an attack. Four days prior to the attack Prentiss confirmed the location of Holmes's army as fifteen miles from Helena and advancing slowly. Indeed, the weather provided numerous delays to the rebel attack, allowing sufficient time for the Federals to prepare a devastating welcome. *O.R.*, vol. 22, pt. 1, 387-388.

team, and that I was unwilling to give him up and take a "crow bait" from the herd which contained only broken down horses. He told me I must obey the order or be reduced to the ranks. I told him I preferred the latter, and I, of course, was reduced and went into the battle a private. [Note: The following sentence was crossed out in the original] (The captain was not an efficient officer, he was a favorite of Gen'l Parsons, who made him captain of the battery in place of Captain Gorham, who was popular but not much of a disciplinarian.)[146]

Living in swamps and drinking swamp water made a great many of our men sick. I had camp sickness for a week and could eat nothing. We finally reached a camp[147] on July 3d about 5 miles from Helena where arrangements were completed for the attack which was to be made the following day. It was decided that we would be unable to use our artillery on account of the topography of the country about Helena but volunteers were called for from the members of our battery to go in with the infantry and serve any guns that might be captured. I was one of the thirty-two volunteers, and under the command of 1st Lieutenant A. A. Lesueur we marched that night with the infantry five miles to the position from which we were to attack at day light the following morning.

Parsons's Brigade[148] was assigned to the center position and ordered to assault Grave Yard Hill. We arrived at our post in the investing line several hours before the time for the assault. The intervening time was spent by most of the men in speculations and jests as to the results of the coming battle and by others in giving messages for loved ones in the event of accidents. I was so weak and worn out by my sickness and long march that I threw myself on the ground and was immediately in a sound sleep and when called to take my place in line, did so feeling greatly refreshed.

I had standing next to me a man named Hagerman [or Hagan].[149] While we

---

[146] The previous paragraph was extracted from pages 78-79 of Bull's manuscript and placed here to allow for a better flow of the narrative. The incident occurred on June 1, 1863 at Bayou Meto. Hoskin diary, 50.

[147] The Confederates camped at the Allen Polk house on July 3, preparatory to the attack on Helena. *O.R.*, vol. 22, pt. 1, 409.

[148] Parsons's Brigade contained 1,868 men and organized as follows:
7th Missouri (became 11th Missouri) Infantry, Levin M. Lewis, commanding.
8th Missouri (became 16th Missouri) Infantry, Samuel P. Burns, commanding.
9th Missouri (became 12th Missouri), James D. White, commanding.
10th Missouri, A. C. Pickett, commanding.
Pindall's Sharpshooters (became 9th Battalion Missouri Sharpshooters), Lebbeus A. Pindall, commanding.
Tilden's Battery, Alexander A. Lesueur, commanding.
Ibid., 420-422, 903.

[149] The compiled service records lists the name as "S. Hagan." See Appendix A for service record.

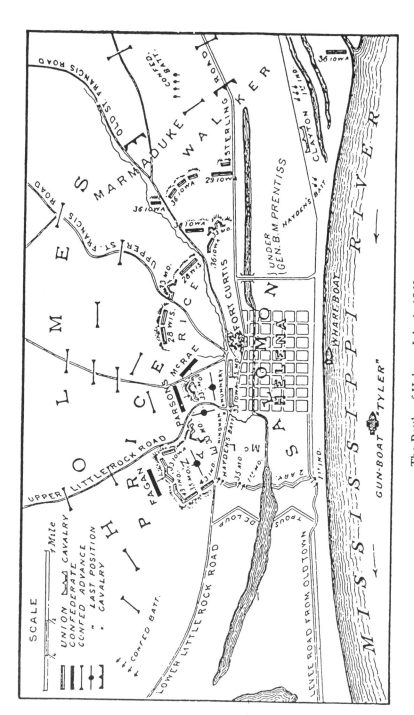

The Battle of Helena, July 4, 1863
(*Battles and Leaders of the Civil War, Vol. 3:455*)

were waiting for the report of a gun on the extreme right of our line, which was to be the signal for a general charge, he talked to me and I found him greatly disposed. He said he had never felt before in going into battle as he felt then. That he could not shake off the feeling that he was going to be shot and would like to make an agreement with me, that if either were shot the other would take care of him. I said I would agree to that and tried ineffectively to cheer him up. Our conversation was interrupted by the signal gun and the order to charge.

The fortifications of the enemy, consisting of well built forts and rifle pits connecting them, were along a very high ridge in rear of and encircling the city of Helena. To reach this ridge it was necessary to pass over three steep and high hills, but not so high as the ridge upon which the fortifications were located. The hills in front of the works had been covered with heavy timber, this had been cut and the trees with their branching limbs allowed to lie where they fell. This made a most excellent abatis.

Our battery boys had been placed on the left of the brigade as it went in. The other units went in columns of divisions, two companies abreast. We were in the first division immediately in the rear of Pindall's Battalion of Sharpshooters,[150] which was deployed as skirmishers.

At the command to charge we made a rush over the top of the first hill, down its opposite side and on to the near side of the next hill where we were halted, in comparative safety, to rest and correct our formation which had become disordered in getting over the felled timber and by the shots of the enemy which was poured upon us from small arms and artillery from the time we appeared on the top of the hill until we were under the protection of the next hill. We did not know the fate of individuals at the time but the gaps in our reformed lines showed the fire had been very disastrous. The dead body of my comrade Hagerman was afterwards found just where he first got under fire, which seemed to confirm, what many believe, that we sometimes have a premonition of approaching death.

After a few minutes rest we were ordered to rush the next hill and then the third and then the fort which was captured. By this time the men of the different companies had become inextricably mixed. I found myself with the infantry and

---

[150] Commanded by Lebbeus Pindall, the sharpshooter battalion was organized on December 2, 1862, with Pindall's appointment to command. At Prairie Grove the battalion contained three companies, adding a fourth company on June 7, 1863 just prior to the Battle of Helena.

Pindall joined the war effort in early 1861, being appointed the Provost Marshal of the Second Division, Missouri State Guard. He was knocked off his horse at the siege of Lexington, Missouri by a cannonball, but recovered. At Pea Ridge, Pindall was a lieutenant colonel, serving in the Third Division, Missouri State Guard. During the summer of 1862 he actively recruited for Missourians, which eventually led to his receiving command of the sharpshooter battalion. Pindall fought at Reed's Mountain (December 6, 1862), Prairie Grove, and all other engagements in which Parsons's Brigade participated during its service in the Civil War. *O.R.*, vol. 3, 193; *O.R.*, vol. 8, 315; *O.R.*, vol. 13, 45; *O.R.*, vol. 53, 458, 460; Wallace diary, June 7, 1863; National Archives, Record Group 109, Muster Rolls, Ninth Battalion Missouri Sharpshooters; Peterson, *Sterling Price's Lieutenants*, 82.

went with them far down into the grave yard, which was located on a ridge running at right angles to the one upon which the forts were located and was being swept by a cross fire of shot and shell from the forts both to the north and to the south of us.

I saw Col. [James D.] White,[151] who commanded one of the regiments of our brigade and seeing none of our battery boys around asked him if he knew where they were. He said he thought they had stopped at the captured fort. While I was talking to him he was shot in the arm. I immediately ran the gauntlet back along the ridge and arrived at the fort uninjured.

I found that an effort had been made to use two pieces of artillery which had been captured but it was found they had been rendered unserviceable by the Federals before abandoning them by "shotting" them—that is by ramming a solid shot into the bore without any powder behind it.[152] In the effort to get one of the guns into position Lieut. Lesueur and several other members of the company were wounded by a Federal shell which burst under the gun they were moving.

The other commands, comprising our army, failed to capture the position they attacked and fell back. Many of our brigade (Parsons) continued the charge into the town of Helena where they were cut off and captured. The remnant of Parsons's Brigade, and some of [Dandridge] McRae's[153] Arkansas Brigade, who had joined us, concentrated in a hollow in front of the captured fort and held it until ordered out by Gen'l Price. Notwithstanding, the fire of the entire Federal line and of the Gun Boat *Tyler*,[154] which was lying in the river, was concentrated

---

[151] James D. White was commissioned a captain in the First Division, Missouri State Guard in May 1861. In October 1861 he was elected colonel, Third Cavalry Regiment of his State Guard division, but mustered out in December 1861. General Hindman appointed White commander of a Missouri Regiment on August 29, 1862. White resigned from the service on February 13, 1863, but his resignation was never accepted. He departed his regiment on August 28, 1863 and went on to become the Provost Marshal of the Second Arkansas District, which encompassed the lower Arkansas River. National Archives, Record Group 109, Confederate Muster Rolls, Twelfth Missouri Infantry; *Sterling Price's Lieutenants*, 53-54; *O.R.*, vol. 48, 249.

[152] Parsons's Brigade captured Battery C of the Helena defenses manned by companies E and H, Thirty-third Missouri Infantry. One gun was shotted as described by Bull, but the other could not be fired due to the lack of "friction primers" which the gunners took with them when they retreated. *O.R.*, vol. 22, pt. 1, 400.

[153] Dandridge McRae was born in Alabama on October 10, 1829, attended college in South Carolina, and moved to Arkansas shortly after he graduated in 1849 to run the family plantation. At the beginning of the Civil War, McRae was the Arkansas Inspector General and then major of the Third Arkansas Infantry Battalion. He fought at Wilson's Creek and was elected colonel of the Twenty-first Arkansas Infantry. After McRae's regiment transferred to east of the Mississippi River, he returned to Arkansas and raised the Twenty-eighth Arkansas Infantry. He was promoted to brigadier general on November 5, 1862, but did not learn of his promotion until after the Battle of Prairie Grove. McRae commanded brigades at Prairie Grove, Helena, the fall of Little Rock (September 10, 1863), and during the Red River Campaign of 1864. He resigned his commission in 1864 and returned to his home in Searcy, Arkansas, where he lived out the remainder of his years. Warner, *Generals in Grey*, 206; Banasik, *Prairie Grove*, 473-474; John M. Harrell, "Arkansas," *Confederate Military History*, 407-408.

[154] The 180-foot *U.S.S. Tyler* was built in 1857 and during the war served on the western

upon that point.

To prevent a charge upon our position we kept up a steady fire. A few of us battery boys got together and would follow one after the other in firing over the top of a stump which stood on the brow of the hill. Just ahead of me was a man named [W. G.] Farris.[155] While in the position to fire, a Federal minnie ball passed through his left hand and lodged in his breast. As he fell back, Bob Young and I caught him and started with him to the bottom of the hill where, we were told, there was a spring.

When we had gotten about half way down the hill there was a rush made by the entire force we had left in front of the fort. We were thrown down and then learned that Gen'l Price had sent in orders for the men to get out as quickly as possible to avoid capture. Young and I went back to our wounded comrade and offered to assist him but he said he could go no further and urged us to leave him and save ourselves by immediate flight. This we reluctantly did.

I was so weak I made slow progress and Young soon left me. Frequently I fell down and would have to rest and must have been killed or captured but for the fact that the enemy seemed not to know, for a long time, that we had fallen back. I finally reached a point of comparative safety where our field hospital had been established and to my amazement found my wounded comrade there, he having gotten out more quickly than I.

Seeing he was in a very bad way I went to an ambulance and asked for some whiskey for him. I was given half a tin cup full but when I took it to him he said he was a son of a preacher and no amount of persuasion would induce him to drink it. So I drank it and it did me much good.

We were urged to hurry on to camp as quickly as possible as an attack from the enemy was momentarily expected. As I started off, fearing in my weakened condition it would be impossible for me to walk the five miles to camp, Harvey Salmon[156] our Brigade Ordnance Officer rode up and seeing my condition gave me his horse to ride to camp. I have ever since had a great fondness for him for his kindness on that occasion.

Farris could not be moved from the field and died in a few days from the effects of his wound. Parsons's Brigade suffered terribly in the battle, losing 800

---

waters. She fought at Belmont, Missouri, forts Henry and Donelson and engaged the rebel ran *Arkansas* on the Yazoo River. The *Tyler* was part of the Western Flotilla and played an important role in defeating the Confederate attack on Helena on July 4, 1863. *O.R.*, vol. 22, pt. 1, 385-386; Tony Gibbons, *Warships and Naval Battles of the Civil War* (New York, 1989), 73.

[155] See Appendix A for service record.

[156] A St. Louisian, Harvey W. Salmon joined the First Regiment, Sixth Division, Missouri State Guard in 1861. He rose to the rank of captain, was captured on December 3, 1861, near Versailles, Missouri, and paroled on February 8, 1862. Salmon was exchanged at Vicksburg on September 20, 1862, and then commanded a company in the First Missouri Cavalry. He was appointed Assistant Ordnance Officer of Parsons's Brigade on February 3, 1864. National Archives, Record Group M322, rolls nos. 7 and 189, Service Records, Missouri State Guard and First Missouri Cavalry; Carylon M. Bartles, *The Forgotten Men: Missouri State Guard* (Shawnee Mission, KS, 1995), 319.

out of 1,800 in killed, wounded, and missing. Out of our 32 battery boys we had 12 casualties.[157]

Our army returned to Little Rock the way we had come. We marched leisurely, no attempt being made by the Federals to follow us. The cavalry under Gen'ls [Lucius Marsh or Marshall] Walker[158] and [John S.] Marmaduke[159] remained in the vicinity of Jacksonport. We were greatly distressed to learn that Vicksburg surrendered on the day we made our attack on Helena.

---

[157] Parsons's Brigade lost 764 men killed, wounded, and missing. *O.R.*, vol. 22, pt. 1, 422.

	Killed	Wounded	Missing	Total
7th Missouri (Lewis)	17	126	54	197
8th Missouri (Burns)	14	82	67	163
9th Missouri (White)	7	53	-	60
10th Missouri (Picket)	11	41	237	289
Pindall's S.S. (Pindall)	9	26	8	43
Tilden's Battery (Lesueur)	1	8	3	12

Grand Total	764

[158] Lucius Marsh or Marshall Walker was born in Tennessee in 1829 and graduated number fifteen of forty-four in the West Point Class of 1850. He served two years in the army and then resigned to pursue the mercantile trade in Memphis. He again entered military service in November 1861, being elected colonel of the Fortieth Tennessee Infantry. After an unsuccessful career east of the Mississippi River, Braxton Bragg transferred Walker to the Trans-Mississippi, noting that Walker could not be trusted with a command. Walker commanded a brigade of cavalry at Helena, after which he had a falling out with John S. Marmaduke over Walker's failure to carry out his perceived mission at Helena on July 4, 1863. The near-sighted Marmaduke killed Walker in a duel near Little Rock on September 6, 1863. Warner, *Generals in Grey*, 322-323; Boatner, *Civil War Dictionary*, 885; Anne Bailey, "Lucius Marshall Walker," *Confederate General*, vol. 6, 92-93.

[159] See Appendix B for biography.

Chapter 10
The Fall of Little Rock

Shortly after our return to Little Rock, Gen'l [John W.] Davidson[160] with about 6000 Federal Cavalry came down Crowley's Ridge, the ridge running in near Helena from Missouri. They finally went to DeValls Bluff on the White River where Gen'l Frederick Steele[161] concentrated a large force whose object was the capture of Little Rock.[162]

The movement on Little Rock commenced about the middle of August and Walker and Marmaduke united their cavalry commands to oppose it, Walker being the senior was in command.[163] Considerable friction and bad feeling was created between these two officers, Marmaduke claiming that Walker failed to give him proper support back at Helena and in resisting the movement on Little Rock. Walker considering that his honor and bravery had been impeached challenged Marmaduke to mortal combat.

They met Sept. 6 on the field of honor and after the exchange of three shots Walker fell with a mortal wound. Col. Bob Crockett[164] was Walker's second and Maj. Henry Ewing[165] acted for Marmaduke. Ewing made an effort to arrange the

---

[160] John Wynn Davidson came from a long line of military officers, with his grandfather being a general officer in the Revolutionary War. John was Virginian, born on August 18, 1824. He graduated from West Point in 1845, number twenty-seven of forty-one. He served in the Mexican War and fought Indians in the pre-Civil War days. Offered a commission in the Confederate Army, Davidson refused, remaining a loyal Unionist. He was appointed a brigadier general on February 3, 1862, and served in the eastern war zone until the August 1862, when he was posted to Missouri. Davidson commanded the District of Missouri (August 6-November 13, 1862) and the District of Southeast Missouri (November 13, 1862-February 23, 1863). During the Little Rock Campaign, he commanded Steele's cavalry division. He left Arkansas on January 30, 1864, and was assigned to duty in the Cavalry Bureau and stationed in St. Louis. In June 1864, the War Department reassigned Davidson to duty as Chief of Cavalry in the Military Division of West Mississippi. He completed his military service on the east side of the Mississippi River. Boatner, *Civil War Dictionary*, 223; Warner, *Generals in Blue*, 112; *O.R.*, vol. 34, pt. 2, 187; *O.R.*, vol. 34, pt. 4, 240-241, 531.

[161] See Appendix B for biography.

[162] Steele's forces consisted of a cavalry division, commanded by John W. Davidson and an infantry division commanded by Colonel S. A. Rice. The command numbered 6,000 cavalry, 6,000 infantry, and 39 pieces of artillery. *O.R.*, vol. 22, pt. 1, 475.

[163] Davidson's division began the Little Rock Campaign from Wittsburg, Arkansas (about fifteen miles north of Madison, on the St. Francis River) on August 1, 1863. The infantry followed from Helena on August 10, 1863. The two forces united at Clarendon, on the White River, on August 17, 1863. *O.R.*, vol. 22, pt. 1, 475, 483-484.

[164] Colonel Robert H. Crockett rose from the rank of major in 1861 to command the Eighteen Arkansas Infantry. Crockett and his regiment were captured at Port Hudson in July 1863. After his exchange, Crockett served in the Trans-Mississippi until the end of the war. Marcus J. Wright, *Arkansas in the War 1861-1865* (Batesville, AR, 1963), 32; Joseph H. Crute, Jr., *Units of the Confederate States Army* (Midlothian, VA, 1987), 52-53; *O.R.*, vol. 15, 934, 1061; *O.R.*, vol. 34, pt. 1, 770; *O.R.*, vol. 41, pt. 3, 944.

[165] Henry Ewing was from Nashville, Tennessee. He served as Marmaduke's Adjutant and

matter amicably but was repulsed by the other side who insisted upon a meeting. Marmaduke was so nearsighted he could not see his adversary when they took their position on the field and it seemed the merest chance that the third shot he fired should have reached a vital point. I knew General Marmaduke intimately in after years and know that the result of this meeting, although not of his making, greatly saddened his life.

Immediately upon the return of the infantry to Little Rock from Helena they were put to work constructing breast-works on the north side of the Arkansas River for the protection of the city. These works extended from the river about five miles back to an impassable swamp [see map]. They were well-constructed with an extensive open space cleared in front, and it would have been extremely difficult, if not impossible, for an enemy to have crossed this open space and capture the works.

The Federals, instead of coming against our strong breast-works as we expected them to do, found a ford below the city and crossed the river at that point. A feeble and ineffective effort was made by some cavalry to prevent this.[166] Being flanked out of our position, to the surprise of everybody, orders were given for the evacuation of the city and as we marched out the Federals marched in and retained possession to the close of the war. I believe the responsibility for the evacuation of Little Rock has never been definitely placed.[167] We left Little Rock Sept. 10, '63, marched through Arkadelphia and

---

Inspector General, a position he maintained throughout the war. After the war he moved to St. Louis, bought and published the newspaper the *St. Louis Times*. A complete biography on Ewing is contained in a book entitled *Tennessee Cavalier in the Missouri Cavalry Major Henry Ewing, C.S.A. of the St. Louis Times. O.R.*, vol. 22, pt. 1, 148, 198; *O.R.*, vol. 22, pt. 2, 1, 113; John S. Marmaduke letters, October 1862, Peter W. Alexander Collection, Columbia University; William J. Crowley, *Tennessee Cavalier in the Missouri Cavalry Major Henry Ewing, C.S.A. of the St. Louis Times* (Columbia, MO, 1978), 167.

[166] In his report of the Little Rock Campaign, General Price stated that there were twelve fords across the Arkansas River, within twelve miles of the city. The Federals selected a horseshoe bend to cross the river just north of Bearskin Lake, about eight miles south of Little Rock. On September 10, 1863, the Unionists placed batteries on the sides of the river bend to protect the crossing. The Confederates opposed the crossing with Chamber B. Etter's four-gun battery and some dismounted cavalry from Archibald Dobbins's Brigade. John Bull, William's brother, commanded the cavalry who opposed the Federal crossing.

In an ensuing action the same day, at Bayou Fourche, the Confederate cavalry fought a delaying action to allow time for the remainder of the Confederate Army to evacuate Little Rock. The Federals lost 18 killed, 118 wounded, and 1 captured in their almost bloodless effort to take Little Rock. The Confederates lost 12 killed, 34 wounded and 18 missing. *O.R.*, vol. 22, pt. 1, 476, 482, 522, 539.

[167] In analyzing the fall of Little Rock, both Albert Castel and Robert E. Shalhope, state that Price did the right thing. Little Rock was impossible to hold given the circumstances of Price's small army and the large area to defend. Contemporaries of the time were not so kind to Price, feeling that the Missourian should have put up a fight for the city. Albert Castel, *General Sterling Price and the Civil War In the West* (Baton Rouge, 1968), 158-160; Robert E. Shalhope, *Sterling Price Portrait of a Southerner* (Columbia, MO, 1971), 243-244.

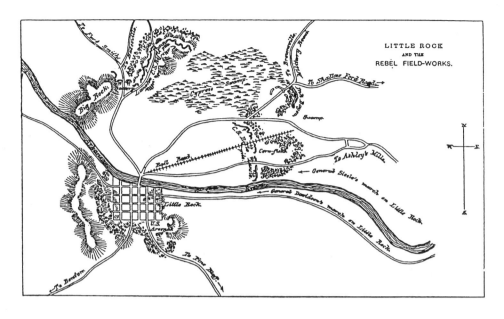

Approaches to Little Rock, August-September, 1863
(*O.R., Series 1, Vol. 22, Part 1:478*)

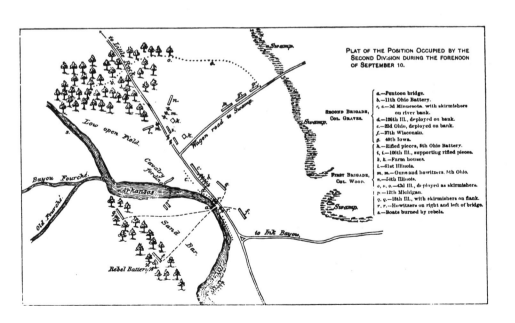

Crossing the Arkansas River at Terry's Ferry, September 10, 1863
(*O.R. Series 1, Vol. 22, Part 1:515*)

established a camp for winter quarters, near Red River, which was known as Camp Bragg. We built log cabins with chimneys and were more comfortable quartered than we had been since we entered the service.

Under the Confederate Army Regulations, all volunteers were entitled to the privilege of electing their officers. Our company had never been allowed to elect its officers. We had an election once but it was not approved at headquarters. This and the fact that the captain did not go into the fight with us at Helena made us determined we would now have an election.

One day we got orders to prepare for an inspection and review. We refused to obey the order. A regiment of infantry marched our entire company to the guard house. Gen'l Price came over in a towering rage and wanted to know what this mutiny meant. One of our men, who had been selected for the purpose, stepped to the front and asked if he might say a few words.

Being given permission, he said in effect, all volunteers in the Confederate service were entitled to select the officers under whom they were to serve. We had been denied this privilege. Notwithstanding, we had sent many petitions to him for an election and that, as we well knew his fondness for his soldiers and his respect for their rights, we suspected our petitions had not reached him. That we had endured patiently what we considered wrong while we were actively campaigning, but that now, being in winter quarters, we thought it the proper time to bring the matter to his attention and had adopted this means of doing so— the usual means having entirely failed.

As our man spoke we saw Gen'l Price's face change from that pained and stern expression which it wore when he called us before him to that of kindness and interest for which he was justly so famous and we knew we had won our case. When he ordered us to our quarters and duty we obeyed most willingly. In a few days an order for an election came which resulted in the election of A. A. Lesueur as Captain and I was elected sergeant to command my old detachment.[168]

---

[168] The mutiny occurred on November 26, 1863. A member of Pindall's Sharpshooter Battalion, James T. Wallace, provided this account of the mutiny. Wallace's account corroborates Bull's story on the matter.

> The battery is in mutiny and refuses to go out on review.
> They are all sent to the guard house and confined there.
> I am on fatigue at the guard house to build chimneys.
> General Parsons makes a speech to the prisoners but it
> does no good. General Price came down and talked to them
> and told them that as they were in a state of mutiny he
> could do nothing for them even if they had been wronged;
> that mutiny must be punished but if they would return to
> duty again he would release them and after that he would
> hear their complaint. They agreed to this and they were
> accordingly released and he promised them that they should
> have an election of officers; this being the cause of
> mutiny not wishing to serve under appointed officers.

December 9, '63 I got a leave of absence for a few days to go to Washington, Ark. to get some clothing sent through the lines to me from home. Old Baurburgo and Max Wells made frequent trips between our army and St. Louis and brought me and others letters and articles of clothing from home. In this way I managed to keep fairly well clothed during the entire war. One of them brought me a uniform at one time, which my father had made by George West[169] in St. Louis. It was about the finest uniform in our army and I was very proud of it.

I found my supplies at Capt. Sanders in Washington—his daughter Zenobia was engaged to be married to my brother John. I had a pleasant visit and at the expiration of my leave of absence, which I still have, I returned to camp.

The election was held on December 18, 1863. A. A. Lesueur was elected captain and B. F. K. Boldridge first lieutenant. Ed Chappell and Lawrence Kingsland were elected second lieutenants. Wallace diary, November 26, 1863; Hoskin diary, vol. 2, 36.

[169] George West commanded Company G (also known as Missouri Guards or Governor's Guard), First Regiment, St. Louis, Missouri Volunteer Militia. West, misspelled as "Wert" in the Official Records, was captured at Camp Jackson, exchanged in November, but never joined either the Missouri State Guard or the Confederate service. West was a veteran of the Mexican War. "Officers of the First Regiment Infantry, Missouri Volunteer Militia," Missouri Militia scrapbook, page 17 of unnumbered pages; "'Volunteer' Reviews History of First Missouri Regiment," News Clippings, 2-4, Camp Jackson Papers; *O.R.*, Series 2, vol. 1, 554.

Chapter 11
Incidents of the War in St. Louis

I have another paper dated January 23d '64 which recalls an interesting incident of the war. It is a permit to go with John Tatum to Magnolia, Arkansas[170] and lead back his horse. Jno. Tatum's family and mine were near neighbors and we went to Wyman's school together when we were little boys and we had been mess and bunk mates since we joined the army—now more than two years.

Reports had been reaching us recently that girls at home, who were engaged to Confederate soldiers, growing tired of their long absence, were in some cases marrying others. These reports made John wild with fear that he might lose the girl whom he was engaged to be married. She lived on 8th Street between Chouteau and Gratiot across the street from my father's residence. He was so unhappy about it that Captain Lesueur succeeded in getting him permission to go to St. Louis, ostensibly to get us clothing and other supplies, but really to see his sweetheart, and he got me the leave of absence, above referred to, to go with him to Magnolia, which was the furthest Confederate outpost, in order that we might be together as long as possible.

We had a sad parting, he to enter the Memphis lines which he knew was full of danger and almost certain death if caught and I to return to camp to the duties and the dangers of the soldier's life.

Tatum had secured a citizens suit of clothes and after many hardships and hair breath escapes, finally reached St. Louis and went to my father's house. A few nights after his arrival he went with his fiancee to Father Ryan's Church and in the presence of a few of his, the young lady's, and my father's families, with no light in the church, except the altar light, they were made man and wife. After a few days stay Tatum started on his return trip.

He took passage on a steam boat going down the river, his intention being to leave the boat at an island near Napoleon, Arkansas. He had been a steam boat clerk and was well known to and well liked by the steam boatmen, most of whom were Southern in their sympathies. Steam boats were allowed to land only at designated points except in an emergency and there were many government spies, special agents. They were called on the boats to see that the regulations were complied with, and particularly that no "aid and comfort" was given to the enemy.

My father had a faithful Irish employee carry Tatum's baggage aboard the boat where it was taken charge of by the engineer and concealed in the engine room. It contained among other things, uniforms for General Price, Captain Lesueur, my brother John and myself. Before the boat reached the island upon which Tatum was to land, the captain told him there were so many Federal spies aboard his boat he did not dare to land and it would be necessary for him to go to

---

[170] Magnolia is located in Columbia County in southwestern Arkansas.

New Orleans, but he would try to land him on his up trip. He left the boat at the stock yards above New Orleans, where the boat stopped to land cattle and went to the home of the engineer where he remained until the boat was ready to make her return trip up the river. Tatum again got aboard and concealed himself.

When the boat arrived near the island, near Napoleon, the engineer in accordance with a prearranged plan, notified the captain that he was short of wood and the captain gave orders to land at the island to take on a supply. It was arranged that when the boat landed, Tatum was to go ashore as though he were the second clerk and measure the wood after which he was to conceal himself in the bushes until the boat had left. He was then to look up the wood choppers on the island, who he was assured were Southern in sympathy and arrange with them to put him over to the Arkansas shore where he would be in easy reach of the Confederate outposts.

While the boat was at the landing the engineer dropped Tatum's baggage overboard through a hole he had cut in the deck, he having attached heavy weights to it to prevent its floating away. When the boat had gone and he had picked his baggage out of the river he found the wood choppers who readily agreed to put him on the Arkansas shore. He returned to his baggage which of course had gotten thoroughly soaked, intending to open it and dry the contents before starting on what might be a long trip. While engaged in this he heard a noise and on looking around found he was surrounded by a Federal guard which demanded his surrender.

The wood choppers had proven treacherous and had gone to the head of the island and signaled a gun boat lying there which sent the guard and made the capture. Tatum was taken aboard the gun boat which was commanded by an officer of the old navy, who had little, if any, animosity against southern soldiers and when he heard Tatum's story and found him to be a gentleman of education & culture, felt a sympathy for him and disinclined to treat him as a prisoner and had him performing clerical duties.[171]

The authorities at Cairo hearing of the capture, gave orders that the prisoner be sent to them. Arriving at Cairo he was thrown into prison, tried by a court martial and sentenced to be hanged as a spy. The authorities offered to spare his life if he would tell who harbored him while in St. Louis. This he refused to do, saying he would rather die than get into trouble those who had befriended him.

His sister, who was married to a Federal officer, hearing of his fate hurried on to Washington City and succeeded in getting a personal interview with President Lincoln, who upon hearing her story ordered Tatum released upon his taking the oath of allegiance. This time he reluctantly accepted as he felt his life belonged to his young wife. He however felt the disgrace of having to abandon the cause he had espoused and it caused him great unhappiness to the day of his

---

[171] Tatum was captured in March 1864 near Honey Island on the Mississippi River by men from the *Marmora*, commanded by Acting Master Thomas Gibson. Tatum's goods were captured and listed as prizes of war, to be sold, with the proceeds going to the crew of the *Marmora*. *N.O.R.*, vol. 26, 15, 581.

death—more than thirty-five years after. The Southern people in St. Louis, notwithstanding they were abused and oppressed and frequently severely punished by imprisonment or banishment by Federal authorities, continued their love for the South to the close of the war and aided the cause in every way in their power. My father, as I have stated lived on Eighth Street between Chouteau Avenue and Gratiot Street.[172] McDowell's Medical College stood at the corner of 8th and Gratiot Streets and was used by the Federals as a military prison.[173]

The Department Commander, Gen'l [John C.] Frémont had his headquarters, and his body guard[174] quartered at the corner of 8th and Chouteau Avenue. Our family and many other families in the neighborhood frequently sent food and other necessities to the prisoners and any that escaped found a place of refuge in my father's house, although if discovered my father's life might have been the penalty.

Col. [William H.] McCowan[175] escaped from the Gratiot Prison through the assistance of a negro man who waited on the officers of the prison. One of the duties of the negro was to remove the ashes from the cellar of the building. He succeeded in getting McCowan into the cellar, blackened his face, dressed him as a negro, put a bucket of ashes on his head and marched him out past the guard. When McCowan got near the guard he hesitated, the negro seeing he was losing his nerve called to him "Come on here with them ashes you black Nigger" and he passed out without the slightest suspicion being aroused. He went to our house and remained there until an opportunity offered to get south.

Colonel [Richard K.] Murrell[176] escaped from the Alton prison and went to

---

[172] The area is now occupied by the Ralston Purina Company, which is south of Busch Stadium and Interstate 64.

[173] The McDowell Medical College Prison was renamed the Gratiot Street Military Prison on May 26, 1862. The Gratiot served as the principal prison facility for prisoners of war or disloyal citizens in the St. Louis area. Special Order No. 279, Provost Marshal General, Department of the Mississippi, May 26 1862, George E. Leighton Collection, box 1, folder 4, Missouri Historical Society.

[174] The bodyguard was known as "Frémont's Guard." The unit was composed of three companies of cavalry, mounted on bay horses, each man armed with a pair of navy revolvers, and commanded by Major Charles Zagonyi. The Guard disbanded on November 28, 1861, less than a month after Frémont was relieved of command. A complete history of the Guard and Frémont's time in Missouri, entitled *The Story of the Guard*, was written by Jessie Benton Frémont, the general's wife, in 1861 (though not published until 1863). McElroy, *Struggle For Missouri*, 227-228; Jessie Benton Frémont, *The Story of the Guard: A Chronicle of the War* (Boston, 1863), 213-214.

[175] McCowan was a member of the Eighth Division, Missouri State Guard. He was wounded at Wilson's Creek on August 10, 1861 and captured on December 26, 1861. Bull's story is supported by the Official Records that speak of McCowan's escape in the manner described. McCowan escaped from Gratiot Prison on October 10, 1862, but was later recaptured. He again escaped on November 6, 1862 and was captured in St. Louis on November 14. He was subsequently exchanged. The incident that Bull refers to occurred on October 10. *O.R.*, Series 2, vol. 4, 668; Bartels, *Forgotten Men*, 243-244; Peterson, *Sterling Price's Lieutenants*, 250.

[176] Richard K. Murrell was elected major of the Eight Cavalry Regiment, Eighth Division,

our house. My father went to Louisville with him and registered the escaped Confederate at the Galt house under the name of a prominent republican of the state. Plans were quickly made for his getting into Confederate lines which after a few days delay he succeeded in doing.

The Southern people in St. Louis who could be trusted were known to each other and they were constantly giving aid and comfort to Confederates and the Confederate cause which, if known to the Federal authorities, would have gotten them into serious trouble. Many who, for business reasons, professed to be loyal to the government were in fact in sympathy with the South. Such as one, a prominent and wealthy man, who gave to my brother and I when we went south, the plan for a shot which he said would easily cut through the iron plates of the gun boats which at the time were being built here [St. Louis].

He also kept a horse, saddle and bridle in Arnot's Livery Stable for any Confederate wishing to get through the lines. When a horse and equipments was taken another was put in its place. His daughters were untiring in rendering "aid and comfort" to the prisoners, and one of them, after the war, married an officer with whom she became acquainted while a prisoner in Gratiot Street Prison.

The Southerners had a secret mode of communicating not only with each other but also with our army. I have said that Mac Wells and Old Bainburger carried letters and supplies, and, I might have added, information, between our army and the city. They would stop outside the city, not daring to come in, and trusted and fearless women would drive out and meet them, receiving what was to be distributed in the city and delivering what was to be taken to the army.

My mother and Mrs. McClure frequently performed this duty. It was considered that women could pass through the lines with more safety than could men. There were many besides those mentioned engaged in the dangerous duty of carrying supplies and information between the city and the army.

One Jim Utly, a school mate of mine, was caught and hanged. Another who frequently brought me supplies and letters, I have forgotten his name, was also hanged. Another, Ab Grimes[177] was caught several times but always managed to

---

Missouri State Guard on July 10, 1861. On October 23 1861 he was elected the lieutenant colonel of the Second Cavalry Regiment of the same division. Murrell was captured in Henry County, Missouri on April 3, 1862, and escaped from Alton, Illinois Prison on July 25, 1862. He was one of thirty-six prisoners who escaped by digging a fifty to sixty foot tunnel from the prisoner's wash-house to a point eight feet beyond the sentinel shack. Peterson, *Sterling Price's Lieutenants*, 247, 270; *O.R.*, Series 2, vol. 4, 317-318.

[177] Absalom Carisle Grimes was born in Kentucky and moved to St. Louis, Missouri in 1859. At the beginning of the war his residence was listed as Ralls County. He was a river boat pilot by trade. He joined the Missouri State Guard in July 1861 and commanded a company which included Lieutenant Samuel Clemens (Mark Twain). He later joined Company K, First Missouri Cavalry as a private. Grimes recorded three escapes from Federal authorities. He was captured a fourth time on November 6, 1863. In an attempted escape in 1864 from Gratiot Street Prison, Grimes was wounded and two other men were killed. After the war he wrote a book of his exploits as a Confederate spy entitled *Confederate Mail Runner, Edited From Captain Grimes' Own Story by M. M. Quaife*, which was published in 1926. Peterson, *Sterling Price's Lieutenants*, 106; *O.R.*, Series 2, vol. 7, 399; National Archives, Record Group M322, roll no. 4, Service

escape and is still living. When it became known that prisoners were to be brought to Gratiot Street Prison, Southerners from all over the city would gather in our neighborhood to see them pass and give them a friendly look if nothing more and to see if there were friends or relatives among them.

There was such a gathering one day. Our house was filled with ladies. One who stood at a third story window had run in from the neighborhood and had on a wrapper with a red border on either side, which, with the white skirt between might easily have been mistaken for a Confederate flag. Such at least a Dutch soldier supposed it to be and reported to the authorities that a Confederate flag had been displayed at our third story window as the prisoners passed the house. The authorities placed a guard around the house and no one was permitted to enter or leave it for a week, the entire family being treated as prisoners and prison fare was issued to them.

There was one person, however who entered the house without permission of the authorities. He was a young man, Basil Elder[178] by name, who lived in the same row and by going through the scuttle in his roof and down through the scuttle in our roof managed to keep our family informed as to what was going on in the outer world. The authorities learning that the Dutch soldier was mistaken and the offending young lady having explained the matter to their satisfaction, the guard was removed. The papers had daily accounts of the imprisoned family. This no doubt was the origin of one of the incidents selected in Winston Churchill's book "The Crisis".[179]

My father was well-known as a Southern man, that he had two sons in the Confederate Army, and he was closely watched. The authorities were more vigilant after this incident to detect him in a disloyal act. He considered his close proximity to the prison where he was constantly under the eye of the guard, was an unsafe place for him and his family so he moved to Carondelet, Missouri[180] and continued to live there until after the war.

It is impossible to relate the suffering endured by the Southern people in St. Louis, the risks they ran to assist their relatives and friends in the Southern Army, nor the outrages committed by the Federal authorities. The crowning outrage was the passage by the Legislature and signing by the Governor, both put in office by Federal bayonets, of what was known as the [Charles] Drake

Records, First Missouri Cavalry.

[178] Basil J. Elder eventually joined Boone's Regiment of Mounted Infantry in 1862. He was captured in Jefferson County on August 18, 1862, exchanged and later enlisted in Company G, Ninth Missouri Infantry (J. B. Clark's Regiment). National Archives, Record Group M322, rolls no. 64 and 146, Service Records, Boone's Mounted Infantry and Ninth Missouri Infantry.

[179] *The Crisis* was written in May 1901 by Winston Churchill (not to be confused with Sir Winston Churchill of World War II fame) and is considered one of the best novels ever written on the Civil War. Churchill was thirty when he wrote the book, which solidified his position as one of America's most popular novelists of the period. The book sold over 320,000 copies when first issued and covered the Civil War in St. Louis during the early days. Winston Churchill, *The Crisis* (introduction by Joseph Mersand, n.p., 1901; reprinted New York, 1961), xiii-xvii.

[180] Now part of modern day St. Louis, located south of Civil War St. Louis.

Constitution.[181] It disenfranchised not only all in so-called rebellion but also those who sympathized with or in any way gave them aid or comfort.

An oath so far-reaching and outrageous in its character was required of those wishing to vote or engage in business, that many Northerners refused to take it. Even ministers of the gospel were required to take this oath before performing their offices and a marriage ceremony performed by a minister who had not taken what was called the list oath was declared illegal. Of course the Southern people would not take the oath and were consequently disenfranchised and found it difficult, if not impossible, to carry on their ordinary associations and were consequently in danger of arrest. After this long digression I will get back to the army.

[181] Missouri's Constitutional Convention opened on January 6, 1865 in St. Louis. Charles Drake was the main proponent of the new Missouri Constitution, which included items like state supported schools and popular ratification of constitutional changes. By far, the most controversial part of the new constitution was the requirement that voters, officeholders, teachers, preachers, and attorneys take an "Ironclad Oath," of support for the government. The oath covered acts and deeds performed during the war years and effectively excluded most rebels or their supporters from Missouri politics. Primm, *Lion in the Valley*, 275-277.

Chapter 12
The War—1864 to the Surrender
(Jenkins' Ferry—April 30, 1864)

Our brigade moved from Camp Bragg to what was known as Camp Sumpter not far from Washington, Arkansas, which was the headquarters for the District of Arkansas. On Feb'y 27, '64, I got a leave of absence which I still have, for a few days to go to Washington to attend the wedding of my brother John to Miss Zenobia Sanders.

After this marriage I was considered, and treated like, a member of the family. The other daughters of Captain Sanders were married; Virginia to Augustus H. Garland, who was in the Confederate Congress and afterwards was governor of the state, United States Senator from Arkansas and Attorney General in President Cleveland's first cabinet; the other Belle to Joe Thomas, who was an officer in the army. It was a delightful household whose factotum was, as nearly all Southern families, was an old Negro mammy, beloved and respected by all, very tall, very black, very thick lips but kind of heart and thoroughly devoted to the family.

While a servant and a slave she had the watchful care of a mother for the girls whose mother died when they were young. The men of the family, as well as the ladies, always kissed old mammy when they went home and when they were leaving. No one ever thought of giving her the unhappiness our failure to do so would have caused. Northern people can never know or understand the real affection which existed between the whites and the blacks in slavery times.

On March 22, '64, Parsons's Division[182] and [Thomas J.] Churchill's

---

[182] When Parsons's command organized in November 1862, it contained five regiments of infantry, a sharpshooter battalion and a four gun battery. By 1864 additional units had been added, allowing the formation of another brigade, thus making Parsons's command a division. On March 26, 1864 the new division was organized as shown below. (James Wallace in his dairy puts the date as March 25, 1864.)

> First Brigade (Col. John B. Clark):
>   8th Missouri Infantry, Col. Charles S. Mitchell
>   9th Missouri Infantry, Col. Richard H. Musser
>   Missouri Battery (four guns), Capt. Samuel T. Ruffner
>
> Second Brigade (Col. Simon Burns):
>   10th Missouri Infantry, Col. William M. Moore
>   11th Missouri Infantry, Lt. Col. Thomas H. Murray
>   12th Missouri Infantry, Col. Willis M. Ponder
>   16th Missouri Infantry, Lt. Col. Pleasant W. H. Cummings
>   9th Missouri Battalion Sharpshooters, Maj. Lebbeus A. Pindall
>   Missouri Battery (four guns), Capt. Alexander A. Lesueur

O.R., vol. 34, pt. 1, 786, 812, 815; Eathan Pinnell diary, March 26, 1864, Missouri Historical Society; Wallace diary, March 25, 1864.

Division[183] were ordered to Shreveport to reinforce Gen'l Dick Taylor,[184] who was charged with the duty of meeting and repulsing the Federal Army under Gen'l [Nathaniel P.] Banks,[185] who had started on his expedition up the Red River. Gen'l Price was left with the cavalry to meet the Federal Army under Gen'l Steele which was marching from Little Rock with the purpose of forming a junction with Banks in an attack on Shreveport.

On April 7, '64, the day before we reached Taylor's army, he saw a good opportunity to attack the Federals at Mansfield, did so and routed them most disastrously.[186] The following day the entire force followed the Federals and on the 9th caught them at Pleasant Hill where another bloody battle was fought.[187] Our battery did not get into the fight as General Parsons held it in reserve and

---

[183] Thomas James Churchill was from Kentucky and studied law until he volunteered for service during the Mexican War. He was captured in January 1847 and not released until Mexico surrendered. After the war he moved to Little Rock. At the beginning of the Civil War, Churchill organized the First Arkansas Mounted Rifles and was elected the unit colonel. He fought at Wilson's Creek and Pea Ridge and for gallant service was promoted to brigadier general on March 6, 1862. He surrendered Arkansas Post in January 1863 and was later exchanged. After a short stay with the Army of Tennessee, Churchill returned to Arkansas, where he commanded an Arkansas division. He participated in the Red River and Camden campaigns. Churchill was promoted to major general on March 18, 1865. After the war he became the governor of Arkansas in 1880 and died in 1905. Churchill's Division was composed of three brigades—James C. Tappan, Alexander T. Hawthorn, and Lucien C. Gause. Anne Bailey, "Thomas James Churchill," *Confederate General*, vol. 1, 186-187; Harrell, "Arkansas," *Confederate Military History*, 394-396; Warner, *Generals in Grey*, 49-50; *O.R.*, vol. 22, pt. 1, 902; *O.R.*, vol. 34, pt. 1, 785.

[184] See Appendix B for biography.

[185] Massachusetts-born Nathaniel P. Banks had no military experience prior to the Civil War. President Lincoln appointed Banks a major general in May 1861 despite objections from his military staff. Banks proved to be an incompetent military commander, performing badly in the East during 1862. In late 1862 he replaced Ben Butler as commander of the Department of the Gulf, headquartered in New Orleans. His most notable military success occurred with the surrender of Port Hudson and this was largely due to the surrender of Vicksburg. Banks's 1864 Red River Campaign was a complete disaster, which only reinforced his status as one of the worst Union generals. Warner, *Generals in Blue*, 17-18; Boatner, *Civil War Dictionary*, 42.

[186] The battle known as Sabine Crossroads by the Federals, or Mansfield by the Confederates, occurred on April 8, 1864 and marked the farthest advance of the Union forces during Banks's campaign. The Federals were routed from the field, losing 2,900-3,200 men, 20 cannon and 200-250 wagons. Confederate losses amounted to about 1,000 of all types. The Official Records listed the Federal losses for April 8, 1864 as 76 killed, 331 wounded, and 1,397 missing. Boatner, *Civil War Dictionary*, 715-716; T. Michael Parrish, *Richard Taylor Soldier Prince of Dixie* (Chapel Hill, NC, 1992), 353-354; *O.R.*, vol. 34, pt. 1, 263-264.

[187] The Battle of Pleasant Hill took place fifteen miles southeast of Mansfield and resulted in a tactical draw, though strategically the battle finished Banks's Red River Campaign. Banks withdrew his command during the night to his base at Grand Ecore. The Confederates left cavalry in the area to hurry the Unionists out of the region while the bulk of the command moved against Frederick Steele's column coming from Little Rock. The Federals lost 1,369 men out of 12,247 engaged at Pleasant Hill while the Confederates lost 1,500 to 1,626 of 14,300. Boatner, *Civil War Dictionary*, 655; John Dimitry, "Louisiana," *Confederate Military History*, vol. 10, 148; Thomas L. Livermore, *Numbers & Losses in the Civil War in America: 1861-1865* (Original Bloomington, 1957; reprinted New York, 1969), 109-110.

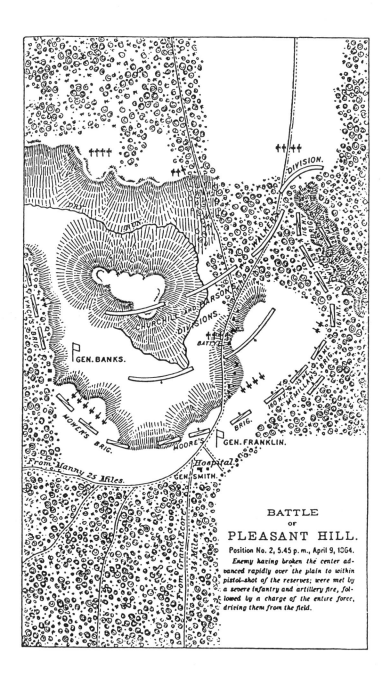

Union Map of the Battle of Pleasant Hill, April 9, 1864
(*O.R., Series 1, Vol. 34, Part 1:231*)

there was no occasion for calling it into action.

We marched over the battlefield of the previous days and I never saw so many dead and wounded and so much artillery and wagons and camp equipage of every kind as the Federals had abandoned.

After the Battle of Pleasant Hill, Gen'l E. Kirby Smith,[188] in command of the Trans-Mississippi Department, fearing Gen'l Steele might prove too strong for the cavalry under Gen'l Price to handle, ordered the divisions of Parsons, Churchill, and [John G.] Walker[189] back into Arkansas to his assistance.

I remember an incident which occurred at about this time, and I will record it here. The Lieutenant, who commanded the section of the battery in which my piece was, and I, on the march, generally rode side by side at the head of the section. Our talk was frequently of home. He was engaged to be married to a young lady in St. Louis.

Speaking of the girls at home getting tired waiting for their Confederate lovers to return and marrying others, he said if his sweetheart should marry, it would not make him unhappy as he could consider her unworthy of him.

One day as we were riding along on the march to Shreveport he asked me if I remembered the conversation we had on this subject. I told him I remembered it very well. He said, "well I have just received a letter from home saying my sweetheart is to be married and I can assure you I feel just as I said I would." After the war he returned home and married her younger sister.

When we got back to Camden we found Price had completely wiped out two large foraging parties of Steele's army, one at Poison Spring and the other at Marks' Mill.[190] Each consisting of several thousand men and had the balance of Steele's army bottled up in Camden behind breastworks which we had constructed.

---

[188] See biography in Appendix B.

[189] John G. Walker was born in Missouri in 1822, attended school in St. Louis and received a direct commission into the U.S. Army in 1846. He served in the Mexican War and resigned his commission in July 1861. He served in the East, where he earned his promotion to major general. In late 1862 Walker transferred to the Trans-Mississippi. Walker commanded a Texas division through the Red River and Camden campaigns. He replaced General Richard Taylor as commander of the District of Western Louisiana in June 1864 and completed his Civil War service commanding the District of Texas, New Mexico, and Arizona. Warner, *Generals in Gray*, 319-320; *O.R.*, vol. 34, pt. 1, 7.

[190] The Battle of Poison Spring occurred on April 18, 1864. It was located about twelve miles west of Camden, Arkansas. The badly outnumbered Federals lost 170 wagons, 4 cannon, and 301 men out of 1,160 present. Confederates lost 114 men.

The Battle of Marks' Mills occurred on April 25, 1864 and proved to be a greater Federal disaster than Poison Spring. Marks' Mills was about twenty-five miles northeast of Camden. Out of about 1,600 effectives the Federals lost about 1,300 men, over 300 wagons, and four pieces of artillery. The Confederates carried about 2,500 men into the battle and lost about 500 men. Edwin C. Bearss, *Steele's Retreat From Camden and the Battle of Jenkins' Ferry* (Little Rock, 1966), 39-41, 76-77; *O.R.*, vol. 34, pt. 1, 786-787.

Our army immediately invested Camden on Ap'l 26 and prepared for an attack.[191] Our battery was in position on the east of the town. Capt. Lesueur had me ride out with him some distance in front of the battery and pointed out a bridge where he said there was an outpost of enemy and ordered me to fire a shot at the bridge. I had my gun moved forward by hand and fired a solid shot. The distance was great and the target seemed small but the following day when we crossed the bridge we found my shot had struck it. When I fired we saw the Federal pickets run from the bridge.[192]

Upon entering the town we found the Federals had burned what they could not carry with them, had crossed the Ouachita River on their pontoon bridge and were on their way to Little Rock, they having hurriedly evacuated the night before.

We started after them as quickly as possible but as they had destroyed their pontoon bridge after crossing, we were delayed in crossing the river.[193] We kept up the pursuit for three days. It rained in torrents all this time and the roads were almost impassable, particularly after the enemy's wagons and artillery had cut them up. But we caught them at Jenkins' Ferry on the Saline River. After a desperate battle in the mud and rain which lasted all day they finally shook themselves loose, crossed the river and continued their hurried flight to Little Rock.

Our battery at the opening of the battle was ordered to a position in a cornfield. It was so muddy the horses had difficulty in pulling the pieces. My piece was the third on the field, but, owing to the superior drill of my detachment, was the first to open fire.

We had no infantry support and after firing a few rounds Gen'l Marmaduke, who had his men dismounted and deployed as skirmishers, ordered us out saying it was no place for artillery. The Federal infantry was in the woods, which concealed them, but so near, they could with good aim have picked us off very easily.[194] Gen'l Marmaduke was the only mounted officer on the field, except ours, every member of his staff having been shot or had his horse shot. As we were going out we met a section of [Samuel T.] Ruffner's Battery,[195] under the command of Lieut. [John O.] Lockhart.[196] Capt. Lesueur

---

[191] Sterling Price's command began the bombardment of Camden on April 22, 1864. E. Kirby Smith's troops arrived between April 20-27 and joined in on the siege of Camden. Parsons's Division arrived on April 23. *O.R.*, vol. 34, pt. 1, 668, 781-782; Pinnell diary, April 23, 1864.

[192] The incident that Bull relates is also covered in Eathan Pinnell's and William Hoskin's diaries, which lists the date as April 23, 1864. It occurred the same day that Parsons's command arrived in the Camden area. Pinnell diary, April 23, 1864; Hoskin diary, April 23, 1864, vol. 2, 57.

[193] Confederates completed a pontoon bridge and crossed the Ouachita River on April 28, 1864. *O.R.*, vol. 34, pt. 1, 782.

[194] The Federal troops were the Second Kansas Colored Infantry. *O.R.*, vol. 34, pt. 1, 669.

[195] Ruffner's Battery (Also known as Roberts's Battery or the Eighth Missouri Battery) was organized on September 7, 1862 near Newtonia, Missouri from two guns captured at Lone Jack, Missouri on August 16, 1862. Westley Roberts was the first captain of the battery and Samuel T.

told him he had better turn back as Gen'l Marmaduke had ordered us out. "No," he said, "I have been ordered in and must obey the order." When he got to the position we had left nearly all of his men and horses were killed or wounded and his guns captured.[197]

Our battery moved back and with several other batteries took position on elevated ground to repel the enemy should he succeed in driving our infantry in the death struggle in which they were engaged in the river bottom, about half a mile away in our front. We had marched day and night through rain and mud in pursuit of Steele and it seemed probable we would have to pursue him further.

It was my habit to get sleep whenever I had the chance. Believing it would be sometime before our infantry could be driven back and we called into action I coiled up on an ammunition chest for a nap telling my gunner to call me if we were needed. Notwithstanding the roar of the musketry and artillery half a mile away I enjoyed a very refreshing sleep.

Both armies suffered very heavy loss, but we fortunately had none in our battery.[198]

Parsons's Division at this time consisted of the following commands:
1st Brigade, Gen'l John B. Clark,[199] Jr. Comd'g

Ruffner the second lieutenant. The battery eventually contained two twelve-pounder James rifles (from Lone Jack) and two six-pounder smoothbore guns (from Fort Smith, Arkansas). The battery fought at Prairie Grove, after which a discouraged Captain Roberts tendered his resignation.

Samuel T. Ruffner enlisted in the Missouri State Guard on July 20, 1862, serving as a private until his election to second lieutenant in September 1862. After Roberts resigned, Ruffner commanded the battery. S. T. Ruffner, "Sketch of First Missouri Battery, C.S.A.," *Confederate Veteran* (Nashville, 1912), vol. 20, 417-418; W. Roberts, Manuscript report on the Battle at Prairie Grove, no date, Francis Herron War Papers, New York Historical Society; National Archives, Record Group 109, Confederate Muster Rolls, Roberts/Ruffner's Battery; National Archives, Record Group M322, roll no. 83, Service Records, Eighth Missouri Battery.

[196] The Virginia born John O. Lockhart lived near Waverly, Lafayette County, Missouri. He was elected second lieutenant of Company C, Second Regiment, Eight Division, Missouri State Guard on September 8, 1861. He subsequently became the first lieutenant of Roberts' Battery on September 7, 1862. Lockhart was wounded at the Battle of Jenkins' Ferry. Peterson, *Sterling Price's Lieutenants*, 224; National Archives, Record Group M322, rolls no. 83 and 185, Service Records, First Field Battery Missouri Artillery and Missouri State Guard.

[197] Lockhart reported his losses as two guns, four killed, six wounded and seven captured or missing out of thirty-two men he carried into the battle. *O.R.*, vol. 34, pt. 1, 813.

[198] The Federals had about 700 casualties of 4,000 engaged, while the Confederates lost Ruffner's two guns and about 1,000 men of 6,000 engaged. Parsons's Division lost 28 killed, 124 wounded and 6 missing of which Lesueur's Battery lost one man wounded. Even though the rebels won the Battle of Jenkins' Ferry they failed to destroy Steele's army, which stumbled back into Little Rock. Bearss, *Steele's Retreat From Camden*, 161; *O.R.*, vol. 34, pt. 1, 810, 816.

[199] A native Missourian, John B. Clark, Jr. was elected captain of Company C, First Infantry Regiment, Third Division, Missouri State Guard in May 1861. He subsequently rose to brigadier general, commanding the division. Clark was appointed a colonel in the Confederate Army on June 28, 1862 and assigned by Thomas C. Hindman to command the Ninth Missouri Infantry in northwest Arkansas. He was promoted to brigadier general on March 8, 1864, having fought in most major engagements west of the Mississippi River. After the war, Clark was elected to the U.S. Congress (1873-1883) from Missouri. He died in 1903. Moore, "Missouri," *Confederate*

8th Mo. Infantry, Col. C. S. Mitchell[200]
9th .. .., Col. R. H. Musser[201]
Ruffner's 4 gun battery
2nd Brigade (Parsons), Col. S. P. Burns,[202] Comd'g
10th Missouri Infantry, Col. W'm M. Moore[203]
11th .. .., Lieut. Col. Tho's H. Murray[204]
12th .. .., Col. Willis M. Ponder[205]

Military History, vol. 9, 206-208; Special Order letter book, Special Order No. 38; Peterson, *Sterling Price's Lieutenants*, 107, 113, 115; Warner, *Generals in Gray*, 52; National Archives, Record Group M322, roll no. 36, Service Records, Ninth Missouri Infantry.

[200] Charles S. Mitchell was born in Wisconsin, moved to Saline County, Missouri, and on August 8, 1862 was elected colonel of the Eighth Missouri Infantry. The Confederate Congress appointed Mitchell a colonel to rank from his election date. He served as colonel of his unit throughout the war. National Archives, Record Group M322, roll. no. 142, Service Records, Seventh/Eighth Missouri Infantry; Pinnell diary, August 7, 1862.

[201] Richard H. Musser was appointed Judge Advocate General of the Third Division, Missouri State Guard on June 23, 1861. He later entered Confederate service, raised a battalion of infantry, which united with other units on January 4 1863 to form John B. Clark's Missouri Infantry Brigade. On September 30, 1863 Musser's Battalion and Clarks' Infantry Regiment consolidated to form a new regiment. On December 15, 1863, per Special Order No. 177, Headquarters, Price's Division, the unit was designated the Ninth Missouri Infantry. Peterson, *Sterling Price's Lieutenants*, 108; National Archives, Record Group 109, Confederate Muster Rolls, Ninth Missouri Infantry; Pinnell diary, January 6, 1863.

[202] Simon P. Burns was born in Ohio, moved to western Missouri and enlisted in DeWitt C. Hunter's cavalry battalion as a private on July 21, 1862. He was elected major of Hunter's command on September 1, 1862 and lieutenant colonel on September 15, 1862. When Hunter resigned on March 24, 1863 Burns was promoted to colonel of the regiment. The Confederate Congress appointed Burns a colonel on January 8, 1864 to rank from March 24, 1863. National Archives, Record Group M322, roll no. 156, Service Records, Eleventh Missouri Infantry.

[203] William M. Moore entered the Missouri State Guard in 1861, being appointed the adjutant of the First Cavalry and later Fifth Cavalry Regiment, Second Division, Missouri State Guard. He was wounded at Lexington in September 1861. Moore was appointed lieutenant colonel of his regiment following the Battle of Pea Ridge. He entered Confederate service in 1862 and organized Company A, Steen's Missouri Infantry (Tenth Missouri) on November 10. Moore was promoted to colonel of the Tenth Missouri on December 2, 1863. He was again wounded at the Battle of Jenkins' Ferry on April 30, 1864. Peterson, *Sterling Price's Lieutenants*, 84, 94; National Archives, Record Group M322, roll no. 154, Service Records, Tenth Missouri Infantry; *O.R.*, vol. 34, pt. 1, 815.

[204] Thomas H. Murray born in Kentucky, moved to Missouri, and entered the Missouri State Guard on July 4, 1861. He subsequently resigned on August 13. On May 30, 1862 he entered Confederate service, being elected a major in DeWitt C. Hunter's Missouri Infantry on September 15, 1862. Murray became the lieutenant colonel of the regiment on March 24, 1863 when S. P. Burns was promoted to colonel. He was wounded at Helena, Arkansas and Pleasant Hill, but recovered. National archives, Record Group M322, roll no. 159, Service Records, Eleventh Missouri Infantry; Peterson, *Sterling Price's Lieutenants*, 232.

[205] Willis Miles Ponder entered the Missouri State Guard on July 8, 1861, being elected major of the Third Infantry Regiment, First Division, Missouri State Guard. He resigned in January 1862. In July 1862 he entered the Confederate service and organized Company A, Twelfth Missouri Infantry. He became the lieutenant colonel of the regiment on February 19, 1863 and

16th .. .., Lieut. Col. P. W. Cumming[206]
Pindall's Battalion Sharpshooters, Maj. L. A. Pindall
Lesueur's 4 gun battery, Capt. A. A. Lesueur

Col. [Levin M.] Lewis[207] and I believe Col. [James D.] White[208] were captured at Helena, the former was afterwards promoted to brigadier general. I do not know what became of the latter.

After the Battle of Jenkins' Ferry our command went into camp near Camden, Ark. About Sep. 6, 1864 Bob Young and I got permission to go before a board which was to meet at Shreveport to examine applicants for commission in the Ordnance Department. We got recommendations from Gen'l Parsons and Capt. Lesueur and I had an item from Governor Trusten Polk and Col. H. Clay Taylor[209].

We left camp in time to reach Shreveport without being hurried, stopping at nice places on the way. One morning after leaving a very pleasant place where we had spent several days, being quite warm, I took off my coat and threw it

---

colonel in August. Peterson, *Sterling Price's Lieutenants*, 65; National Archives, Record Group M861, roll no. 36, Records of Confederate Movements and Activities, Twelfth Missouri Infantry; National Archives, Record Group M109, Confederate Muster Rolls, Twelfth Missouri Infantry.

[206] Pleasant W. H. Cummings was born in Tennessee, and moved to McDonald Country, Missouri. He joined the Missouri State Guard, being elected captain of Company D, Sixth Cavalry Regiment, Eighth Division on September 28, 1861. He resigned in December 1861 and entered Confederate service on July 19, 1862 as a private in Sidney D. Jackman's Missouri Regiment (became the Sixteenth Missouri). Cummings was elected major of the command on August 31, 1862, and lieutenant colonel on March 24, 1863 after Levin Lewis was promoted to colonel. Assumed command of the regiment after Lewis was captured at Helena and retained the command until the end of the war. Cummings was wounded at Helena. Peterson, *Sterling Price's Lieutenants*, 265; National Archives, Record Group M322, roll. no. 167, Service Records, Sixteenth Missouri Infantry.

[207] Levin M. Lewis was born in Maryland in 1832, attended the Maryland Military Academy, Wesleyan University, and studied law from 1851-1855 at Cambridge, Maryland. He moved to Missouri in 1855 and settled in Clay County. In April 1861, Governor Jackson appointed Lewis colonel of the Third Regiment, Fifth Division, Missouri State Guard. He fought at the Battle of Pea Ridge and later joined the Confederate service. Lewis organized Company A, Sixteenth Missouri Infantry on June 18, 1862, and became the colonel of the regiment in March 1863. He was captured at the Battle of Helena and exchanged in August or September 1864. He rejoined the Trans-Mississippi Department in late 1864, and on May 16, 1865, General E. Kirby Smith promoted him to brigadier general. After the war Lewis taught at various colleges or preached the gospel. He died in 1887 while in California. Peterson, *Sterling Price's Lieutenants*, 163; Arthur Bergeron, Jr., "Levin M. Lewis," *Confederate General*, vol. 6, 188-189; National Archives, Record Group M322, roll no. 1690, Service Records, Sixteenth Missouri Infantry; National Archives, Record Group 109, Confederate Muster Rolls, Sixteenth Missouri Infantry.

[208] White was not captured at Helena. See note no. 151.

[209] Taylor joined the Missouri State Guard in 1861 as the aide-de-camp to Major General Sterling Price. On June 6, 1863, Price appointed Taylor his Chief of Artillery and Ordnance. Taylor later became the Chief of Ordnance for the District of Arkansas, serving in the position to the end of the war. Peterson, *Sterling Price's Lieutenants*, 62; *O.R.*, vol. 8, 794; *O.R.*, vol. 22, pt. 2, 860; *O.R.*, vol. 41, pt. 4, 1,099.

across my saddle. After riding several hours I happened to think of our papers which I carried in my coat pockets. To our dismay and great distress we found they were gone. We rode back some distance but could not find them. We knew it was almost useless to go before the board of strangers without recommendations but concluded to take the chance.

We stopped at a hotel opposite Shreveport where we could cross the river[210] to the city on a pontoon bridge. The hotel was filled with refugees from New Orleans and other places. One evening I finished my supper more quickly than the other quests and went to the upper veranda on the third floor to have my smoke. While sitting there alone I saw a very bright light through the window of one of the front rooms. I went immediately to investigate the cause and met a little negro girl running from the room crying fire.

I rushed into the room and found the mosquito bar covering the bed, in flames and a little child lying asleep on the bed—burning cinders of the mosquito bar were falling on it. I took the child in my arms, tore down the mosquito bar and extinguished the fire.

The cries of the negro girl had by this time alarmed the household and the guests came running upstairs, the mother of the child in the lead. She was greatly relieved to find her baby uninjured and was most profuse in her thanks to me. The incident was of little importance but served to make me acquainted, and I may say popular, with the ladies of the house.

The examination was held on a steamboat in the Red River. I think we both passed good examinations but as there were only about half a dozen appointments to make and about one hundred and fifty applicants, we, of course, with no recommendations, got left.

I received, and still have, a pass back to my command from Gen'l E. Kirby Smith dated Sep. 6, 1864. We returned quite crestfallen but Col. Clay Taylor, who was Col. of Ordnance, raised my hopes somewhat when he told me at Camden he heard that I had passed and that he had made application to have me assigned to duty with him. It must have been a mistake as I heard nothing more of it.

Gen'l Price started on his raid into Missouri from Camden on Sep. 6, '64. He did great damage to the enemy but his soldiers endured great suffering and hardships and had much hard fighting to do before he got back in November. As he only took cavalry and the artillery attached to cavalry with him, we of course, did not go but remained in camp at Camden.

My brother John went as Lieut. Col. of a cavalry regiment in [William L.] Cabell's[211] Brigade. In a fight near St. Louis he was wounded in the knee. He

---

[210] The Red River flowed by Shreveport.

[211] William L. Cabell was born in Danville, Virginia on January 1, 1827, attended West Point and graduated in 1850, number thirty-three of forty-four. At the beginning of the Civil War he served primarily in the Quartermaster Department, east of the Mississippi River. Cabell commanded a brigade under Earl Van Dorn and was wounded at Corinth in October 1862. Back in Arkansas in November 1862, General Holmes appointed him the inspecting officer of the

had a very faithful negro servant named Sam, who had but one serious fault, that of drinking too much at times. When he heard that John was wounded and was being brought to camp he ran out and met the ambulance and begged John to get on his back that he might carry him to camp. He did so to please the faithful fellow but he had not gone far when he fell and hurt John badly. John then discovered that Sam had been drinking. Becoming very angry he told Sam if he ever came into his presence again in that condition he would shoot him.

Sam was very penitent and kept sober for some time but one day after Gen'l Price had started on his retreat from Missouri he got whiskey and took too much again. He was afraid that John might shoot him if he went into camp so he laid out in a fence corner all night. Price's army moved early the following morning and the Federals coming along in close pursuit found Sam still asleep and made him a prisoner. He was sent with other prisoners to Gratiot Street Prison in St. Louis. There he was told as he was a negro he could take the oath of allegiance and be released. He said, "No sir, my master is a Confederate and I'se a Confederate and I ain't going to take your oath." So they put him back in prison and we found him there on our return home after the close of the war the next year.

November 14, '64, I received a letter from my sister-in-law, Zenobia, which I still have, in which she says she had one from John at Cane Hill dated November 2. It is a nice sweet letter and shows the great struggle in the breasts of Southern women between their duty to their Government and their anxiety regarding the loved ones in the army.

On December 1, '64, at Camden I received written order from Capt. Lesueur, which I still have, to report to Capt. [Chambers B.] Etter,[212] Chief of Artillery, Defenses of Camden, as artillery drill master. He assigned me to drill the battery in the fort on Point Lookout. I have a letter from Captain Etter, dated December 9, '64 calling for a report as to which supplies and equipment were needed also an outline of my report.

I had always taken a great interest in drilling and in the study of the tactics and had the best drilled detachment in the battery and it was always called upon to drill on show occasions. This was no doubt as the reason for my assignment as

---

Quartermaster Department. He was promoted to brigadier general on April 23, 1863 and again commanded troops, participating in an attack on Fayetteville, Arkansas in April 1863 and the Camden Campaign of 1864. Cabell was captured during Price's 1864 Missouri Raid at Mine Creek, Kansas on October 25, 1864. He died in Dallas, Texas on February 22, 1911 after serving four terms as mayor. *O.R.*, vol. 13, 915; Boatner, *Civil War Dictionary*, 111-112; Anne Bailey, William Lewis Cabell," *Confederate General*, vol. 1, 154-157; Warner, *Generals in Gray*, 41-42.

[212] Chambers B. Etter organized an artillery company on June 14, 1862 at Washington, Arkansas as part of the Confederates attempt to reorganize the Trans-Mississippi following the departure of Van Dorn's army in April 1862. Initially issued six, ten-pounder Parrot rifled guns, Etter's Battery was issued new guns in October 1862. Etter participated in the Little Rock Campaign of 1863 and the Red River Campaign of 1864. "Artillery," *Washington Telegraph* (Washington, Arkansas), June 18, 1862; Copy letter book, June-December 1862, 66-67, 206; *O.R.*, vol. 22, pt. 1, 529; *O.R.*, vol. 34, pt. 1, 566.

artillery drill master. I have an order from Gen'l Parsons dated December 11, '64, confirming my appointment. I have an order dated January 7, '65, to report back to my company but instead was sent to drill the battery in Fort Southland [Southerland] and continued in that position until our troops were ordered to evacuate Camden and march to Shreveport where they surrendered May 26, '65.

Before leaving Camden, I, in obedience with orders disabled the guns in Fort Southland [Southerland] and exploded the magazine. This was necessary as we had no horses to move the guns. I received a leave of absence to visit Washington on the way to Shreveport to get some supplies brought me through the lines by Miss Eliza A. Dean.[213] While there I learned of the surrender and after a few days started for home via Little Rock.

---

[213] Miss Dean passed through the Union lines on February 28, 1865. Her party consisted of several ladies carrying letters from and to prisoners of war and, it would appear, supplies for selected members of the Confederate Army. *O.R.*, vol. 48, 1, 139-140.

Chapter 13[214]
The Road Home and the End of Service

Flemming[215] of Ruffner's battery, who was also visiting in Washington went with me that far. I gave a new silk handkerchief, which was among the articles brought me through the lines to have our horses shod.

Our trip was uneventful until we got near Little Rock. There we met a mover from whom we enquired, and wisely, as to how the Federals would treat us if we went into the city. He said, they would treat us all right but they would take my horse from me as it had the C.S. brand showing it belonged to the Confederate Government. He had a spirited team to his wagon, consisting of two oxen and a very small pony. He suggested that I trade my horse for his pony. The trade was finally consummated, he giving me ten dollars in green backs to boot.

This was the first green back I had ever owned and I was glad to get it as I hadn't a cent except Confederate money. I felt too, I would rather the mover would have my little horse than the Federal Government as I was sure he would receive better treatment. I was attached to the horse as we had been constant companions for several years and it was the horse about which I had the trouble with the officer just before the Battle of Helena.

We soon reached the outpost and after the exchanges of a few pleasant words we passed on and into the city. Upon enquiry I found where Capt. Fulton lived and went immediately to his house where I received a cordial welcome. I gave Flemming my pony, saddle and bridle and he went to his brother's plantation on the Arkansas River.

I telegraphed home, but afterwards learned that the lines were so busy with official business that my message was not sent. Jim Marr, who was a neighbor and friend in Carondelet before the war, learning I was in the city, called to see me. He was a Lieutenant in a Federal artillery company and was most cordial in his greeting and kind and attentive during my stay in Little Rock. A few days after my arrival he asked me if I had seen Mr. Tucker. I asked him, who Mr. Tucker was. He told me, he was the president of one of the banks in the city and that he wanted to see me.

I immediately called on him and to my delight was told he had received a

---

[214] This chapter is presented to give the reader a flavor of post-war St. Louis and not highly annotated as the other chapters. Many of the names associated with this chapter had no clear connection with the Civil War years or had no significance other than what Bull writes about in his account.

[215] This Flemming should not be confused with John Flemming, who served in Lesueur's Battery. There were two Flemings in Ruffner's Battery, Patrick and Nicholas. Both listed their residence as Bossier Parish, Louisiana, which could have been a lie. They gave the data to Federal authorities upon their parole in June 1865 and may have feared the consequences of having served in the rebel army. National Archives, Record Group M322, roll. no. 83, Service Records, First Field Battery Missouri Artillery.

letter from my father enclosing $300.00, which he was to give to John and me to get home. I took $100.00 and left the balance for John who was to follow soon with his wife. This money not only enabled me to get home comfortably but also to assist others in doing so.

I took a train to Memphis where I found our father had sent John and me clothing. I also procured transportation there from the Government officials to St. Louis, but as it was only good on Government transportation I did not use it, preferring to go on a regular passenger steamer and pay my way. I still have the order for transportation dated June 16, 1865.

It is impossible to describe the joy which filled our hearts upon my reaching home safe and sound after an absence of more than three and a half years which had been filled with dangers and hardships not only to John and me but also to the loved ones at home who were in constant danger of punishment if not death for their efforts in behalf of the cause we all loved so much. Our cup of happiness was entirely filled when a short time later, John arrived with his wife.

My father thinking it desirable to get us into business as quickly as possible in order to divert our minds from the failure of our cause, suggested that I take a shipment of such articles as were most needed in the South to Camden, Ark. where I had been stationed so long and knew the people so well. I readily consented, believing it would be a good business venture but that is another story and need not be related here. Sufficient to say in order to engage in business it was necessary for me to take the oath of allegiance which I did on June 19, '65 and still have a copy of it.

I had not even given my parole since entering the Federal lines and disliked to take the oath although it had no dishonor attached to it as our armies had all surrendered and the war was over beyond any question. I have always respected that oath and have ever been ready to defend the Government against domestic or foreign foes and I believe every Confederate soldier has felt the same way.

My military ardor had not been entirely destroyed and in about 1870 I joined in a movement to reorganize the old Engineer Corp to which I belonged at and before Camp Jackson. We succeeded in enlisting about one hundred of the most prominent young men, socially and in business circles, in the city. Colonel J. N. Pritchard[216] was our first captain. He was succeeded by J. H. Slocum. The lieutenants were Maj. Henry W. Ewing, who was on Marmaduke's staff and Geo. Chapman,[217] who was a lieutenant in the Confederate Army. The sergeants

---

[216] J. N. Pritchard was a founding member of the First National Guard Company, St. Louis, Missouri Volunteer Militia and a strong Unionist. At the first company election, Pritchard was elected first lieutenant. In 1854 he became the captain of the National Guards. In 1858 Pritchard was elected the lieutenant colonel of the First Regiment, Missouri State Militia, and prior to the Civil War was the colonel of the regiment. He resigned from the militia in April 1861 because of his support for the Union. Snead, *Fight For Missouri*, 154; "The National Guards," Missouri Militia scrapbook, page 5 of unnumbered pages.

[217] George J. Chapman was a founding member of the Second National Guard Company, St. Louis, Missouri. Volunteer Militia which was organized in 1858. He was captured at Camp Jackson on May 10, 1861 and paroled in November 1861. He was appointed a first lieutenant in a

were C. P. Ellenbe, H. H. Marmaduke, Thomas H. Larkin, Bob Sickles and myself. Among the corporals and privates were D. R. Francis, Chas. W. Knapp, W. C. Marshall, the Laker brothers, Vernon Knapp, Phil Chew, Geo. Hynes and my brother Lal.

Francis has since been mayor of the city, Governor of the State, Sect'y of the Interior in the cabinet of President Grover Cleveland and President of the Louisiana Purchase Exposition. C. W. Knapp is President and general manager of the St. Louis *Republican* and Marshall is on the Supreme Court of the State and many of the other members of the company have been prominent in the community.

The sentiment of the company was decidedly Southern, which was shown by the adoption of gray as the color of the uniform. The armory was on the south west corner of 4th and Washington Ave. where balls were given which were considered the greatest social features for several seasons. The company finally disbanded as did all other military organizations in the city for want of State financial aid.

In 1877 the great Rail Road Strike, with its accompanying lawlessness, extended from the east, where it started, to St. Louis. The criminal element, taking advantage of the disorder which prevailed, committed all sorts of outrages. The police force was inadequate to deal with the situation and the militia, as I have stated, had been disbanded for want of state financial aid assistance.

The condition becoming intolerable a meeting of citizens was called to devise a means for the preservation of the peace and the protection of property of the city. The meeting was held at the 4 Courts and all law-abiding citizens were invited to attend. The meeting resulted in the appointment by Major Overstoltz of Generals Marmaduke and Smith, to command a military force to be raised immediately and used in restoring order.

My brother John and I attended the meeting. When I entered the door, some one told me Gen'l Marmaduke had been enquiring for me. I found him and he requested me to recruit a company for the protection of the person of the mayor, who would make his headquarters in the 4 Courts Building.

I soon recruited my company and reported for duty. From the nature of the service for which it was organized it became known as the "Mayors Guard" and has been that name for many years, although it never performed any bodyguard duty. The following day I continued receiving recruits for my company until it numbered 165 men. It, as I have said, did no bodyguard duty but was kept on outside duty all the time.

J. Cabbell [Cabel] Breckenridge [Breckinridge], the son of Gen'l Jno. C.

Tennessee battery defending New Madrid in 1861 and in August 1862, Chapman joined Sanders Tennessee Cavalry Battalion (17th Battalion Tennessee Cavalry). This Chapman is not the same as the one who enlisted in the unit that William Bull joined. Exchanged prisoners of Camp Jackson, Camp Jackson Papers; "Military companies of St. Louis—No. 4, National Guard Company—2nd Company," Missouri Militia scrapbook, page 6 of unnumbered pages; Moore, "Missouri," *Confederate Military History Extended*, vol. 12, 255-256.

Breckenridge, who was on his father's staff during the war, was my First Lieutenant and Charles Minnegarode [Minnigerode], who was on Fitzhugh Lee's staff during the war, was my Second Lieutenant. The ranks were filled with young Capitalists and Mechanics—all eager to do their full duty.

One night I sent a platoon to guard the Laclede Gas Works which, with the water works, was threatened with devastation by the mob. With the other platoon I escorted a wagon load of arms to the Republic Building, which was also threatened and in which was stationed a company composed of Rail Road officials and clerks. My brother John, being an officer in the company for which the arms were intended. My brother Lal was a member of my company.

On Friday my company was of the force which captured Schulers Hall, the strikers headquarters, at the corner of 5th and Biddle Streets. Friday night my company was ordered to Carondelet by Gen'l Smith to whom Col. Super, the Gen'l Superintendent of the Iron Mountain Rail Road reported he had reliable information that the buildings of the road were to be destroyed that night.

I marched my company to the Iron Mountain Depot at the corner of Main and Plum Streets where I found a train waiting for me. I went into the telegraph office and directed the operator to ascertain the exact condition at Carondelet. The answer came back there were six thousand rail road strikers and iron workers waiting to receive me. By direction of Gen'l Smith I stopped at the arsenal and took on a piece of artillery which had been under the command of Captain Murphy.[218]

With this on a flat car I proceeded to Carondelet and on my arrival found the strikers and their friends had dispersed. I quartered my men in the round house and placed sentinels around the entire group of buildings.

The following morning the crowd again assembled about the station. I sent a platoon to the police station to relieve the entire police force from duty there and with the other platoon supported the police who went into the crowd and arrested the ring leaders. The Rail Road then with our protection started up their trains.

In the afternoon I was relieved by a battalion from the city and returned to headquarters with our prisoners and received congratulations upon the success of the expedition. That night the members of my company, after having been on duty continuously for three days and nights, got much needed rest.

In a few days, order was restored but my company remained on duty for a week after the other companies were relieved. I had a beautiful camp in Washington Park, diagonally across from the 4 Courts. The tents were furnished by the U.S. Government through Maj. [Edward] Grimes, who was the Quartermaster stationed here.

Realizing the importance of having a well-drilled and disciplined force for such emergencies as I have just described, two regiments were formed from the companies that had been on duty—One as National Guards under the State law,

[218] See note 129.

the other as Police Reserves under the police law. I and others preferred the latter form of organization as under it we would not be required to do duty outside the city.

Col. Jas. G. Butler was elected Colonel and E. H. Meir Lieutenant Col. of our organization. The companies drawing lots for position, mine became Co. "E." The companies soon became thoroughly proficient in drill and discipline and it was generally admitted that mine was the best in both respects.

I took my company to Washington to the inauguration of President [James] Garfield[219] and was overwhelmed with compliments from militia and Regular Army officers upon the wonderful perfection of its drill.

The Police Reserve Regiment continued its organization for several years but we finally concluded it would be better for many reasons to be organized under the State laws and were mustered in as the 3d Regiment National Guard of Missouri. I received and still have my commission as Captain from T. T. Crittenden the Governor at that time.

I commanded the company, altogether, eight years when I was promoted to Inspector General of the State with the rank of Colonel by Gen'l Jno. S. Marmaduke, who had been elected Governor of the State. I was continued in the position for eight years by Governors Marmaduke and Francis. My last commission as Inspector General, which I still have, is particularly prized by me, from the fact that it bears the signatures of two former comrades in arms—D.R. Francis as governor, who was a member of the reorganized Engineer Corp in 1870 and A. A. Lesueur, as Secretary of State, who was the gallant commander of our battery in the Confederate service.

My military career, of twenty years in all, ended with the going out of office, as Governor, of David R. Francis, but many other positions of distinction awaited him all of which he filled with the most consummate skill and ability.

---

[219] Union general from Ohio and twentieth President of the United States. He served primarily east of the Mississippi River. Boatner, *Civil War Dictionary*, 323-324.

Part II

Letters To Home
By William J. Bull and John P. Bull

Introduction

In addition to William Bull's manuscript, the Missouri Historical Society preserved several Civil War letters written by William and his brother John. Unfortunately, many of the brothers' letters never reached home, being lost or destroyed during the war. The surviving letters provide a different look at the life of two Confederate soldiers of the Trans-Mississippi Department. A more personal side is revealed that shows the bravado of the early war and the resoluteness of the latter years of conflict, when the glamour of war had disappeared.

Of the two brothers, John attained the greatest success, serving as an aid to Colonel Emmett MacDonald in MacDonald's Missouri Cavalry Regiment and then as a field officer in Robert C. Newton's Fifth Arkansas Cavalry Regiment. John's letters are of particular interest since they remain one of the few sets of letters that detail any type of cavalry activity in the Trans-Mississippi area.

Notes have been added to give the reader a better appreciation of the action and personalities in the Civil War west of the Mississippi River. These letters are presented to further support the interest in the Trans-Mississippi region and are not intended as genealogical history of the Bull family and as such no attempt has been made to provide detailed information on the relatives or friends of the two brothers.

Items contained within [ ] were added by the editor for the sake of clarity. Paragraphing has been added in some of the letters, which generally used none. The content and spelling are as written by the Bull brothers.

* * * * * *

Letter, William to Mother:

Steamer "Iatan"
December 3rd 1861

My Dear Mother[220]
I avail myself of an opportunity to send you a few lines. We left St. Louis on the above named boat at about 5 o'clock yesterday evening and thus far have had a very pleasant trip. The idea of soon being from under the rule of

[220] Following the Union surrender of Lexington, Missouri, on September 20, 1861, the two warring factions agreed to a prisoner exchange for the men captured at Camp Jackson. An exchange was agreed to on November 2, 1861 by the two commanders, John C. Frémont and Sterling Price. General Order Number 4, Headquarters Department of Missouri, issued on November 22, 1861, allowed the 530-man prisoner exchange to proceeded. On December 2, 1861 sixty-six men, including the Bull brothers and Brigadier General Daniel M. Frost, departed St. Louis on the steamer *Iatan* bound for Columbus, Kentucky and the rebel lines. (For a complete list of *Iatan* passengers see Appendix D) *O.R.*, Series 2, vol. 1, 551-559; "The Camp Jackson Prisoners," *Missouri Republican*, December 3, 1861; Frost letter book, Mesker Papers, Box 2, Missouri Historical Society, 11-12.

Frank Blair[221] puts us all in the best spirits imaginable.

Nothing of interest has transpired yet. I will write to you again from Cairo. We are about to land at Cape Girardau [Girardeau] where we will lay during the night. I must close now and send my letter up to the post office. Give my love to all my friends.

Affectionately
Your son
Willie

* * * * * *

Letter, William to Mother:

Camp Sterling Price
Jacksonport, Ark.
December 26th, 1861

My Dear Mother[222]

We arrived at Columbus, Ky. the Wednesday [December 3, 1861] after we left St. Louis. On Friday evening, much to our joy, we found that Aunt Lizzie (Uncle Ben's wife) was on the st'r [steamer] "Kentucky" which had that day arrived at the warf. She and a younger sister had come up on a pleasant trip with their father, Capt. Warman, who was one of the pilots on the boat. They all manifested great pleasure at meeting us & insisted upon our taking quarters on the boat, which we gladly accepted.

We all left Columbus the following Saturday December 7, 1861 & reached Memphis on Monday [December 9, 1861]. Capt. Warman would not think of us going into quarters with the rest of the boys but would have us go to his house, where we remained during our stay in Memphis. Uncle Ben is staying at the Capt's. He is much better and is in business. He may live several years.

---

[221] Francis (Frank) Preston Blair, Jr. was a Kentuckian by birth and a Missouri Congressman (1856-1858 and 1860-1862). He helped organize the Union forces and secured the appointment of Nathaniel Lyon to command in Missouri following the outbreak of hostilities. Blair commanded the First Missouri Infantry in the early part of the war and just prior to Wilson's Creek he returned to Washington to resume his seat in the U. S. Congress. In November 1861, Blair used his political influence to force John C. Frémont out as the Union commander in Missouri. He returned to active military service in 1862, being appointed a brigadier general on August 7, 1862. Blair served east of the Mississippi River, commanding a corps during the Atlanta Campaign in 1864 as a major general. *O.R.*, vol. 3, 429; *O.R.*, vol. 38, pt. 4, 33; Peckham, *Missouri in 1861*, 119; Dino A. Brugioni, *The Civil War in Missouri as Seen from the Capital City* (Jefferson City, 1987), 16-17, 77-78; Boatner, *Civil War Dictionary*, 67.

[222] After their exchange the Bull brothers moved to Memphis, Tennessee. The men of Camp Jackson next boarded a boat and completed their return to the Trans-Mississippi area, establishing a camp at Jacksonport, Arkansas on the White River. In the meantime, the brothers joined Captain Henry Guibor's artillery company and began their instruction in artillery drill. William Bull Reminiscence and Diary, Bull Family Papers, Missouri Historical Society, 22-26.

We met a good many old friends and made a great many new ones. Everybody treated us all very kindly and we had a very pleasant stay in Memphis & left there on Tuesday, 17th [December 1861].

We are all well & expect to be in St. Louis before a great while. We are in camp here & expect to remain for some time. Have no fears for the success of the South. She will be free. I wish I could tell you all.

You know I am very poor hand to write so you will please excuse me from writing any more. Johnie[223] will write a P.S. Give my love to all my friends & remember me as

Ever your Affectionate Son
W'm Bull

P.S. Johnie will not have time to write as I have to send this immediately. He is well & will write the next chance we have.

W'm B.

* * * * * *

Letter William to Mother:

Camp Churchill Clark[224]
near Corinth, Miss.
May 21, 1862

My Dear Mother[225]

I well know the anxiety you must feel to hear from us. I therefore avail myself of the present opportunity of writing to you. This is the first time since

---

[223] John Bull, William's older brother, was captured with Will at Camp Jackson and later exchanged with his brother as part of the Frémont-Price deal of November 1861. The two brothers served together in the same artillery company until December 1862 when John joined Emmett MacDonald's Missouri Cavalry (Tenth Missouri). John remained in the cavalry until the end of the war, rising to the rank of lieutenant colonel. The remaining letters, from this point on, contain a mix of correspondence from the two brothers as they continue their wartime exploits.

[224] Camp Churchill Clark was named after Captain Samuel Churchill Clark, who died at Pea Ridge, while resisting the enemy's last charge. Clark was a St. Louisian and a grandson of explorer William Clark. He was in West Point at the beginning of the Civil War, but resigned and returned to Missouri. He joined the army in August 1861 and commanded a Missouri State Guard Battery at the siege of Lexington and at the Battle of Pea Ridge. *O.R.*, vol. 3, 186; *O.R.*, vol. 8, 327, 329; Peterson, *Sterling Price's Lieutenants*, 151.

[225] Departing Jacksonport in late January 1862 the Bulls returned to Missouri, arriving at Springfield on February 11, just in time to join Price's retreat from the state. After one day's rest the battery moved southward toward Arkansas and the concentration of Major General Earl Van Dorn's Confederate Army. John and William participated in the Battle of Pea Ridge on March 6-8, 1862. Despite the defeat, the Bull brothers crossed the Mississippi River and joined the Confederate Army that was forming to defeat General Grant at Pittsburg Landing. Van Dorn's army did not arrive in time for the Battle of Shiloh. Next, Will and John's command moved to Corinth, Mississippi which proved to be the focal point of the Union advance in April and May 1862 following the Battle of Shiloh. While east of the Mississippi River the Bulls transferred to Gorham's Missouri Battery. Bull diary, 28-37.

I left home that I have felt that I could write without reserve. I wrote you a few lines from Memphis telling you that we were well and indicated that we had orders to move to this place.

We got to Memphis on the 21st of April [1862]. We had a delightful time there, everybody was so kind to us. Our company (we were in Guibor's Battery then) camped at Fort Pickering, near the city & Johnie and myself were allowed to spend most of our time at Captain Warman's house. I cannot say too much in praise of him, or his family, for the kind manner in which they treated us. They could not have done more for us had we been their own children.

Aunt Lizzie made us each two hickory overcoats which will soon be a very pleasant substitute for the flannel ones which you made us as the weather is becoming very warm. I merely give this single instance of her kindness, I might give many more. The rest of the family were equally kind. They all made us promise that in case we got sick or wounded we would come immediately to their house and let them take care of us. This we will certainly do and I know that we will receive the very best of care.

We made many friends in Memphis among the number several very nice young ladies. How I did dislike to leave there! It seemed like leaving home again. But finally order came & we had to leave upon very short notice. Before leaving, however, we left "Guibor's Battery" and joined "Gorham's." Ed Chappel, Ed B___l, John L___m and Bob Y___g joined with us. We all mess & tent together and call ourselves the "Shirks." I think we have the best mess in the army. It would amuse you to look upon us some day and see us at work.

Ed B___l is 1st cook, Bob Young 2nd Do. [cook], Jno. L___m assistant, the rest of us do heavy work such as pitch & strike tent, get wood and water, etc. We get along finely, notwithstanding our name implies the contrary. The officers say we are the best workers in the company. We all had our hair cut off just as short as it could possibly be cut. You can imagine what queer looking objects we are, but it is very comfortable and I think I will always wear my hair so.

We are all privates or cannoneers except Johnie who still has his position as sergeant. We are all delighted with the artillery service & wouldn't think of exchanging it for any other, even if we could get commissions. Capt. Gorham & his Lts. are all good soldiers and perfect gentlemen. They associate with our mess upon terms of perfect equality and do all in their power to make us comfortable & contented. Any little delicacy they get they share with us, we do the same with them.

We left Memphis on the 2nd of May. We met with a warm reception all along the road. Right here I will state that the Mo. troops & especially those from St. Louis have a "big name" all through the South and in the army. At every house we passed we found a lot of young ladies assembled who threw us bouquets & sent us buckets of milk. At one little town we passed through the ladies had a fine dinner ready for us. The table was set in the street & was loaded with all sorts of nice eatables. They gave us each a bouquet with a nice pair of socks tied to it.

We got here on the 10th of May (anniversary of Camp Jackson). How we did wish the Yankees would attack us on that day. We are all anxious for a fight and expect one every day but are afraid the Feds will not give us one. They have a great many more men than we have but we know that we can whip them if they will come out of their entrenchments.

The Shirks are well supplied with every thing they need. We have a large wall tent with fly. We have a large mess chest containing cooking utensils & table ware of every kind. The rations issued to us are very good—generally flour, pork, fresh beef, sugar, molasses, rice, beans, & until recently coffee. They now give us rye as a substitute. Besides this we send to the country for hams, chickens, butter, and eggs. We have plenty of money to keep our table well supplied.[226]

We have received full pay from "Camp Jackson" to the 15th April last. Hereafter we will be paid every two months.[227] We will be paid again in a few days. Besides this we received $50.00 bounty when we enter the Confederate service. None of our mess have gone into it yet & perhaps will not go into it at all as we love the old M.S.G. [Missouri State Guard][228] and don't like to leave it.

I have seen a great many of my old friends since I have been here. I saw Mr. P___k frequently in Memphis. He was very well. I see Messrs L___r & J___n frequently also Sammy T___r. They are all well. Sammy was slightly wounded at Elk Horn but has entirely recovered. He is a private in the 1st Missouri Brigade.

I visited Bowen's Camp[229] a few days since and found the boys all well. Among the rest Sam E___e, John N___n, Sam K___d, Charley H___k and young Thompson, who used to stay in Pa's office. I suppose you have heard of the death of Joe Draw, he was on Gen'l John S. Bowen's staff & dearly beloved by the whole brigade. He was wounded at the Battle of Shiloh and died at Memphis while we were there. Parker Dunnica also died at Memphis

---

[226] The rations received by the men from Missouri would be the best the command ever received. By November 1862 the unit's daily ration would be beef and corn meal and little more. Pinnell diary, November 1862.

[227] Pay in the Confederate Trans-Mississippi was erratic at best. If funds were available they went to buy food, forage, arms, or quartermaster supplies for the army. Paying troops was among the last item to be funded west of the Mississippi River. The Bulls counted themselves lucky if they got paid every six months. The Bulls were paid in August and September 1862, for service to August 15, 1862, but received no further pay until March 1863. Bull diary, August 17 and September 18, 1862; Pinnell diary, March 2, 1863.

[228] In response to the capture of Camp Jackson on May 10, 1861, the Missouri legislature passed the Military Bill on May 11 which disbanded the former state militia and organized the Missouri State Guard. The Military Bill divided Missouri into nine districts and appointed Sterling Price the commander of the State Guard. Peterson, *Sterling Price's Lieutenants*, 5.

[229] Named after John S. Bowen. See biography in Appendix B.

while we were there from a wound received at Shiloh. Dr. Shelton died in New Orleans recently from consumption. I think he left our army in Arkansas on account of bad health.

I saw cousin Burr frequently while in Memphis, but he left us there & started back to Mo. and I hear was taken prisoner on his way back. He was a very good soldier and had rank of Lt Col. I see your young friend Capt. Billy occasionally. He is a fine fellow and I like him very much. He never ceases to praise you & his other lady friends in St. Louis for the favors they did him.

We have just received orders to move to a position about 8 or 9 miles from here to guard a R.R. bridge over the Tuscumbia River. I will have to close for the present.

Will

* * * * * *

Letter, John to Mother:

June 6th 1862
40 miles from Corinth

My Darling Mother

Your welcome letter of 26th May 1862 has just been received by me, and although short, it was none the less appreciated. I am surprised that you have received so few letters from us, as we have written at least 30 times. The reason is, I suppose, on account of those by whom we send them getting frightened & destroying them for fear of detection. About the only news we can communicate is that we are as perfectly well and confident of success as the day we left home. Willie has changed very much, he has grown in height as well as weight, but, as regards laziness he is the same slow Willie as when he left home.

. I have changed more I believe than Willie[;] we both, as well as my whole detachment of 25 men wear our hair as close as the scissors would clip it, and a rounder faced, jollier, fatter set you never saw. We are all very rough looking, though as every one expresses "The Missourians are the finest looking & best dressed soldiers in the Confederacy." The reason is, we were all paid up to the day, in Memphis and one years pay accumulating is quite a sum. I have in my pocket $1050.00 and one of the finest horses, saddle, bridle & accouterments, in the army.

The "Camp Jackson" boys are all paid off from the 6th of May [1861] one year ago and I (although you know) received $160.00, Willie, Jno. Tatum, Bob, Ed Chappel, Ed B. & Lieut. [Charles B.] Tilden are all sitting in front of my tent while I am writing sporting their 50 & 100 dollar bills and speculating how they will outlay their money when they get home, which I hope will not be long hence.

Gen'l [John B.] Clark, [Jr.] told me this evening that France had acknowledged the independence of the Confederacy, and negotiations were on in the Federal Congress for peace and that in two months we would all return once more to our houses. May God grant it be so.

Ma, if I should be spared to reach home once more I could engage you for days with narratives of our adventures. Six months service in our army where we have fought 4 battles and ten or eleven skirmishes, has given us an opportunity to see the "elephant"[230] in his most stupendous proportions. Gen'l B[eauregard] issued an order the other evening, that he would confer a "Badge of the Legion of Honor" upon every one who distinguished himself in the coming battle.

I am drilling my detachment constantly 6 hours a day, with the intention of winning one for myself & boys and they have all entered into the spirit heartily, and if we should be fortunate to march into St. Louis don't be surprised to see the cannoneers of the brass 6 pounders "Jennie M" and "Maurnie Bull" each with a "Beauregard"[231] on the lapel of his coat. Gen'l B. has issued 3 already and all of them to Gen'l Price's Missourians.

One was a little boy only 13 years old, who had lost one of his legs at the Battle of Farmington[232] the other day. The regiment to which he belonged was ordered to charge the enemy, who were in full flight and when within reach of them almost, were fired on by some men in ambush. He fell and the Gen'l rode up and asked him if he suffered much from his wound. The little fellow raised on his arm and saluting Gen'l B. remarked with tears in his eyes, "Gen'l, I do not miss my leg near so much as I do the privilege of following the Feds." "Brave boy" exclaimed the Gen'l. "In the presence of my Gen'ls I confer upon you the badge of the Legion of Honor, and may God spare you many years to be proud of your gallantry upon the field of Farmington." He then ordered the surgeon to remove him to his own quarters where he could supervise the treatment himself.

Ma, I would have been willing to have given two legs to have been in that little hero's place. I had a splendid daguerreotype[233] taken of myself in Memphis which I will send you the first opportunity. Hereafter Ma, if you should not receive letters from us, rest assured it is not our fault as we write them at every opportunity that presents and besides the opportunities are not so good in an army of two or three hundred thousand men, as it was in Missouri when we were all together and knew one who we could send by.

I see Willie is writing and I will not weary you with a longer epistle.

---

[230] Term used by green troops to refer to their first time under fire.

[231] Term troops used to refer to the "Legion of Honor" conferred by General Beauregard to soldiers for bravery.

[232] Battle of Farmington (May 9, 1862) was one of the few engagements during the Union advance on Corinth. It occurred when Daniel Ruggles's Confederates, of Van Dorn's Corps, encountered two brigades of Union troops on the road to Farmington, Mississippi. After a short battle the Union troops withdrew. Union losses totaled 178 killed, wounded and missing, while Confederate losses numbered 99. *O.R.*, vol. 10, pt. 1, 805, 811.

[233] Daguerreotype—Early type of photograph.

Give my love to Jennie, Fannie, Mary, Cornelia, & Anna and all other friends who may feel interested in us and also to the Misses Cordelia and Dora. God bless them. I have heard how kind they have been. Bob joins in love to all as also all the "mess." Tell Pa the next time you write to drop a line if it is not treason. His hand-writing on your envelope was a pleasure to see. Give my love to him and all the family. Give my love to Aunt Ness when you write. Good bye, God Bless you dear Mother.

Your Son John

* * * * * *

Letter William to Mother:
[Note: This letter is the continuation of the May 21, 1862 letter which Will ended abruptly when orders came to march.]

Camp Price
Tupelo, Mississippi
June 10, 1862

Mother[234]

Since writing the above [May 21 letter], many movements have taken place in the army which would perhaps interest you, but as I am in a great hurry to finish my letter I will not take time to mention any except the last and most important, the evacuation of Corinth.

Of course I know nothing of the private reasons of Gen'l Beauregard for this move, but I believe the principal one to have been to get to good water and a more healthy location.[235] Notwithstanding, it was a retreat, it is regarded by the entire army as equal to a victory.

It is ridiculous the reports the Federals give of this affair. I saw the other day Gen'l [Henry W.] Halleck's official report, saying he had taken 10,000

---

[234] This would be the last Bull letter from the east side of the Mississippi River as the Missouri State Guard received permission to return to the west side of the river on July 18, 1862. The Bull brothers spent a little less than four months in the Department of the West and would spend the remaining years of the war attempting to return Missouri. Of the two brothers only John would ever enter Missouri again while in a Confederate uniform. *O.R.*, vol. 13, 855; *O.R.*, vol. 17, pt. 2, 610. (Note: Special Order No. 117 was incorrectly dated and should read July instead of June 18, 1862.)

[235] In his official report, Beauregard stated "the purposes and ends for which I had occupied and held Corinth having been accomplished...and having ascertained definitely that the enemy had received large accessions to his already superior force, while ours had been reduced day by day by disease, resulting from bad water and inferior food, I felt it clearly my duty to evacuate" Corinth. Later in his report, Beauregard clarified what he meant by "purposes and ends for which I occupied and held Corinth"—the Federals were attempting to cut off Beauregard from his support base and by retreating toward their support the Confederates defeated the Union purposes and ends. Beauregard could not handle the pressure and repeatedly asked Jefferson Davis to relieve him of command. Following the fall of Corinth, Beauregard gave up the command to General Braxton Bragg. *O.R.*, vol. 10, pt. 1, 762-763.

prisoners, among the number Gen'l Price and his entire army.[236] This is an infamous lie. They were afraid to attack us & did not molest us in the least.

The headquarters of the army for the present is at Tupelo [Mississippi] a little village on the Mobile & Ohio rail road, about fifty-six miles from Corinth. Arrangements are being made for a protracted stay at this point. Previous to the retreat from Corinth there was a good deal of sickness in the army. Two of our mess were quite sick—Ed B___l [Bridell] and Bob Y___g [Young] but they have entirely recovered. The health of the army is improving very much, there not being one third the sick at this new encampment as we had in Corinth.

The water is better, the location more healthy and food and provender much easier to obtain. Our loss while at Corinth was very serious but the loss of the enemy must have been five times as heavy. The men being afflicted with almost every disease known to camp life, this we know to be a fact.

I have no doubt but that our friends in St. Louis feel somewhat discouraged at our recent defeats (as the Feds call them—we consider them victories). I wish all such could be in this army and hear our men talk, then they would believe as I do that the South can never be conquered. We believe she is destined to be an independent power, "a Nation among nations" and that no earthly power can prevent it. We know we will have to undergo many hardships to gain her independence, but this we are willing to do, for what would our freedom be worth. How could we properly appreciate its blessings without undergoing hardships to gain it.

This feeling prevails throughout the army and it matters not what reverses we meet with, it never [will] forsake us. You may be sure of one thing, I will remain in the army as long as the war lasts, [even] if it lasts ten years.

A good many changes have taken place in the "Shirks Mess" recently. In the first place we have a negro boy who does our cooking, washing and all the other work about the mess. He is a faithful servant and an excellent cook. Almost all of the Shirks have been promoted. Ed B___l [Bridell] got an appointment as aid to Gen'l [Charles W.] Phifer,[237] rank 1st Lt. Ed C___l

---

[236] Bull is basically correct in his comment on Halleck's report, though there is no mention of Price's capture. General Halleck reported that he received a dispatch from General John Pope, reporting "10,000 prisoners and deserters" and "15,000 arms captured." Five days later the reported Confederate losses rose to "between 20,000 and 30,000." At the war's end General Pope called into question Halleck's highly exaggerated report, but received no satisfaction from the politically sensitive Halleck who replied to Pope, "I never reported to the Secretary of War dispatches received from you which were not received." The actual losses on both sides were negligible from actual combat as both sides suffered more by sickness and disease. Ibid., 669-670; *O.R.*, vol. 17, pt. 2, 635-637.

[237] Charles W. Phifer was appointed a brigadier general from Texas on May 25, 1862. He was never confirmed by the Confederate Congress. In the summer of 1862 he commanded the Third Brigade, Third Division (D. H. Maury) in Van Dorn's Army of the West. Boatner, *Civil War Dictionary*, 650; *O.R.*, vol. 10, pt.1, 789-790; Charles C. Jones, Jr., "A Roster of General Officers, Heads of Departments, Senators, Representatives, Military Organizations, etc., etc. in Confederate Service During the War Between the States," *Southern Historical Society Papers* (original, Richmond, VA, 1876; reprinted Wilmington, NC, 1990) vol. 2, No. 6, 380-381.

promoted to orderly sergeant. Bob Y___g [Young] to Commissary and I to corporal or gunner. I sight & command the piece while in action. Johnie still has his position as sergeant, or Chief of Piece. You may think these offices very trifling, but they are not. We all rank as high as commissioned officers in any other service.

I see Charley Mc every day, he is in Wade's Battery[238] acting color bearer. He is well & perfectly satisfied. I heard from Mr.P___k yesterday, he was well. Mr. L___r came over to see us today. He wishes you to write to his wife & tell her that he and Sammy are well. He thinks the prospects of the South are brighter now than have ever been before. He expects to be at home before a great while. Our brigade [Parsons's Missouri State Guard] has marching orders.

Will

* * * * * *

Letter John to Mother:

Camp on Ark. River
near Van Buren, Arkansas
Nov. 28, 1862

My Dear, Dear Mother[239]

I have an opportunity of writing a letter but there is really so little news which I can communicate. I scarcely know what to say or write. There is one piece of news which I am sorry to record. Dave Tatum died at Pitman's Ferry on the Ark. River on the 1st of this month of chronic Dhiarhea. Poor fellow he never had the pleasure of seeing John [his bother] or any of his old friends but died among strangers.

Those strangers gave him though all the kind attention his own dear home folks would and gave him a decent though humble burial. His grave is marked and John and myself know where it is. Poor John takes the death of his brother very hard but bears up under it as well as would be expected.

He & Willie and I share each other's blankets and make a common fund of each other's effects. We have been together for eight months and have never

---

[238] Wade's Missouri Battery was commanded by Captain William Wade. The unit formed in the Spring of 1862 from elements of the Missouri State Guard, Third Division. The battery saw action at Pea Ridge and then was transferred to the east side of the Mississippi River as part of the Confederate movement from Arkansas to Mississippi. *O.R.*, vol. 8, 284-285; Peterson, *Sterling Price's Lieutenants*, 132; Crute, *Units of the Confederate Army*, 210.

[239] The Bulls returned to the Trans-Mississippi area on July 31, 1862. They moved with the Missouri State Guard to Arkansas Post, then to Clarendon on the White River. Next the Missouri troops headed northwest toward Yellville, Arkansas where they joined other Missouri troops who were concentrating for their return to Missouri. On October 29, 1862 the Missourians travelled south to Van Buren on the Arkansas River and General Hindman's army. Bull diary, 41-56; Parsons letters, October 29, 1862.

yet passed an angry word. We are well and as hearty as men could be. Plenty of blankets & clothes but scanty rations.

There is a great deal of talk now in camp about an armistice. I hope it is untrue, for I will say this much, we have the best and strongest army now on the border that we have ever had and before many weeks we will make a noise that will be heard all over this land so be hopeful dear Ma, all will yet be well with my dear Confederacy. The world was not made in one day but it took time and with time and God's blessing we will yet be free. Young boys yearn for the day when they will once more embrace their dear ones at home, but never, until it can be said of them "Well done good and faithful servants thou hast finished the work I have given you to do." Then all will be well and we will return never to leave you again and try and repay you by kindness for our past [illegible]. Give my love to Dear Father, sister, & brothers and all enquiring friends. Tell Fannie I dreamed of her last night. I would like so much to receive the photograph you spoke of in your last letter. Give my love to Jennie. I wrote her a letter by ___. Good bye.

Your Son John[240]

* * * * * *

Letter Will to Mother:

Nov. 28th, 1862

My Dear Mother

I only have time to say we are all well and in good spirits. We think there is a good chance for peace to be made in the next 6 months. We are still in the battery now commanded by C. B. Tilden,[241] formally 1st Lieut. I have taken another step and am now Serg't of a piece. John is still Serg't. I think he would have been a Lieut. if we could have had an election, but the officers were all appointed.

Here is something I want circulated. Hearing that Ed Chappel had been appointed jnr. [junior] 1st Lieut., we got up a petition, signed by every non-commissioned officer & private to have him removed. This was refused. Chappel saw the petition & had there been anything of the gentleman about him he would have refused the appointment, but he accepted and is now hated & dispised by every man in the company & considered too contemptible to be noticed.

---

[240] Four days after John wrote this letter he transferred to Colonel Emmett MacDonald's cavalry brigade with the rank of captain. John served his remaining days in the Confederate service as a cavalryman. Bull diary, 59; *O.R.*, vol. 22, pt. 1, 58, 146.

[241] Bull's unit reorganized on November 10, 1862. Charles B. Tilden was appointed commander of the battery and the unit assigned to Colonel Alexander Steen's Missouri Brigade, Parsons' Third Division, First Corps Trans-Mississippi Army. Special Order letter book, Special Order No. 38, 109-110.

[John] Dunk [Duncan] Holliday is Ord. [Ordnance] Serg't, Jno. Tatum gunner on Johnie's piece. I was sorry indeed to hear of the death of Dave Tatum. He died about a week ago near Clarksville. We are all well. Love to all. Write soon.

Ever your affectionate Son
W. B.

P.S. Tell Cal Howard his brother Will[242] is here in the battery. We have a first rate company—4 guns and 130 men. All fine fellows

Will

* * * * * *

Letter, John to Mother:

On the Battle Field
Dec 8th, 1862

My Dear, Dear Mother[243]

I have an opportunity to write this by a friendly fed. Willie & myself are safe and all the St. Louis boys I now know of. I am now on Gen. [Colonel] Emmett McDonald's staff (aide-de-camp) & Willie is promoted to a Sergeant in the battery. Gen. McDonald is safe & well. We charged the enemy yesterday for 10 miles. Gen. Hindman has named our brigade McDonald's Lighting Brigade. We have won laurels. Good bye and God bless you all. Your son Johnie.

My love to Jenni

---

[242] William Howard enlisted in the company on November 10, 1862 while the unit was camped at Mullberry Creek, Arkansas. He deserted on December 10, 1863 while on the march in southwest Arkansas. National Archives, Record Group M322, roll no. 85, Third Field Battery Missouri Artillery.

[243]. On December 7, 1862 the Confederate forces under Major General Thomas C. Hindman engaged the Army of the Frontier, commanded by Brigadier General James G. Blunt in the Battle of Prairie Grove, Arkansas. The battle began at dawn when the Confederate cavalry, including Emmett MacDonald's cavalry brigade, surprised elements of the Union Seventh Missouri and First Arkansas Cavalry. The Union troops routed from the field followed in close pursuit by the Confederate cavalry. Meanwhile, the rebel infantry established a strong position on a wooded ridge near Prairie Grove church. By early afternoon the two forces were heavily engaged. When the Confederates seemed to have the upper hand, Union reinforcements under General Blunt arrived and stemmed the rebel tide. Night ended the battle with neither side gaining a significant advantage. The rebels withdrew, during the lull, citing a lack of ammunition. On December 8 a truce was in effect while the wounded were removed from the field, which gave John Bull a chance to send this short note. Confederate losses from the battle were 164 killed, 817 wounded and 336 missing while the Union command suffered 175 killed, 813 wounded and 263 missing. Both of the Bull brothers were in the battle, but only John played an active part. Will came under fire several times but his battery, Tilden's, never fired a shot. *O.R.*, vol. 22, pt. 1, 68-158; Bull diary, 60.

* * * * * *

Letter, John to Father:

[Dec 1862]

My Dear, Dear Father[244]

My friend is about leaving and as I have sent several letters by Federals who I met on the field after the battle, I will make my epistle short. My friend will inform you of my promotion and present position which I know Dear Father will be pleasant to you and all my Dear ones at home. Oh for one short hour's conversation & communion with you all. But it is impossible and therefore I am contented with my lot.

Is Ma satisfied, is she contented with our being here or does she grieve. Tell her we will both live to embrace her after these troubles are over. Pa, will you please give this gentleman, the bearer of this, an overshirt and cap for me. I would send you money but I know you cannot use it. Give my love to all my friends Jennie, Fannie, the Misses H—E's, and P's. Kiss all the family for me. Farewell. Yours, Affectionately

Johnie

P.S. If you are able, furnish the bearer with what articles I have sent for. My love to Bob.

Yours

Johnie

* * * * * *

Letter, John to Mother:

Dover, Ark. December 22 '62
At Mrs. Judge Wards

My own Dear, Dear Mother[245]

---

[244] The December 1862 date is estimated based on the content of the letter and Will's December 2, 1862 diary entry which mentions John's new position and unit. The battle mentioned here is Prairie Grove. Bull diary, 59.

[245] Following the Battle of Prairie Grove the Confederates withdrew to Fort Smith. Within weeks General Hindman dispersed his army to gain better access to food and forage. John's cavalry unit moved to Lewisburg (on the Arkansas River midway between modern day Conway and Morrilton, Arkansas) on December 12 to recoup for a movement east. James F. Fagan's Division departed western Arkansas on December 26. Daniel M. Frost's Division was scheduled to move eastward on December 28 but circumstances delayed the march for several hours when the Federals attacked nearby Van Buren on the scheduled date of their march. William was in Frost's command.

The Union raid was led by General Blunt who took Hindman's command completely by surprise and captured Van Buren. Hindman offered little resistance, ordering Will's unit to march late on December 28. *O.R.*, vol. 22, pt. 1, 171-172, 905; Telegram, December 12, 1862, Hindman to Holmes, Peter W. Alexander Collection, Columbia University.

Although I have written you seven times since our last two battles[246] I cannot feel contented as long as an opportunity remains to communicate with you. And then to night of all times I feel inclined to hold private communion with you dear ones at home.

I am now sitting and writing this in the house and in the presence of one of Pa's old Playmates Mrs. Judge Ward, formerly Miss Charity Green of Harrodsburg. She and her family are refugees from Missouri. She has an interesting family of two sons and one beautiful daughter. As soon as Mrs. Ward discovered who I was she had me to come down and spend the night & evening with them and all evening she had been regaling me with their adventures of long ago. She is an excellent lady and has made me promise her if I should get wounded or be sick or if Willie should need her assistance to send on, come to her and she would take care of us as she would one of her own sons. Her husband died some days or months ago and one of her sons is now lying with wounds received at Newtonia.[247] Poor old lady, she has had enough to prostrate one of stronger frame than she. Our God has given her fortitude to bear it and every Missourian who has been fortunate enough to shelter under her hospitable roof will when in after years recalling incidents of his soldier's life craft to her memory a heartful God bless her. She and her daughter Miss Mary send their love to you all.

I suppose ere this you will have heard of my promotion. I am now Aid-de-Camp to Col. Emmett McDonald with rank of Captain. My promotion has been a long time coming but it has come at last and if the war should last one year longer I hope to come home to you a Colonel commanding a cavalry regiment and then my ambition will be satisfied and I will come home to you willing to rest contented upon what every laurel I may have won.

Of one thing Ma you should rest contented, your son will never disgrace his name or family on the field. Col. McD. gave me a very handsome notice in his two last reports[248] and if I was in camp I would send you them, but I must close now. Farewell dear Mother. Give my love to Jennie Yannie and all the family & rest of my enquiring friends.

I send by a friend for a uniform. If you are able to send me one I want a

---

[246] John is referring to Cane Hill and Prairie Grove.

[247] Battle of Newtonia—On September 30, 1862 the First and Second brigades of James G. Blunt's Kansas Division engaged a 4,000-man Confederate cavalry force commanded by Colonel Douglas H. Cooper. The engagement took place near Newtonia in Newton County of southwest Missouri. Beginning shortly after dawn, the battle continued throughout the day. The Unionists withdrew, having suffered 50 killed, 80 wounded, and 113 captured while the Confederates lost 12 killed, 63 wounded, and 3 missing.

The Battle of Newtonia marked the beginning of the Prairie Grove Campaign. Within days of the engagement three Union divisions drove the rebels out of southwest Missouri. These same forces settled the campaign on December 7, 1862 at Prairie Grove. *O.R.*, vol. 13, 286-307; Report of Troops, Douglas Cooper's Command, September 1862, Peter W. Alexander Collection, Columbia University, New York; Dyer, *Compendium of the Civil War*, 804.

[248] MacDonald thanked John for his "cool and gallant manner in which he carried" his orders throughout the Battle of Prairie Grove. *O.R.*, vol. 22, pt. 1, 156.

cavalry captains uniform; the coat double breasted with gold lace on the sleeves to the elbows. The coat to be grey and pants blue and of very heavy cloth with broad gold lace stripe and if you can send me some socks and under clothing. I need boots very much too and a hat like the one Capt. Mc had.

Good bye again
Your Johnie

P.S. I also need a yellow or buff cavalry sash. Make one of our Patriotic lady friends send one for me and one for Col. Mc D.

* * * * * *

Letter, John to Mother:

January 25th, 1863

Our Dear Mother

An opportunity affords us of writing you & we eagerly embrace it. Although during the last five weeks we have fought five battles, traveled nearly one thousand miles[249]—half of the time nearly starved & already dying for want of rest and hundreds of our companions falling neath the leaden hail, we are still well and hearty. Brother Willie is also well and all the St. Louis boys except those whose deaths you see in the papers. You will find enclosed a letter from my particular friend Lt. Arthur C. MacCoy to his wife. I wish you would call on Mrs. MacCoy & tell her, her husband is well. I wish you would get a letter from Mrs. MacC. & send it the first opportunity & enclosed in mine.

Yours
John P. Bull
H. P. McClure

* * * * * *

---

[249] Following the Confederate evacuation of the Fort Smith-Van Buren area, it took three weeks for Marmaduke's cavalry division to recover sufficiently to launch a raid into Missouri. Marmaduke mustered 1,600 men of Joe Shelby's brigade, 600 men of Joe Porter's brigade and 270 men of Emmett MacDonald's regiment (John Bull's unit). The force moved northward on December 31, 1862 and ended their raid at Batesville in northeast Arkansas on January 25, 1863.
John's unit was engaged at the Missouri towns of Fort Lawrence (January 6, 1863), Springfield (January 8, 1863), Marshfield (January 9, 1863), and Hartville (January 9 and 11, 1863). Confederate losses totaled 32 killed, 201 wounded and 29 missing. John's unit lost 6 killed, 23 wounded and 17 missing, including Colonel Emmett MacDonald, who was killed at Hartville on January 11, 1863. The Federals recorded their losses at Springfield and Hartville as 21 killed, 210 wounded and 7 missing. Ibid., 178, 181, 191, 194-199, 207-211.

Letter, John to Mother and Father:

February 20, 1863

My Dear, Dear Father & Mother[250]

Your letter enclosing one from Lal & Mamie were duly received by me and I am unable to express to you my thanks for writing so promptly. I also received your letters with articles sent—viz; Boots, underclothes, dressing case, etc for which I am also grateful. Your letter father has given me more encouragement than anything I have received since the war commenced and you cannot imagine how pleasant it was to me in this my hour of prosperity to have those whom I love dearer than all else or everything, encouraging me.

Since last May I have not taken two drinks of spirituous liquors and I have no desire for it. My health though all the miarads [myriads] of the swamps and mountain rains & snows, in the rain, hail & mud has been better than ever it was. I am as robust and as rough as a grizzly bear and I doubt if my very nice dandy friends would know their old friend Johnie Bull if he were some fine day to charge their fine city at the head of some thousand of Indians & Mexicans.

I have just received an appointment as Major & with Col. Charlie Harrison, an old Indian fighter & trader, ordered upon the plains for duty.[251] My star which 2 months ago was but dimly seen is gradually rising and ere this war closes I hope to make you my Dear Parents proud of the name of your once unworthy son. I am ambitious Father as Napoleon was, and with perseverance and attention I can accomplish almost anything.

I was tendered the command of the finest battery in Marmaduke's command a week ago and I declined it on account of my very field of service. You will hear of us before many moons and in a way that will strike awe into our enemies inmost souls. Then pray for me that I may be spared to enjoy your "Well done good & faithful servant."

Emmett's watch ring & pocket book with several locks of hair, which I cut from his head after his death, I sent to his Sisters but the messenger returned & I will send them as soon as possible. He talked a great deal about his Brother & Sister but more particularly about Mrs. Dean. His last words were, "God bless my poor brothers & sisters" and then quietly as the setting of a summer evening sun the spirit of our depositary then passed away. Poor

---

[250] Following Marmaduke's Missouri raid, John's regiment went into a long period of inactivity as they wintered in northeast Arkansas. Will's battery also experienced the same lack of activity as his unit wintered in Little Rock. Ibid., pt. 2, 786, 789, 808, 811-812; Bull diary, 68.

[251] John's appointment to major and new assignment appear to have been premature. In a subsequent letter John will note his promotion date as May 1, 1863. See John's letter of July 20, 1863. Charles Harrison commanded Company A, MacDonald's Regiment. He resigned from the army on January 15, 1863 and organized a guerrilla band in southwest Missouri. He was killed on May 18, 1863 near Newtonia, Missouri. *O.R.*, vol. 22, pt. 1, 328-329; *O.R.*, Series 2, vol. 5, 502-503; National Archives, Record Group M322, roll no. 57, Service Records, Tenth Missouri Cavalry.

Emmett, God will pardon the faults & bless you for your many kind deeds when with us and as long as one of your old Legion remain, they will never cease to sing your praise & exalt over your gallant deeds.[252]

But I must close. Farewell Dear ones & may God bless you & preserve me for you. My love to all.

Your Aff. Affectionate Son
Johnie

P.S. Tell Jennie I received her letter & will answer it soon.

* * * * * *

Letter, William to Mother

Little Rock, Arkansas
May 9th, 1863

My Dear Mother,

I have received two letters recently from some <u>unknown</u> friend informing me of the good health of the family. These letters were dated 6 & 22 April. I have not got a letter from any of the family for a long, long while but I assure you I fully appreciate your reason for not writing. Under the circumstances I think it would be wrong for you to write, but hope I shall hear from my <u>unknown</u> friend frequently.

There is not a particle of news, and I hardly know how to fill up my sheet, but will do so by speaking of our friends telling you where they are, and what they are doing. But first let me tell you of our battery, "Tilden's 1st Mo.[253]" We have four pieces, two six pdr. [pounder] guns and two 12 pdr. howitzers. The guns were taken from Jefferson City by Gen'l Parsons just about two years ago, and were the first that <u>opened</u> upon the Feds in the State of Mo. The howitzers belonged to Braxton Bragg's famous Battery (the one he had in Mexico). Gen'l Earl Van Dorn gave them to us at Tupelo in exchange for two which we captured at "Elk Horn."[254] Our pieces were all made long before the war and are of the very best quality. We have a caisson we think a great deal of. We took it at "Elk Horn." It has the inscription on it "Dubuque Battery Light Artillery, 9th Iowa Reg't."[255]

---

[252] The Emmett that John talks about is Colonel Emmett McDonald, who commanded John's unit during the Battle of Prairie Grove and the January 1863 Missouri raid.

[253] The unit was actually the Third Field Battery Missouri Artillery.

[254] Elk Horn Tavern was also known as the Battle of Pea Ridge. This battle seriously damaged Confederate dreams of reclaiming Missouri for the southern cause. After a three-day battle the Confederates withdrew leaving the Union command in possession of the field. Earl Van Dorn commanded the rebels while Samuel R. Curtis led the Unionists. *O.R.*, vol. 8, 191-204.

[255] The "Dubuque Battery" was the Third Independent Battery Iowa Light Artillery. The battery organized in September 1861 in Dubuque, Iowa and was initially attached to the Ninth Iowa Infantry. The Battle of Pea Ridge was the first engagement for the battery. In addition to the caisson, the battery lost three guns, two men killed, and seventeen men wounded. S. H. M. Byers, *Iowa In War*

We have about 125 men, mostly from St. Louis all from Mo. As a lot they are the most gentlemanly set of fellows and best fighters in the army. We are camped about half a mile from the river back of town. All the batteries are camped together and form an Artillery Battalion.[256] We have a beautiful drill ground. We have field drill every morning and have become very well drilled. It seems to be the opinion throughout the North that the "Rebels" are starving to death. This is a good joke on the "Yanks." The truth of the matter is we live better now than even before since the war began. They issue us full rations, daily, of flour, corn-meal, beef, pork, beans, sugar, molasses, etc. Besides this we can buy all kinds of vegetables. We have become so fastidious of late, we won't eat corn bread, we feed the meal to the horses. We are in fine health. There is not a sick man in the battery.

Jim Edwards is aid to Gen'l Parsons. He is a gallant little fellow. I want Lal to get acquainted with his brother Joe, who lives at St. Charles [Missouri] and forward any thing he may wish to send to Jim. Sam Rayburn is a private in Parsons Brigade. He is a clever fellow and a good soldier. Maj. [Thomas L.] Snead[257] is Adj't for Gen'l Price. Leo Boyle[258] is a clerk in his office. Pete Sorgrain is Adj't of some regiment here ([James R.] Shalers[259] I believe). Frank Von Phul[260] is aid to Gen'l [Daniel M.] Frost, Ben [Von Phul] is Lieut. in a temporary battery.[261] Jim Douglas[262] is a Lieut. in the same. Jim Otey is

Times (Des Moines, 1888), 601-602.

[256] The battalion referred to here is G. H. Hill's Arkansas Artillery Battalion. The battalion was composed of Tilden's Missouri Battery, Blocher's Arkansas Battery, Marshall's Arkansas Battery, Etter's Arkansas Battery, and Ruffner's Missouri Battery. *O.R.*, vol. 22, pt. 2, 781, 832.

[257] Thomas Lowndes Snead was born in Virginia and moved to St. Louis in 1850, where he worked on a St. Louis newspaper. During the Civil War, he was an aide to Governor Jackson, then Sterling Price's adjutant, and finally became a Missouri Congressmen for the Second Secession of the Confederate Congress. Peterson, *Sterling Price's Lieutenants*, 28; Moore, "Missouri," *Confederate Military History Extended*, vol. 12, 407.

[258] Leonidas H. Boyle was from Bolivar, Polk County, Missouri, and a preacher by trade. He enlisted in the Missouri State Guard regiment, which became the Fifth Missouri Infantry, on January 11, 1862. He participated in the battles of Pea Ridge and Farmington. On December 12, 1862 he was detailed to Price's escort and in January 1863 he was made a permanent member of Price's staff, serving as a clerk in various departments. National Archives, Record Group M322, roll. no. 127, Service Records, Fifth Missouri Infantry.

[259]. Shaler's Regiment—Also know as the Twenty-seventh Arkansas Infantry, the regiment was commanded by Colonel James R. Shaler. Despised by his command as a strict disciplinarian, Shaler never attained any great stature in the Trans-Mississippi area or the Confederate service. Turnbo, *History of the 27th Arkansas Regiment.*

[260] Frank later joined the staff of John B. Clark, Jr. *O.R.*, vol. 22, pt. 2, 969; *O.R.*, vol. 41, pt. 2, 1,094.

[261] Von Phul's battery organized from details of men from Daniel Frost's Brigade in February 1863. The six-gun battery was stationed at Fort Pleasants, six miles above Pine Bluff, guarding the river approaches to Little Rock. On November 22, 1863 the battery officially organized, per Special Order No. 215, District of Arkansas and disbanded on December 2, 1863 per Special Order No. 222 of the same headquarters. National Archives, Record Group M322, roll. no. 90, Service Records, Von Phul's Battery.

[262] James Douglas was a member of the St. Louis, Missouri Volunteer Militia. He was captured at

Serg't Maj. of [Charles S.] Mitchell's Reg't,[263] Frost's Brigade. [Lawrence] Doug[las] Kingsland[264] is Adj't of the same regiment. Geo. Kerr is ordnance officer of Frost's Brigade. Mr. Marvin is here, he has rec'd [received] no appointment yet, but will be Chaplain of Price's Div. Mr. P [Trusten Polk] is also here, he is President of the Military Court, his rank is Colonel. Mr. Jim Mitchell[265] is here. Whenever he hears of my getting a letter he comes to me to see if it said anything about his family. He seems to be very anxious about them. Please mention them in your next. Arthur McCoy[266] is here safe & sound. Please let the Lounegans know this.

All the above named persons are well, so also are Capt. Tilden, Lesueur, Chappel, Holliday, Tatum, [Stephen] Spellan,[267] Lal [Lawrence] Kingsland,[268]

Camp Jackson on May 10, 1861. After his exchange he joined Guibor's Battery. Douglas later became the first lieutenant in Van Phul's temporary battery. Exchanged prisoner list, Camp Jackson Papers; *O.R.*, Series 2, vol. 1, 555.

[263] Mitchell's Regiment—Also known as the Eighth Missouri Infantry, this unit was commanded by Colonel Charles S. Mitchell. The unit formed in late November 1862, combining Major W. L. H. Frazier's Battalion and Mitchell's Battalion into one command of nine companies. A tenth company was added on December 23, 1862. On January 28, 1863, per Special Order No. 27, Headquarters Trans-Mississippi Department, Mitchell's Regiment was formed. The unit saw action at Prairie Grove, Pleasant Hill, and Jenkins' Ferry. Pinnell diary, December 7 and 23 1862, April 9 and 30, 1864; Parsons letters, December 23, 1862; National Archives, Record Group 109, Confederate Muster Rolls, Eighth Missouri Infantry.

[264] Lawrence Douglas Kingsland graduated from the Western Military Academy, Nashville, Tennessee. He is a different Kingsland than listed in Appendix A. He was commissioned a second lieutenant of the Provost Marshal's Company, Second Division, Missouri State Guard on December 13, 1861. He later organized a company of cavalry, which became the general's escort of the Second Division. He returned to St. Louis in the summer of 1862, seeking recruits for the Missouri units serving in Mississippi, but was stymied in his mission. Instead, he joined Mitchell's Missouri Regiment, serving as the unit's adjutant. He departed the unit on furlough in 1864 to Mexico, and went to New York to obtain a blockade running ship. Failing in his efforts, Kingsland sat out the rest of the war. He returned to St. Louis, after the war, to become a prominent businessman. Peterson, *Sterling Price's Lieutenants*, 83; Moore, "Missouri," *Confederate Military History Extended*, vol. 12, 335-336.

[265] Several James or J. or with various middle initials Mitchells are listed in the compiled service records. The most likely one that Bull is referring to is James M. Mitchell, who enlisted in the Sixteenth Missouri Infantry on August 21, 1862. National Archives, Record Group M322, roll. no. 169, Service Records, Sixteenth Missouri Infantry.

[266] Arthur C. McCoy was born in Virginia and moved to western Missouri. He enlisted in the Missouri State Guard and followed Joe Shelby to Corinth and back to Arkansas. On July 1, 1862 McCoy entered the Confederate Service as a private. McCoy helped Shelby recruit a cavalry regiment in western Missouri, being elected second lieutenant of Company A, Fifth Missouri Cavalry on August 1, 1862. He was promoted to first lieutenant in January 1863 and subsequently joined Shelby's staff. McCoy was captured on February 6, 1864, near Arkansas Post, while searching for deserters. National Archives, Record Group M322, roll no. 39, Service Records, Fifth Missouri Cavalry; *O.R.*, vol. 34, pt. 2, 321; *O.R.*, vol. 41, 1, 657; *O.R.*, Series 2, vol. 7, 414.

[267] Stephen Spellan or Spellen or Spellin was a member of the St. Louis, Missouri Volunteer Militia and captured at Camp Jackson on May 10, 1861. He was exchanged in November 1861 and boarded the steamship *Iatan* on December 1861 for a trip to Columbus, Kentucky. He entered Confederate Service on September 1, 1862 at Des Arc, Ark. Spellan was captured at Helena, Ark. on July 4, 1863. Exchanged prisoner list, Camp Jackson Papers; "The Camp Jackson Prisoners,"

[A.] Schib[269] and all the rest of the battery boys. We have been here nearly four months and have had a first rate time. Tatum & I have got acquainted with a number of fine families and lots of nice young ladies. Mrs. Fulton of St. Louis has been very kind to us. But we want to leave here and go into the field again. We are anxious to go into Mo. and wake up the Feds once more. We are not as sick of this war as they think we are. We can fight them two or three years longer just as well as not. The only trouble is we don't like to be kept from home so long.

Mr. P wishes me to say that he does not want his houses rebuilt as he will make some changes in them when he gets home.

Huff [James C. Hough], our Sr. 2nd Lieut., is being Court Marshaled. He will be cashiered.[270] The officers assure me that I will be appointed in his place. It lays between Lal Kingsland & myself & Lal says he would not accept it, as he is not satisfied with the service.[271] He wants to get into the cav'y [cavalry]. So you see my chances are very good. This makes me the more anxious to get the uniform which I wrote to you for. I would not trouble you with it but it is impossible to get one here. A friend of mine happened to find one a few days ago, but had to pay $400 for it. At that rate I could not buy one if I could find it for sale. Learning the letter was lost containing a description of the uniform I want, I will write it over.

I want it made of <u>Cadet Grey</u> cloth. The coat double breasted, Mo. buttons, if they can be had, if not Federal Staff buttons. Cuffs, collar & tail pockets trimmed with red. Pants & vest trimmed with red, in the usual style.

I am sorry to say my boots have turned out badly. They are made of very inferior leather. They are almost gone. If you ever send me another pair have them made. If you can not do this send the McClelland cav'y boots, they are the best I have seen. Boots are very high here. They ask $75.00 for such as I used to pay $7.00.

I have not heard from Johnie for a long time. He was well at last accounts. I suppose you hear from him oftener than I do. I write every opportunity. Love to all the family, also to Miss Belle___, the Misses P___s, H___s' K___s, E___s, Miss E__D & all the rest. Remember me to Robb, Dr. Mc and all my friends.

I remain as ever
Your Affectionate Son
Will

P.S. When you send the uniform, please send gold lace to trim sleeves, etc. Please send a pair of cross cannon (the artillery badge). The bearer promised

---

Missouri Republican, December 3, 1861; See Appendix A for service record.

[268] See Appendix A for service record.

[269] A. Schib or Shebb—see Appendix A for service record.

[270] Hough elected to resign, citing his age as the reason he desired to leave the army. He was forty years old, born in England, and a resident of St. Louis. See Appendix A for service record.

[271] Lal accepted the promotion in December 1863 when the battery elected their officers for the first time. See Appendix A for service record.

me to bring out any thing you may wish to send.

Will

* * * * * *

Letter, Will to Mother:

May 16th, 1863

My Dear Mother

I have an opportunity to write to you and cannot think of allowing it to pass unimproved, notwithstanding, I have written you several letters recently. I gave you all the news in my last and think there is no doubt about your getting it as it is in the charge of a good, trusty, fellow. I have heard from Johnie. I understand he has been app'td [appointed] Major of the Reg. to which he belongs.[272] This was told me by a gentleman just from the command. I cannot vouch for the truthfulness of it. Johnie was well.

The Court Martial has not decided the case of our Second Lieut. My chances for his position are very good. Our friends are all well. Jno. Tatum & Cpt. Lesueur wish to be remembered. Messrs P___, U___n, Lon B___l, and all the rest are well. Remember me to all my friends. Love to the family, also to Misses P___k's, H___'s, K___'s, J___'s, Miss Belle & Miss E. D. We all (the shirks) wrote a letter to Bob. I hope he may get it. Write every opportunity.

I remain as ever
Affectionately Your Son
Will

P.S. The bearer says he will bring anything you may wish to send. W.

* * * * * *

Letter, John to Mother:

July 20th, 1863
Near Helena, Ark.

My Dear Mother[273]

Knowing the penalty of your communicating with your rebel son I have

---

[272] John Bull was promoted to Major in Colonel Robert C. Newton's Fifth Arkansas Cavalry on May 1, 1863 and remained in Newton's unit until war's end. Bull letters, July 20, 1863.

[273] Following a long period of inactivity, the Confederate Army made a desperate attack on Helena on July 4, 1863. The attack was designed to relieve the pressure on Vicksburg but failed miserably. Confederate losses totaled 173 killed, 645 wounded, and 772 captured or missing. Union losses amounted to only 239 killed, wounded and missing. Ironically, the day the Helena assault was made, Vicksburg surrendered. District of Arkansas commander, Lieutenant General Theophilus H. Holmes led the rebel command while Major General Benjamin M. Prentiss led the Federals. *O.R.*, vol. 22, pt. 1, 384-391, 408-412.

withheld on several occasions when opportunity offered of writing to you. Now however, I think I have a safe plan by which we can communicate with each other.

You will perceive this letter comes from Helena. The young lady who so kindly sends this letter to you will receive any letter from you to me and transmit them through "our line." Her address is "Miss R. Fannie Stayton, Helena, Ark." She is a beautiful young lady and she & her sister with several ladies from this vicinity were upon the field and under fire during the fight of the 4th of July 1863 ready and willing to do any service in their power for the good of our Dixie. God bless them, they will have their reward for their charity & goodness, if not here, in a world to come.

I suppose ere this you have heard many tales with regard to the fight at Helena in which not only my portion but Willie's Division of the army were also engaged. Before I go further, Willie and I escaped without injury and are both now as well and hearty as we ever were before. I will give you a kind synopsis of the battle.

On the evening of the 2nd of July, every thing being in readiness, the final orders were read to the effect that Gen'l Price would attack the enemy on the right & take what is termed Grave Yard Hill while Marmaduke on the center would take Fort Reiter [Rightor] and Walker's Cavalry on the left would skirmish the enemy to prevent a flank movement and at a given signal from Price, Marmaduke to charge the town & take possession.

At daylight on the morning of the 4th, the old 12 pound steel parrot guns of Shelby's Brigade exclaimed the anniversary of American Independence by several rounds of shell on the forts of the Federals. In a few moments it was taken up by the enemy and then by Price, [James F.] Fagan,[274] [Dandridge] McRae, Marmaduke & Walker and then pop, pop, pop, pop went the small arms and in a less space than it has taken me to write it the whole line was one complete blaze of light.

I had been left in command of all the mounted cavalry and ordered to hold myself in readiness to charge at a moment's notice. I rode to the front and ascended an eminence overlooking the entire field of action and I never beheld any thing as beautiful in my life. I could stand it no longer. I rode back & dismounting one hundred & fifty picked men, went forward as skirmishers.

The Yankees very bold at first but when I ordered my skirmishers to charge they gave back like sheep. I fought them about an hour and one half

---

[274] James F. Fagan was born in Kentucky and at the age of ten moved to Little Rock, Arkansas. He served in the Mexican War as a second lieutenant. At the outbreak of the Civil War, Fagan raised a company of volunteers and was elected colonel of the First Arkansas Infantry. On September 12, 1862 he was promoted to brigadier general and assigned to command a brigade in Arkansas. Fagan fought at Prairie Grove, Helena, Marks Mills during the Camden Campaign, and participated in Price's 1864 Missouri Raid. Following the war Fagan settled in Little Rock where he died on September 1, 1893. *O.R.*, vol. 22, pt. 1, 142, 412, 423-427; "Arkansas", *Confederate Military History*, vol. 10, 399-400; Warner, *Generals in Gray*, 85-86; Banasik, *Prairie Grove Campaign*, 472-473.

when they left and I retired & remounted. I had the satisfaction of hearing from one of their Lieutenants on the next day, under a flag of truce, that where my men fought there were eighteen bit the dust. I lost eight men killed & wounded.

The battery in which Willie & John Tatum are in found it impossible to get position and he and John with thirty other brave boys volunteered to go in with muskets. When the command was given to charge, the thirty two brave battery men led it & John & Willie were among the first to mount the ramparts, into the rifle pits where they captured seven prisoners. Next, over the redoubts, never stopping until they had reached and taken the enemy's artillery and the famous Grave Yard Hill. Only nine out of the 32 escaped, among that number was Willie & John.[275]

Every thing was working finely when about one o'clock much to the astonishment of everyone, Gen'l [Theophilus H.] Holmes[276] ordered the engagement to cease and the line withdrawn. Our loss was quite heavy, 800 I think is the highest estimate. Since then our (Walker's Brigade) has been the advance pickets of the army in this direction.

I suppose you have heard of my promotion to Major of [Robert C.] Newton's Regiment[277]. It occurred on the 1st of May. The Lieut. Colonel resigned the other day which again promotes me. If the war lasts long enough there is no telling what you may call your son Johnie when he comes home.

I saw in the *Republican*[278] the announcement of the marriage of Fannie Grover. Poor devil, who ever he is, I pity him. The old woman & the family will completely grind him. How is Pa getting along and Bob!

On our last raid[279] in Mo. my orderly was captured & sent to St. Louis. His name was Thomas McHugh. If he is still there do all you can for him. He is a good man. I will close. All of our acquaintances in the army here are well.

Give my love to Pa & Robert and kiss the children for me.

Farewell, Your son
Johnie

P.S. The young lady I speak of in the beginning of my letter has a brother

---

[275] At Helena the battery lost one killed, eight wounded, and three missing. *O.R.*, vol. 22, pt. 1, 422.

[276] See Appendix B for biography.

[277] Newton's Regiment also known as the Fifth Arkansas Cavalry. The regiment formed in the spring of 1862 and was commanded by Robert C. Newton, former adjutant general for General Thomas C. Hindman. Crute, *Units of the Confederate Army*, 45.

[278] The *Missouri Republican* was a daily newspaper published in St Louis, Missouri (1822-1919). The paper was, despite its name, the most democratic paper in Missouri. Library of Congress, *Newspapers in Microfilm, United States, 1948-1983* (Washington, 1984), vol. 1, 563.

[279] On April 17, 1863 Marmaduke launched his second Missouri raid with the objective being the capture of Rolla. His forces consisted of 5,000 men divided into four brigades. John's unit was part of John Q. Burbridge's brigade. A number of engagements occurred during the expedition, the most note worthy being the action at Cape Girardeau, Missouri on April 26, 1863. On May 2 Marmaduke returned to Arkansas, having lost 161 men. The Union losses totaled 120 troops. *O.R.*, vol. 22, pt. 1, 253, 286-287.

checking with Mr. Markhand. Hunt him up Ma & get acquainted with him. I do not know him myself but he must be clever. Ma, could you not so arrange it that you cold could come down & see me! If you could come to Helena you could get through their line if you would come with any one from Helena. If you can come, do so.

Yours
Johnie

* * * * * *

Letter, Will to Mother:

Nov 10th, 1863

My dear Mother[280]

I received a letter from you a few days ago written about the 10th of last month. I am glad you write every opportunity and hope you will continue to do so as the greatest pleasure I now have is that of receiving letters from home.

The exile got through "all right." He wishes to be remembered to you and the rest of his friends. I hope you may soon have an opportunity to send the things you have for us. Please send me a pair of heavy top boots No. 7. It is impossible to get any thing of the kind here. There was a pair sold here the other day at auction. I bid a $100 for them but failed to get them. They were sold for $110.

John T___[Tatum] left the other day for Red River. He has a 30 day furlough. See his mother & tell her he is well. Our friends here are all well. I have rec'd two letters from Cornelia since she has been at school in N.O. [New Orleans]. I wrote to her a few days ago. Remember me to all my friends. Love to all the family. Kiss little Lillie for me. How I should like to

---

[280] After Holmes defeat at Helena the Confederate Army returned to Little Rock. On August 1, 1863, Major General Frederick Steele began his movement on the Arkansas capital. Opposing Steele's 12,000-man force were about 8,000 troops, commanded by Sterling Price, Holmes being sick. The Little Rock Campaign involved a series of maneuvers with very little fighting. On September 10, 1863 Price abandoned Little Rock, having been flanked by Steele's army. During the forty-one day campaign both sides suffered only a few hundred casualties.

Both of the Bull brothers were evolved in the Little Rock Campaign, with John being heavily engaged throughout the Union advance. Will on the other hand spent his time in the trenches, north of Little Rock, and saw virtually no action.

John's unit fought skirmishes at Brownsville (August 25, 1863), and Bayou Meto-Shallow Ford (August 26 and 27, 1863). By September 7, 1863 John commanded his regiment as a major shuffle occurred in the Confederate cavalry, catapulting him to prominence. On September 10, 1863, John's regiment attempted to prevent a Union crossing of the Arkansas River. The federal pressure proved too great and John was forced to execute a fighting withdrawal. This final engagement for Little Rock was at Bayou Fourche.

John's actions during the advance on Little Rock were praised by his brigade commander who noted, "I cannot too strongly commend the bravery and dash of Major John P. Bull." Ibid., 475, 482, 521, 523, 535-540.

see the little creature. Johnie was well the last I heard from him.

Your Affc't [Affectionate] Son

Will

P.S. To Bob—Alex Lesueur is Capt. of the battery.[281] We had an election, Buck was thrown out. Alex, Edward F. Chappel, Lawrence Kingsland, John Duncan Holliday and all the boys are well. See their friends and let them know this. Get letters from their friends for them. Write every opportunity. We are always anxious to hear from you

Affectionately Yours

Will

* * * * * *

Letter, John to Mother:

Head Quarters Newton's Cavalry Brigade

"Bivouacking in the Woods"

November 19th 1863

My own Dearest Mother,

I have this moment received your letter and "devoured" its contents in a manner I know would have amused you. My transports at it reception would admit of no bounds and I manifested my delight in an up roaring yell, a bound, several somersaults, and indeed at this moment am hardly able to record what did happen but when I fully recovered my equanimity I found my Adjutant & Inspector General with orderlies, negroes & attaches generally standing around ready to give assistance in case the poor Major should need it. The Sergeant of the guard was standing at a respectful distance with several grim looking Rebels at an order arms, their bristling bayonets ready at a moments notice to end the career of any refractory who should bid defiance to authority & law broken.

I at last came to myself & related to them I had received a letter from home at which the Adjutant & Inspector pricked up their ears for news. The orderly & negroes retired to their quarters. The officer commanded—Attention guard—Shoulder arms— Right face—Forward, quick time march and in a few moments I was left in silent possession of my tent where without interruption I could pause & enjoy "Secret news from home."

Oh Mother, you could imagine the pleasure I enjoyed at that minute. Your kind compliments so sincere to me. To know that I have received the approbation of my Mother is sufficient compensation for all the hardships & privations I have endured since I left you.

You say I never make mention of Little Syde! I have written to you several times since I heard the news & have always aimed to mention the fact

---

[281] See pages 64-65 for Bull's comments on the election process.

of knowing it. You ask me, Ma, if I need any thing. I need every thing which we cannot procure for love or money. On the first place, indeed a pair of boots, some shirts, socks, gloves, etc. which my friend Funics led lent me. Confederate money would be of no use to him in passing & repassing and I have given him an order on Pa for some money.

I need a suit of clothes and if you will purchase the cloth & trimmings he will let you know where to leave them & he will bring them out. He could not bring them made up but could in the piece. Don't neglect sending buttons, lace, thread, lining, and every thing requisite to make the suit as we can procure nothing of the kind here.

My Dear Ma, I could write you for hours of what has happened since I left. I could detail to you some of the most interesting news of battle scenes where your Johnie has flourished conspicuously. I could relate to you scenes of bloodshed that would make your woman's heart freeze almost. But tis not my aim in this letter for my friend is standing by hurrying me so I cannot possibly concentrate my thoughts sufficient to tell all these things. Never mind Ma, I will return before long and then if cold winters evening, I will nestle close to "Ma in her nursery and under her protective wing" seek security from the outside world & recount to her all that has passed from beginning to end.

Mother, I never appreciated you or Pa at home as I do now. I always loved you both and attempted to be obedient from honor (for I always had a keen sense of honor) but had an unfortunate way of getting into difficulties but should I ever return I will devote myself entirely to your comfort & your happiness. I have never since I left you been under the influence of liquor. It was an obligation I made with myself upon leaving home & I have strictly, honestly kept it. But I must close.

Give my love & this little note enclosed to Jennie. To all those who have remembered the wandering Rebel "Johnie Bull" present my most affectionate regards. I am sorry Syde is named after Hoppel. He's the only one of our name & blood the least tainted with "Vreis v'lisure." Hoppel is black as tar & I had almost said, I respected Aunt Penelope the less on account of the ties that bind her to him but I will not. Those ties were formed before the break between North and South was so great. But I must close.

Farewell. May God ever bless you is the prayer of your son

Johnie

* * * * * *

Letter, Will to Mother:

December 23d 1863

My dear Mother,

Notwithstanding I have written you several letters recently, I have concluded to write another as I have a good opportunity to send it. Mrs. Dr. S___ got through safely. I have seen her several times since she came down and was very much pleased with her indeed. She gave me all the family news. After talking to her I felt, almost, as though I had been at home. She brought Johnie & I each likeness of Lal & Mary. We were delighted to get them but surprised to find how much they had changed. They have grown so. Why Lal is as large as either of us and is much better looking. Mary, too, has grown very much and is the prettiest creature I ever saw.

Mrs. S. told me you had sent us a likeness of Little Lillie. It is singular what has become of them. We have not rec'd them. She told me of a number of things that you had sent which we have not rec'd, among the number three prs [pairs] of boots for me. I only received the first pair. There was a coat brought through recently for us. Johnie seemed to be in doubt as to who it was for. The person who brought it through said it was for him but it was an artillery coat made I think as I requested mine to be made so I insisted it was mine. Please state in your next who it was for.

Mrs. S___ told me you were very much disturbed that I had not received a commission. That you think great injustice has been done me etc, etc. I was very much amused at the idea. I will tell you how this has happened.

My first object, as a soldier, is to serve my country to the best of my ability. My second is to have as easy a time as possible (I imagine I hear you laugh & call me lazy, well I plead guilty to the charge). I thought I could accomplish both of these objects best in the artillery. This is considered the most dangerous branch of the service and it has always been difficult to keep the batterys full. On the other hand we are allowed more transportation than any other service.

I, as chief of piece, have a horse to ride and can have as much baggage as I wish. The cavalry have no transportation, scarcely, and the infantry, officers & all have to walk. But then promotion in artillery is very slow on account of their being so few batterys in our army. I have been offered promotions in the infantry frequently, but have always preferred remaining present position. I was offered a 1st Lieutenancy in Infantry yesterday. I will accept it if Tatum & Holliday will go with me. I think they will do it.[282]

I saw Johnie about a week ago. He was well. He is a gallant officer, dearly beloved by officers & men. He will be Lieut. Col. before long. I feel very proud of him.

Ma, the bearer of this will, I think, bring out any thing you may wish to send. Please send me a pair of boots, a pair of Gauntlets and a nice saber belt.

---

[282] Will never accepted the position and remained in the artillery service throughout the war.

I need these more than any thing else.

If you have a likeness of little Lillie please send it to me as I should like to have it so much. Remember me to all friends. Love to Bob and all the family. God bless you my dear Mother and all the family.

Your Affec. Son
Will

* * * * * *

Letter, John to Mother:

Colombia, Chicot County Ark.
Head Quarters Cavalry Div.
In the field June 5th 1864

My Darling Mother

Since the Spring Campaign[283] I have written several letters & sent them to be forwarded by "Flag of Truce" but whether they have ever reached you I know not. I received Pa's letter by, "Flag of Truce," dated 21st of April and thank him a thousand times for his congratulations upon my marriage. I expect when the war is over to bring my little wife with me to Missouri and I know you all can not but love her.

Willie thinks there is no one on earth like his Sister Nobie and is as devotedly attached to her as if she were his own blood sister.

I received a letter from her on yesterday and she told me if an opportunity offered, she would write to you all. Ma, I never had an object in life before, I never felt really happy until I found my little Nobie. She is so industrious, so pious, so entirely devoted to me and my interests....Indeed,...she is every thing my heart could desire in a partner....I think fortune has particularly smiled on me in choosing one for me so well adapted to making me happy.

You know, when at home, dancing was my great hobby. She never dances and I have entirely ignored the habit. Her father, like Pa, knows nothing but Methodism and is equally as devoted. I think by the time I get home I will be so comfortably settled down you will hardly recognize me.

I am now encamped within three hundred yards of R. R. Sessions Plantation. Say to Mrs. Sessions, her husband started for Shreveport a few days ago and was very well. Mrs. Sessions is at her father's, Dr. Gibson.

Willie is quite well and I know if he were here he would be pleased to add a post script to my letter. I hear from him every day or two. He nor myself have ever been sick for a moment.[284] Wright Shaurnberg, the Von Phul's[285] and all our St. Louis friends are very well. I saw Dr. Leabt week or

---

[283] Bull is referring to Banks's Red River Campaign and Steele's Camden Expedition.

[284] Not true. Will was sick shortly after the unit returned to Arkansas in August 1862.

[285] John is referring to Francis or Frank Van Phul and his brother Benjamin. Ben commanded a

two ago and he was as very well. Frank Von Phul was wounded in one of our recent engagements but has entirely recovered.

The bugle is sounding to horse and I must be off. Give my love & Nobie's to the whole family and accept for yourself a very large portion my Dear Ma. Farewell & God bless you all. Your Aff. son

Johnie

P.S. I received my promotion to Lt. Colonel the night I was married.[286] Send me my marriage notice from the paper in which it was published in St. Louis.

Yours   J.

* * * * * *

Letter, John to Father:

Franklin Mo
Oct. 1st, 1864

My own Darling Mother and Father[287]

Here I am within forty miles of you & no chance at present of seeing you. I hope however it will not be many days before the Stars & Bars of our glorious Confederacy will wave over the spires of my dear home. I saw Willie just before leaving Ark. and he was very well. Since I left you I have ever been well and always preserved by a Kind Providence. My Nobie was well when I last heard from her. This is all I can write.

Yours Devotedly
Johnie

P. S. My courier will give you an account of us.

* * * * * *

Letter, Will to Mother:

Oct. 1st, 1864

My dear Mother,

I received by flag of truce Pa's letter of date 27th May. I have not heard

---

temporary battery and Frank was on Daniel M. Frost's staff as an aide and later on John B. Clark's, Jr. staff. *O.R.*, vol. 22, pt. 2, 969; *O.R.*, vol. 41, pt. 2, 1,094.

[286] John married Miss Zanobia Sanders in early March 1864. Bull diary, 92.

[287] By the time John wrote this letter he was in the middle of Price's 1864 Missouri Raid. Price launched his invasion on August 28, 1864 and terminated the campaign on December 3, 1864. John was wounded during the campaign, but remained with the army, serving as the army's Provost Marshal. Returning to Arkansas, John waited with his brother for the surrender of the Trans-Mississippi Department which occurred in May 1865. *O.R.*, vol. 41, pt. 1, 642-648.

a word from home since. We received also the likeness of our little sister. I have just returned from Washington where I spent a very pleasant week at Capt. Sanders. Nobie took great interest in making shirts & other articles of clothing which I needed very much. She was as kind and attentive to me as she could possibly have been to an own brother. She is one of the best little souls in the world. I know you will love her.

I received a letter from Cornelia a few days ago written from Atlanta, Ga.[288] She was well & said she had succeeded in getting a pass port to go to her mother in Del. [Delaware]. She said she would make you a visit as soon as she got north.

Love to each member of the family & remember me kindly to all my friends. Write every opportunity & direct as before. I remain, my dear Mother

Your Affectionate Son

Will

* * * * * *

Letter, Will to Mother:

Dec. 13th 1864

My dear Mother[289]

I have not received a letter from home for many months and frequently ask myself the question "Why do they not write?" I am disposed to attribute this to the irregularity of our "mails." I cannot believe that my <u>Mother</u> has forgotten me. No, No <u>perish</u> the thought. Its entertainment would distract me. <u>Do</u> write often. My only anxiety is on your account. Could I hear occasionally that the family were all well & doing well, I think I would be perfectly contented. I have written you repeatedly since I rec'd received your last letter & have sent you verbal messages by several persons & hope you have received all.

I am well, indeed, I have enjoyed excellent health ever since I left home. I heard from Johnie a few days ago. He was well and at home with his wife. Nobie was also well. I expect to spend Christmas with them. How I would love to spend it at home!! This will be the fourth Christmas I have spent from home. Well I will spend the fifth with you if I am spared.

I rec'd a letter from Cornelia sometime ago in which she said she expected to go to Del. soon to meet her mother. Have you heard any thing from her? Please write to her for me & ask her to send me her likeness. I have one of her, but it was taken a long while ago & is not good.

---

[288] Atlanta was occupied by Federal forces on September 2, 1864. *O.R.*, vol. 38, pt. 1, 54.

[289] Four months later, on April 9, 1865, Lee's army surrendered at Appomattox Court House. The remaining rebel forces in the Trans-Mississippi Department, excepting General Stand Watie's in the Indian Territory, surrendered on May 26th, 1865. With the war's end, the long journey home, to rebuild their lives, began for John and William Bull. *O.R.*, vol. 48, 600.

I am very pleasantly situated here, that is, as much as so as could be expected. I have many good friends who will never see me want for anything. I have a very good supply of clothing for the winter. I only lack an overcoat & pr. pair of boots. If you should have good opportunity to send these articles I wish very much you would do so. Probably Judge Smizer would bring them. Don't send them unless you have a first rate chance because I can do without them.

I never have, for one moment, regretted having come here, & am now as I always have been, determined to remain until that, which I come to assist in accomplishing, has been accomplished.

What has become of John T. [Tatum]?[290] We did not think he would act as he has. Do write often & tell me about all my friends. Give my love to each member of the family & to friends inquiring. I remain my dear Mother

Your Affectionate Son

Will

---

[290] Tatum was captured while on furlough in 1864. He was charged with being a spy, and scheduled to be hanged. Upon intervention by his new wife, John agreed to take the oath of allegiance and was spared. Bull diary, 85.

Appendix A
Roster of Gorham's/Tilden's/Lesueur's/Third Missouri Field Battery[291]

NOTE: * indicates the men who accepted parole on June 8, 1865 at Shreveport, Louisiana.

Name/ Entry Into Confederate Service/ Highest Rank// Remarks

Allen, R./ Oct. 28, 1862 (Yellville, Ark.)/ Private// Deserted May 2, 1863 at Little Rock, Ark.

Arndt, F./ Sept. 1, 1862 (Mulberry Creek, Ark.)/ Private.

Baldridge, Benjamin F. K: See Boldridge.

Baldridge, Joseph: See Boldridge.

Barron, J. F./ Oct. 29, 1862 (Yellville, Ark.)/ Private// Discharged for disability on April 23, 1863, probably in Little Rock, Ark.

Beaty, G. W./ Nov. 10, 1862 (Mulberry Creek, Ark.)/ Private// Died in Little Rock, Ark. on March 22, 1863.

Blue, A./ Nov. 11, 1862 (Mulberry Creek, Ark.)/ Private// Deserted on Nov. 12, 1863 from Camp Bragg which was near Red River, 23 miles from Camden, Ark., on the road between Camden and Shreveport, La.

*Boldridge [or Baldridge], Benjamin F. K./ Sept. 1, 1862 (Des Arc, Ark.)/ First Lieutenant (Dec. 18, 1863)// From Marion Co., Mo.

*Boldridge [or Baldridge], Joseph/ Sept. 1, 1862 (Des Arc, Ark.)/ Second Lieutenant// From Marion Co., Mo.; On recruiting duty March 12, 1863, turned back by order of General Holmes on March 17; Returned to recruiting service on April 7, 1863; Wounded at Helena, Ark. on July 4, 1863.

Boling, J [or Bowling J. S.]/ Private/ July 1, 1862 (Mississippi)// Deserted on

[291] National Archives, Record Group M322, rolls no. 85 and 90, Service Records, Third Field Battery Missouri Artillery and Von Phul's Battery (see Ben Von Phul service record); Hoskin diary, vol. 1, 22-23, 35-36, 42 and vol. 2, 35-36, 40-41, 70, 72, 77, 92-94, 427; "Military Companies of St. Louis—No. 4 National guards—2nd Company," Missouri Militia scrapbook, page 6 of unnumbered pages; "Non-Commissioned Officers of the First Regiment of Infantry," Missouri Militia scrapbook, page 17 of unnumbered pages; "Company C—City Guards," and "Washington Blues—company E," Missouri Militia scrapbook, page 18 of unnumbered pages; Exchanged prisoner list, Camp Jackson Papers; "The Camp Jackson Prisoners," *Missouri Republican*, December 3, 1861.

Feb. 26, 1863 from Little Rock, Ark.

Borland, E./ Sept. 1, 1862 (Des Arc, Ark.)/ Private// Died Sept. 25, 1862 at Clinton, Ark. while unit was en route to Yellville.

Bowling J. S.: See Boling.

Brady, John/ Nov. 9, 1862 (Mulberry Creek, Ark.)/ Private.

*Brown, Oscar/ After Oct. 10, 1863/ Private// From Saline Co., Mo.

Bull, John P./ Sept. 1, 1862 (Des Arc, Ark.)/ Sergeant// From St. Louis, Mo.; Founding member Second National Guard Company, St. Louis, Mo. Volunteer Militia; Captured at Camp Jackson, exchanged in Nov. 1861; Went south aboard the steamship *Iatan* in Dec. 1861; Transferred and promoted to staff of Col. Emmett MacDonald on Dec. 2, 1862.

Bull, William J./ Sept. 1, 1862 (Des Arc, Ark.)/ Sergeant// From St. Louis, Mo.; Member Second National Guard Company St. Louis, Missouri Volunteer Militia; Captured at Camp Jackson, exchanged in Nov. 1861; Went south aboard the steamship *Iatan* in Dec. 1861.

*Burton, W. V. [or W. W.]/ After Oct. 10, 1863/ Private// From Van Buren Co., Iowa.

Byrgan, L./ Nov. 10, 1862 (Mulberry Creek, Ark.)/ Private// Died Jan. 9, 1863 at Fort Smith, Ark.; Left behind when the army marched to Little Rock.

Casey, A./ Oct. 28, 1862/ Sergeant// From Atchison Co., Mo.; Wounded in the eye in a camp accident, when a shell exploded on July 7, 1864.

*Chapman, George/ Sept. 1, 1862 (Des Arc, Ark.)/ Private// From Atchison, Atchison County, Mo.

*Chapman, J. M./ Oct. 13, 1862 (Yellville, Ark.)/ Private// From Saline Co., Mo.; Transferred to battery on Nov. 10, 1862 from Pindall's Missouri Sharpshooters.

Chappell, Edward F./ Sept. 1, 1862 (Des Arc)/ Second lieutenant (November 19, 1862) and again (December 18, 1863)// From St.Louis, Mo.; Born in Maryland; Captured at Camp Jackson, exchanged in Nov. 1861; Went south aboard the *Iatan* on Dec. 2, 1861 for Columbus, Ky.; Assigned as Chief of Ordnance of Steen's (Parsons's) Brigade on October 22, 1862; Elected second lieutenant upon battery reorganization in December 1863; Returned from furlough on July 24, 1864 and arrested for failing to report his return.

Childers, E. P./ Sept. 1, 1862 (Des Arc, Ark.)/ Private// Granted furlough of fifteen days in January 1864.

*Chrisman, Granville/ Jan. 5, 1863 (Clarksville, Ark.)/ Private// From Savannah, Andrew Co., Mo.

Cobb, R./ Nov. 7, 1862 (Mulberry Creek, Ark.)/ Private// Died on Sept. 14, 1863 at Little Rock, Ark.

*Conyers, A. L./ After Oct. 10, 1863/ Private// From Scott Co., Mo.

*Cummiskey, John W./ Sept. 1, 1862 (Des Arc, Ark.)/ Quartermaster Sergeant// From St. Louis, Mo.; A corporal in the Sarfield's Guards, St. Louis, Mo. Volunteer Militia; Captured at Camp Jackson, exchanged in Nov. 1861.

*Dawes, W. C./ unknown/ Private// From Saline Co., Mo.

*Dawson, C./ Sept. 1, 1862 (Des Arc, Ark.)/ Sergeant// From Ralls, Co., Mo.

*Decker, John B./ Nov. 9, 1862 (Mulberry Creek, Ark.)/ Private// From St. Louis, Mo.

Dickerson, John/ Sept. 1, 1862 (Des Arc, Ark.)/ Private// Died on May 23, 1863 at Little Rock, Ark.

Donaldson [or Donnelson], James/ Sept. 1, 1862 (Des Arc, Ark.)/ Private// From Lafayette Co., Mo.

Donnelson, James: See Donaldson.

*Duncan, A. T./ After Oct. 10, 1863/ Private// From Jackson Co., Mo.; Moved to Carrollton, Carroll Co., Mo. after the war.

*Dunlap, James T./ Sept. 1, 1862 (Des Arc, Ark.)/ Private// From Marion Co., Mo.

Engleman, John B./ Oct. 28, 1862 (Yellville, Ark.)/ Private// Deserted on Feb. 26, 1863 at Little Rock, Ark.

Ent, Joseph B./ Sept. 1, 1862 (Des Arc, Ark.)/ Private// From Andrew Co., Mo.; Born in Ohio; Transferred to recruiting service on April 9, 1863; Captured on May 28, 1863 en route to home.

Farmer, William/ Sept. 1, 1862 (Des Arc, Ark.)// From Calloway Co., Mo.; Wounded at Helena, Ark. on July 4, 1863.

Farris, W. G./ Dec. 18, 1862 (Van Buren, Ark.)/ Private// Killed at Helena, Ark. on July 4, 1863.

*Flanagan, William A./ Sept. 1, 1862 (Des Arc, Ark.)/ Private// From Saline Co., Mo.

Flanigan, Marshall W./After Oct. 10, 1863/ Probably a Private// From Saline Co., Mo.

Fleming, J./ Nov. 1, 1862 (Carrollton, Ark.)/ Private// From St. Louis, Mo.; Member Washington Blues, St. Louis, Mo. Volunteer Militia.

Forney, Frank A.: See Fourney.

Fourney [or Forney or Tourney or Toomey], Frank A./ unknown/ Private.

Franklin, E. St. J./ Sept. 1, 1862 (Des Arc, Ark.)/ Sergeant.

Freiez [or Freeze], J./ Before Oct. 10, 1863/ Probably Private.

*Gallaway [or Galloway], J. S./ Oct. 29, 1862 (Yellville, Ark.)/ Private// From Boone Co., Mo.

*Galloway [or Gallaway], James M./ Oct. 29, 1862 (Yellville, Ark.)/ Private// From Columbia, Boone Co., Mo.

Garner, W. A./ Before Oct. 10, 1863/ Probably a Private.

*Gausney, G./ unknown/ Private// From Jackson Co., Mo.

Gibson, G. W./ Nov. 9, 1862 (Mulberry Creek, Ark.)/ Private// From St. Louis, Mo.; Member City Guards, St. Louis, Mo. Volunteer Militia.

*Gibson, W. P./ unknown/ Probably Private// From Jackson Co., Mo.

Gillespie, J. H./ Sept. 1, 1862 (Des Arc, Ark.)/ Private.

*Goff, James/ Oct. 29, 1862 (Yellville, Ark.)/ Private// Deserted on April 20, 1863, later returned for the war; From Saline Co., Mo.

Gorham, James C./In 1861/ Captain (Sept. 1862)// From Marshall, Saline Co.,

Mo.; Thrown out as unit commander on November 10, 1862 upon reorganization of the battery; Placed in command of six gun battery defending the water approaches to Little Rock; Resigned in January 1863.

Gorin, H. J./ August 14, 1862 (Arkansas Post, Ark.)/ Private// Discharged for disability on April 27, 1863 at Little Rock, Ark.

Gristy [or Christy], J. B./ Sept. 1, 1862 (Des Arc, Ark.)/ Private// From Scott Co., Mo.

Grove, E./ Sept. 1, 1862 (Des Arc., Ark.)/ Private// Died on Nov. 16, 1862 at camp on Mulberry Creek, Ark.

Hagan, S./ Sept. 1, 1862 (Des Arc, Ark.)/ Corporal// Mortally wounded at Helena, Ark. on July 4, 1863.

Hallam [or Hollam], H. T./ unknown/ Private// From Jackson Co., Mo.

*Hammer, R. M./ unknown/ Private// Scott Co., Mo.

Hanes, T./ Before Oct. 10, 1863/ Probably a Private.

Harris, H. H./ Nov. 10, 1862 (Mulberry Creek, Ark./ Private// Deserted on Jan. 11, 1863 at Lewisburg, Ark. while en route to Little Rock, Ark.

*Hawkinsmith, D./ After Oct. 10, 1863/ Private// From Lexington, Jackson Co., Mo.

*Hedges, Robert/ unknown/ Private// From Jackson Co., Mo.

*Hill, W. N./ After Oct. 10, 1863/ Private// From Johnson Co., Mo.; Moved to Chapple Hill, Lafayette Co., Mo. after the war.

Holland, Thomas/ Sept. 1, 1862 (Des Arc, Ark.)/ Private// Detailed to Quartermaster Department; On Aug. 1, 1863 reported as a deserter.

*Holliday, John Duncan/ Nov. 10, 1862 (Mulberry Creek, Ark.)/ First Sergeant// From St. Louis, Mo.; Founding member Second National Guard Company, St. Louis, Mo. Volunteer Militia; Captured at Camp Jackson, exchanged in Nov. 1861; Went south aboard the steamship *Iatan* in Dec. 1861; Promoted to Lieutenant of Ordnance on Feb. 3, 1864 and left unit.

*Hoskin [or Haskin], William N./ Sept. 1, 1862 (Des Arc, Ark.)/ Corporal// From Marion Co., Mo.; Born Feb. 11, 1841; Granted fifteen-day furlough, beginning Jan. 15, 1864.

Hough [or Huff], James C./ Aug. 18, 1862 (Arkansas Post, Ark.)/ Second Lieutenant (Nov. 19, 1862)// From St. Louis, Mo.; Born in England; Resigned on July 17, 1863 because of age (he was 40).

Howard, W. R./ Nov. 10, 1862 (Mulberry Creek, Ark.)/ Private// Deserted on Dec. 10, 1863 in southwest Arkansas while on the march.

Huff, James C.: See Hough, James C.

Irwin, Joseph, Sept. 1, 1862 (Des Arc, Ark.)/ Private.

*Jackson, John M./ Nov. 11, 1862 (Mulberry Creek, Ark.)/ Bugler// From Saline City, Saline Co., Mo.

*Johnson, C. P./ unknown/ Private// From Jackson, Co., Mo.

Jones, J. C./ Dec. 18, 1862 (Van Buren, Ark.)/ Private// Deserted on May 2, 1863 at Little Rock, Ark.

*Kabeich [or Kabrick], H. P. F. [or H. P. T.] / unknown/ Private// From Jackson Co., Mo.

*Kabrick, H. P. T.: See Kabeich.

Kavanaugh, Thomas H./ Nov. 10, 1862 (Mulberry Creek, Ark.)/ Ass't Surgeon// From Independence, Jackson Co., Mo.; Born in Kentucky; Returned from furlough on July 24, 1864 and arrested for failing to report his return.

*Keith, G. P./ unknown/ Private// From St. Francois Co., Mo.

*Keith, James/ unknown/ Private// From St. Francois Co., Mo.

*Kilgore, E./ Sept. 1, 1863 (Des Arc, Ark.)/ Private// From Audrain Co., Mo.

Kingsland, Lawrence/ Sept. 1, 1862 (Des Arc, Ark.)/ Second Lieutenant (Dec. 18, 1863).

*Kirkpatrick, A. C. [or I. J.]/ unknown/ Private// From Scott Co., Mo.

*Kirkpatrick, S./ unknown/ Private// From Mississippi Co., Mo.

Larimore, Robert/ Oct. 29, 1862 (Yellville)/ Private// From Marshall, Mo.

(Saline Co.); Deserted on Sept. 10, 1863 at Jacksonport, Ark.; Captured in Green Co., Mo. Sept. 18, 1863; Died in a Federal Hospital on April 19, 1864 of "Variola"—Smallpox.

Laton, T./ Sept. 1, 1862 (Des Arc, Ark.)/ Private.

Lesueur, Alexander A./ Missouri State Guard in May 1861; Confederate Service unknown/ First Lieutenant (Nov. 10, 1862); Captain (Dec. 18, 1863)// From St. Louis, Mo.; Born in 1842; Member Joseph Kelly's St. Louis, Mo. Volunteer Militia Company; Participated in early 1861 battles in Missouri, Prairie Grove, Helena, Red River and Camden campaigns; Wounded at Wilson's Creek on August 10, 1861; Wounded at Helena, Ark. on July 4, 1863.

Lewis, J. C./ Sept. 1, 1862 (Des Arc, Ark.)/ Private.

*Lewis, T. S./ Sept. 1, 1862 (Des Arc, Ark.)/ Private// From Marion Co., Mo.; Wounded at Helena, Ark. on July 4, 1863.

Mason, J. W./ Nov. 11, 1862 (Mulberry Creek, Ark.)/ Private// Deserted on Dec. 9, 1862 at Oliver's, Ark. following the Battle of Prairie Grove, Ark.

McAllister, John/ Sept. 1, 1862 (Des Arc, Ark.)/ Private.

McClure (?), W. C./ Before Oct. 10, 1863/ Probably a Private.

*McElwee [or McElwell], J. H./ unknown/ Private// From Louisiana, Pike Co., Mo.

*McElwee [or McIlwee or McElwell], W. B. [or W. C.]/ Sept. 1, 1862 (Des Arc, Ark.)/ Private// From Louisiana, Pike Co., Mo.

McElwell, J. H.: See McElwee.

McElwell, W. B.: See McElwee.

McIlwee, W. B.: See McElwee.

McFarland, Dan/ Sept. 27, 1862 (Searcy, Ark.)/ Private// Deserted on June 23, 1863 at Jacksonport, Ark.

McGinnis, T./ Nov. 10, 1862 (Mulberry Creek, Ark.)/ Private// Deserted on Feb. 26, 1863 at Little Rock, Ark.

*McKibben [or McKibbin or McKibbey], George/ May 1, 1863 (Little Rock,

Ark.)// From St. Louis Co., Mo.

McKibbey, George: See McKibben.

McKibbin, George: See McKibben.

*Melay [Meley], Albert/ Sept. 1, 1862 (Des Arc, Ark.)/ Private// From St. Louis Co., Mo.

Meley, Albert: See Melay.

*Meley, John, Sept. 1, 1862 (Des Arc, Ark.)/ Private// From Moniteau Co., Mo.

Michael [or Mitchel], James/ Oct. 29, 1862 (Yellville, Ark.)/ Private// From Cole Co., Mo.

*Miller, Peter/ unknown/ Private// From Saline Co., Mo.

*Milstead, James/ Sept. 1, 1862 (Des Arc, Ark.)/ Private// From Ray Co., Mo.

Moss, J. T/ Dec. 18, 1862 (Van Buren, Ark.)/ Private// Mortally wounded at Helena, Ark. on July 4, 1863.

*Nelson, J. L. / After Oct. 10, 1863/ Private// From Johnson Co., Mo.; Moved to Chapple Hill, Lafayette Co., Mo. after the war.

*Norris, Andrew W. [or P.]/ Feb. 7, 1863 (Little Rock, Ark.)/ First Lieutenant (Oct. 21, 1863)// From Clark Co., Mo.

Norval, C. H./ Oct. 28, 1862 (Yellville, Ark.)/ Private.

O'Donnal, Daniel: See O'Donnell.

*O'Donnell [or O'Donnal], Daniel/ unknown/ Private// From Saline Co., Mo.

O'Donnell, J. M./ Nov. 10, 1862 (Mulberry Creek, Ark.)/ Private// Deserted on Feb. 26, 1863 at Little Rock, Ark.

O'Donnell, John [or James]/ Sept. 1, 1862 (Des Arc, Ark.)/ Private// Deserted on May 2, 1863 at Little Rock, Ark.

Palmer, J. H./ Oct. 28, 1862 (Yellville, Ark.)/ Private// Discharged on May 3, 1863 for disability, probably at Little Rock, Ark.

Parr, A./ Sept. 1, 1862 (Des Arc, Ark.)/ Private// Transferred to William D. Blocher's Ark. Battery on May 16, 1863.

Pemberton, F. M./ Sept. 1, 1862/ Private.

*Peterson, J. B. [or G. B.]/ Before Oct. 10, 1863/ Private// From Saline Co., Mo.

Phul, Benjamin/ Probably Sept. 1, 1862 (Des Arc, Ark.)/ Private// Left the battery in Feb. 1863 to command temporary battery as first lieutenant.

*Polk, E. B./ unknown/ Private// From Platt Co., Mo.

Powell, S [or J.]/ Sept. 1, 1862/ Private.

Quigley, William/ Sept. 1, 1862 (Des Arc, Ark.)/ Corporal// From Walnut Hills, Ark. (Lafayette, Co.); Wounded at Helena, Ark. on July 4, 1863.

Richards, P. M./Nov. 10, 1863 (Mulberry Creek, Ark.)/ Private// Deserted on Dec. 24, 1862 at Van Buren, Ark.

Roberts, J. C./ Feb. 20, 1863 (Little Rock, Ark.)/ Private// Captured while on furlough in Aug. 1863.

*Roden, L. [or S.] / unknown/ Private// From Laclede Co., Mo.

Ross, John/ Joined after Oct. 10, 1863/ Private// Deserted on August 31, 1864, stealing a horse.

Rootes, George F./ Sept. 1, 1862 (Des Arc, Ark.)/ Private// Detailed to Commissary Dept. in Nov. 1862.

Rutherford, F./ Oct. 29, 1862 (Yellville, Ark.)/ Private// Deserted on Feb. 26, 1863 at Little Rock, Ark.

Ryan, Thomas/ Sept. 1, 1862 (Des Arc, Ark.)/ Private// From St. Louis, Mo.; Captured at Camp Jackson, exchanged in Nov. 1861; Went south aboard the *Iatan* on Dec. 2, 1861; Detailed to Quartermaster Department in Oct. 1862.

*Ryen, John/ unknown/ Private// From Saline Co., Mo.

*Samuel, J. M./ unknown/ Private// From St. Francois Co., Mo.

Sandage, Robert: See Standage.

Schib, A: See Shebb.

Schley [or Schly], William/ Sept. 1, 1862 (Des Arc, Ark.)/ Private// From St. Louis, Mo.; Captured at Camp Jackson, exchanged in Nov. 1861; Went south aboard the *Iatan* on Dec. 2, 1861; Died on Sept. 25, 1862 at Clinton, Ark. while unit was en route to Yellville, Ark.

Schly, William: See Schley.

Schultz [or Shitz], N. P./ After Oct. 10, 1863/ Probably a Private// From Pleasant Hill, Cass Co., Mo.

Schultz [or Shitz], Thomas/ After Oct. 10, 1863/ Probably a Private// From Pleasant Hill, Cass Co., Mo.

Scripture, A. W./ Sept. 1, 1862 (Des Arc, Ark.)/ Corporal// From Howard Co., Mo.; Moved to Saline City, Saline Co. Mo. after the war.

Scudder, Thomas D./ Nov. 10, 1862 (Mulberry Creek, Ark.)/ Private// Discharged for disability on July 21, 1863 at Little Rock, Ark.; Captured in St. Louis on April 25 1864; Took oath of allegiance on May 5, 1864 and released.

Seig, J. [or Sieg, J. F.]/ Oct. 28, 1862 (Yellville, Ark.)/ Private.

Shajack, G. M.: See Shrylock.

*Sharpe, A. H./ unknown/ Private// From Nodaway Co., Mo.

*Sharpe, Daniel/ unknown/ Private// From Nodaway Co., Mo.

*Sharpe, Nicholas/ unknown/ Private// From Maryville, Nodaway Co., Mo.

*Shebb [or Schib], A./ Sept. 1, 1862 (Des Arc, Ark.)/ Corporal.

Shiflet, C./ Sept. 1, 1862 (Des Arc, Ark.)/ Private// Discharged for disability on Dec. 31, 1863, probably at Camp Bragg, Ark.

*Shropshire, J. H./ Sept. 1, 1862 (Des Arc, Ark.)/ Private// From Marion Co., Mo.

*Shropshire, J. W./ Sept. 1, 1862 (Des Arc, Ark.)/ Private// From Howard Co., Mo.; Granted fifteen day furlough, beginning Jan. 15, 1864.

Shrylock [or Shajack or Shyrock], G. [or G. M. or M.]/ Sept. 1, 1862 (Des Arc,

Ark.)/ Sergeant// From Marion Co., Mo.; Granted fifteen-day furlough in Jan. 1864.

Shyrock, G. [or G. M. or M.]: See Shrylock.

Sieg, J. F.: See Seig.

Silkmore, John/ Sept. 1, 1862 (Des Arc, Ark.)/ Private.

Simpson, William/ Sept. 23, 1862 (Des Arc, Ark.)/ Private// Promoted to S. P. Burns's Reg't (11th Missouri Infantry) on May 1, 1863.

Slaughter, Phillip/ June 1, 1863 (Little Rock, Ark.)// Wounded at Helena, Ark. on July 4, 1863 and captured.

Smith, J. C./ Sept. 1, 1862 (Des Arc, Ark.)/ Private.

Smith, John/ Sept. 1, 1862 (Des Arc, Ark.)/ Private// Deserted on Dec. 29, 1862 while on the march to Little Rock, Ark.

Smith, N./ unknown/ Private// From Dade Co., Mo.

Sneider, R. M. [or F. R.]/ Sept. 1, 1862 (Des Arc, Ark.)/ Private.

Sparks, S. H./ Sept. 1, 1862 (Des Arc, Ark.)/ Private.

Spellan, Stephen B: See Spellin.

Spellen, Stephen B.: See Spellin.

Spellin [or Spellan or Spellen], Stephen B./ Sept. 1, 1862 (Des Arc, Ark.)/ Sergeant// From St. Louis, Mo.; Captured at Camp Jackson, exchanged in Nov. 1861; Went south aboard the steamship *Iatan* in Dec. 1861; Captured at Helena, Ark. on July 4, 1863.

*St. John, William/ Sept. 1, 1862 (Des Arc, Ark.)/ Private// From Lewis Co., Mo.

*Stacy or [Stasey or Stasy], A. J./ Sept. 23, 1862 (Des Arc, Ark.)/ Private// From Marion Co., Mo.; Transferred from Pindall's Missouri Sharpshooters on Aug. 15, 1863; Conveyed about $800.00 in donations to a Missouri women who lost her husband in the war, left on Feb. 27 and returned Mar. 5, 1864.

Standage [or Sandage], Robert/ unknown/ Private// From Webster Co., Mo.

Stasey, A. J.: See Stacy.

Stasy, A. J.: See Stacy.

Steare [or Steave], Charles/ Sept. 1, 1862 (Des Arc, Ark.)/ Private// Captured at Helena, Ark. on July 4, 1863.

Steave, Charles: See Steare.

Stephenson, M.: See Stevenson.

*Stevenson [or Stephenson], M./ Sept. 1, 1862 (Des Arc, Ark.)/ Private// From Audrain Co., Mo.

Sullivan, M./ Sept. 1, 1862 (Des Arc, Ark.)/ Private.

*Tarrant, A./ unknown/ Private// From Cass Co., Mo.

Tatum, John/ Sept. 1, 1862 (Des Arc, Ark.)/ Sergeant// From St. Louis, Mo.; Founding member Second National Guard Company St. Louis, Mo. Volunteer Militia; Captured at Camp Jackson, exchanged in Nov. 1861; Captured in March 1864, charged as a spy and scheduled to hang; Released from sentence after appeal to President Lincoln and Tatum's taking the oath of allegiance.

*Thomas, Smith [or S. G.]/ Sept. 1, 1862 (Des Arc, Ark.)/ Corporal// From Fulton, Calloway Co., Mo.; Wounded at Helena, Ark. on July 4, 1863; Had his arm operated on, without anesthesia, on Dec. 10, 1863, survived the operation.

Thorton, A. J./ Oct. 28, 1862 (Yellville, Ark.)/ Private// Killed at Helena, Ark. on July 4, 1863.

Tilden, Charles B. [or Buck]/ In 1861/ First Lieutenant (Sept. 24, 1862; Captain (Nov. 10, 1862)// From St. Louis, Mo.; Born in Maryland; Thrown out as captain on Dec. 18, 1863.

Tiner, C. L./ After Oct. 10, 1863/ Private// Pocahontas, Randolph, Co., Ark.

Tolenings, James/ Before Oct. 10, 1863/ Probably a Private.

Toomey, Frank A.: See Fourney.

Tourney, Frank A.: See Fourney.

*Turnbough, John/ Sept. 1, 1862 (Des Arc, Ark.)/ Corporal// From Florida,

Monroe, Co., Mo.

Turnbough, Joseph/ Nov. 29, 1862 (Van Buren, Ark.)/ Private.

Varum, J. B./ Sept. 1, 1862 (Des Arc, Ark.)/ Private.

Votan, A./ Nov. 10, 1862 (Mulberry Creek, Ark.)/ Private// Deserted on Dec. 29, 1862 while on the march to Little Rock, Ark.

*Walker, John W./ After Oct. 10, 1863/ Private// From Pleasant Hill, Cass Co., Mo.

*Walker, J. W./ unknown/ Private// From Macon Co., Mo.

*Walker [or Waller], J. D./ Nov. 9, 1862 (Mulberry Creek, Ark.)/ Private// From Warren Co., Mo.

*Ware, W. S. [or J. S.]/ After Oct. 10, 1863/ Private// From Jackson Co., Mo.; Moved to Chapple Hill, Lafayette Co., Mo. after the war.

Weis, J. R./ Nov. 10, 1862 (Mulberry Creek, Ark,)/ Private// Died on Jan. 27, 1863 at Fort Smith, Ark. while unit was en route to Little Rock, Ark.

West, F. W./ Nov. 10, 1862 (Mulberry Creek, Ark.)/ Private// Deserted on Feb. 26, 1863 at Little Rock, Ark.

*Wilson, John W./ unknown/ Private// From Webster Co., Mo.

Winn, J [or S.]/ Sept. 1, 1862 (Des Arc, Ark.)/ Private// Court marshaled on January 8, 1864, sentenced to wear ball and chain for thirty days while on hard labor.

Winn, James B./ July 26, 1862 (probably while in Mississippi)/ Private// From Howard Co., Mo.

Woods, James [or J. M.]/ Sept. 1, 1862 (Des Arc, Ark.)/ Sergeant// From Rosehill, Johnson Co., Mo.

Woodson, S. J./ Nov. 10, 1862 (Mulberry Creek, Ark.)/ Corporal// Deserted on Feb. 26, 1863 at Little Rock, Ark.

*Young, J. H./ Nov. 10, 1862 (Mulberry Creek, Ark.)/ Private// From Atchison Co., Mo.

*Young, Robert E./ Missouri State Guard on May 12, 1861; Confederate Service June 4, 1862 (Baldwin, Miss.)/ Sergeant// From Jefferson City, Cole Co., Mo.; Served in McCulloch's and Kelly's Missouri State Guard regiments; Cited for gallantry at Battle of Wilson's Creek (August 10, 1861); Transferred into battery on June 4, 1862; In Spring of 1865 detailed as sergeant to command Camden Arsenal; Became a doctor after the war.

Appendix B
Selected Biographies

Major General John S. Bowen:

Born at Bowen's Creek, Georgia in 1830, Bowen graduated from the United States Military Academy in 1853, being commissioned a brevet second lieutenant in the Mounted Rifles. Bowen ranked thirteenth of fifty-one in a class which included James B. McPherson. In 1856, Bowen resigned his commission, returned to Savannah for a short time to become an architect, and then moved to St. Louis. In April 1861 he commanded the Second Regiment St. Louis, Missouri Volunteer Militia, which was captured at Camp Jackson on May 10, 1861. Bowen journeyed to Memphis, Tennessee in May 1861 where he organized the First Missouri Infantry on June 11. He appears to have been one of several officers who felt that he was illegally captured at Camp Jackson and felt no compulsion to await the exchange that occurred in November 1861. Bowen's name was not on the exchange list prepared by General John C. Frémont, which suggests that he was exchanged earlier.

On March 14, 1862, Bowen was promoted to brigadier general and at the Battle of Shiloh in April commanded a brigade of infantry. After recovering from a wound that he received at Shiloh, General Bowen rejoined his command at Corinth, Mississippi. Captured at Vicksburg on July 4, 1863, General Bowen died nine days later from the effects of dysentery contracted while in the siege. John S. Bowen died a major general, receiving his promotion on May 25, 1863.[292]

* * * * * *

Major General John Charles Frémont:

John C. Frémont was born in Savannah, Georgia on January 21, 1813. He attended Charleston College in South Carolina, but was expelled in 1831. He taught mathematics on the warship *U.S. Natchez* until his appointment as a second lieutenant in the topographical engineers. From 1838-1842, Frémont flourished in the mapping service of the government, leading several important expeditions that mapped the western United States. He earned the title as "Pathfinder" for his prowess in land exploration. During the Mexican War, Frémont played an important role in securing California to the United States. He

---

[292] Moore, "Missouri", *Confederate Military History*, vol. 9, 205-206; Warner, *Generals in Gray*, 29-30; Edwin C. Bearss, "John Stevens Bowen," *Confederate General*, vol. 1, 110-111; Boatner, *Civil War Dictionary*, 75.

Major General John S. Bowen
(*Courtesy of Special Collections, LSU Libraries,*
Hill Memorial Library, Baton Rouge, LA)

Brigadier General Daniel M. Frost
(*Courtesy of Special Collections, LSU Libraries,
Hill Memorial Library, Baton Rouge, LA*)

resigned from the army in 1848, following his conviction on mutiny and insubordination charges, arising from a conflict with Stephen Kearny, who was sent to establish a government in California. Frémont was elected to the U.S. Senate from California in 1850 and became the Republican Party's first nominee for president in 1856. He lost the 1856 Presidential Election to James Buchanan. On July 3, 1861, Lincoln appointed Frémont a major general, to rank from May 14, 1861, and assigned him to command the Western Department, which embraced Missouri. Following a myriad of difficulties, including accusations of corruption and incompetence, Frémont was relived from command in November 1861. He served the remaining days of the Civil War east of the Mississippi River.[293]

* * * * * *

Brigadier General Daniel M. Frost:

A native of New York, the twenty-one-year old Frost graduated from the United States Military Academy in 1844, number four of twenty-five. As a brevet second lieutenant of Mounted Rifles, Frost served in the Mexican War, where he was cited for gallantry and earned a promotion to brevet first lieutenant. Frost resigned his commission in 1853 and returned to St Louis, Missouri (the home of his wife Elizabeth Brown Graham) a private citizen. He joined the St. Louis, Missouri Volunteer Militia and was elected captain of the Washington Guards on December 12, 1853. He became the colonel of the First Missouri Volunteer Militia Regiment in July 1858 and a brigadier general in August, commanding the Missouri First Military District of Missouri. At the outbreak of the Civil War, Frost suffered one of the earliest Confederate defeats, surrendering Camp Jackson on May 10, 1861, to Captain Nathaniel Lyon.

After his exchange in November 1861 Frost journeyed to Columbus, Kentucky aboard the steam boat *Iatan*. The Confederate Congress appointed him a brigadier general on March 3, 1862, just prior to the Battle of Pea Ridge, where he led a small Missouri brigade. After a brief trip to the east side of the Mississippi River, he returned to Arkansas and on November 17, 1862, General Theophilus H. Holmes assigned him to Thomas C. Hindman's First Corps, where he commanded a division. At Prairie Grove Frost's division held the Confederate left and performed admirably. Following the 1863 Little Rock Campaign, Frost submitted his resignation and escorted his wife to Texas to board a steamer bound for Canada. Frost accompanied his wife northward. His resignation was never officially accepted and he was listed as a deserter on December 9, 1863. At the close of the war he remained the only Confederate general officer listed as a deserter. He returned to Missouri following the war and became a farmer near St. Louis.[294]

---

[293] Boatner, *Civil War Dictionary*, 314-315; Warner, *Generals in Blue*, 160-161.

[294] Moore, "Missouri", *Confederate Military History*, vol. 9, 211-213; Warner, *Generals in Gray*,

* * * * * *

Major General Thomas C. Hindman:

Hindman was born in Knoxville, Tennessee on January 28, 1828, and in 1841 moved to Mississippi, where he studied law. He fought in the Mexican War with a Mississippi regiment and was promoted to first lieutenant for gallantry. This early military training was the only formal military education Hindman received.

After the war Hindman returned to Mississippi, completed his law degree, and was elected to the state legislature. In 1856 he relocated to Helena, Arkansas. Hindman used his military experience and his prominence in the Democratic Party, to be elected to the United States Congress in 1858 and 1860. He was an "ambitious politician, rather overbearing in expression, and self-sufficient and self-controlling, uncompromising in everything." "While in Congress, Hindman was regarded the most brilliant speaker and the most forcible reasoner of his age." With the coming of civil war, Thomas resigned from Congress and raised an Arkansas regiment for the Confederacy.

On September 28, 1861, Hindman was promoted to brigadier general and later earned a promotion to major general for his battlefield performance at Shiloh. With the Union pressure building in Arkansas, General P. G. T. Beauregard ordered Hindman back to Arkansas to command the Trans-Mississippi District. He arrived in Little Rock on May 31, 1862, and assumed command of a state under siege.

Hindman was five foot one, blue-eyed, and of fair complexion. He walked with a slight limp—the result of a broken left leg. To compensate, General Hindman used a special high heeled-boot.

His men had mixed feelings about him as a leader. Some considered him "a strict disciplinarian, but a good organizer"; others thought him a dictator. One regimental commander wrote, "I have a growing confidence in Genl. Hindman and feel that he can accomplish as much as anyone with his means." But this, from another commander: "You have never seen men reduced to perfect abjection and slavery until you see them under Gen. Hindman and his sycophantic tools. He's a man without patriotism or principles himself, makes everything animate and inanimate subservient to his own private, selfish ends and personal political aggrandizement."

94-95; Banasik, *Prairie Grove*, 475-476; William F. McLaughlin, "Artifacts of a Confederate General: Daniel Marsh Frost," *North South Trader's Civil War* (July-August 1993), vol. 20, no. 4, 18-25; Daniel M. Frost, Certificates of appointments to captain, colonel and brigadier general, Fordyce Collection, Missouri Historical Society; Boatner, *Civil War Dictionary*, 318; "The Camp Jackson Prisoners," *Missouri Republican*, December 3, 1861.

Major General Thomas C. Hindman
(*Courtesy of the Arkansas History Commission*)

The general feeling of the corps seemed to be summed up by Adjutant N. A. Taylor of the Thirty-first Texas Cavalry Regiment: "I have great confidence in Hindman. He is a superior man and everyone must receive this impression who comes in contact with him. He issues occasionally some exceedingly stringent orders and consequently the army generally dislikes him. It is all the fashion to 'cuss' him but very few seem to doubt his ability."

Hindman rebuilt the Confederate Army in the northern Trans-Mississippi during the summer and early fall 1862. On December 7, 1862, he fought and lost the Battle of Prairie Grove. Hindman became distraught over the loss, asked to be relieved and moved to the east side of the Mississippi River. He served in the Army of Tennessee and at war's end fled to Mexico, but returned in 1867. He was shot and killed by night riders in 1868 while sitting in his parlor.[295]

* * * * * *

Lieutenant General Theophilus H. Holmes:

A North Carolinian by birth, Holmes found a life long friend in Jefferson Davis as he progressed in the military service. Holmes graduated from West Point in 1829 at the age of twenty-four, number forty-four of forty-six. He spent the years prior to the Civil War serving in the west, including a successful tour during the Mexican War. Holmes resigned his commission on April 22, 1861, and joined the Confederacy. He advanced quickly to major general, being appointed brigadier general on June 5, 1861, and major general in October.

Holmes' early military activities included the command of a brigade at First Bull Run (July 21, 1861) and a division during the Seven Days' Battles (June and July 1862) for Richmond. Having failed to distinguish himself in the Richmond battles, Holmes was placed in command of the Department of North Carolina. On July 16, 1862, he was appointed commander of the newly created Trans-Mississippi Department. In October 1862, Holmes was appointed a lieutenant general, despite his lack of demonstrated ability. Feeling uncomfortable in command of the department, Holmes requested to be relieved of his command, and in March 1863, E. Kirby Smith assumed command of the department. Holmes remained in Arkansas and commanded the District of Arkansas. During his time west of the Mississippi River, Holmes only action was his defeat at Helena on July 4, 1863.

Holmes departed the Trans-Mississippi in March 1864 and returned to North Carolina where he spent the remaining months of the war. At war's end Holmes

---

[295] This biography is substantially the same one I wrote for my Prairie Grove book, but corrects the erroneous birth date which I listed as 1818. New data was also added. Banasik, *Prairie Grove*, 470-471; Warner, *Generals in Gray*, 137-138.

Lieutenant General Theophilus H. Holmes
(*Courtesy of the Library of Congress*)

retired to Fayetteville, North Carolina where he died on June 21, 1880.[296]

* * * * * *

Colonel Emmett MacDonald:

A St. Louisian, he commanded a squadron of cavalry during the Camp Jackson affair. After his capture MacDonald refused parole. He subsequently obtained his unconditional release after an Illinois judge, Samuel Treat, ruled that he could not be a prisoner of war since he was legally assembled at Camp Jackson. Emmett then joined Brigadier General James S. Rains's Missouri State Guard unit. MacDonald participated in the Siege of Lexington, Missouri, Battle of Pea Ridge, and numerous skirmishes in northwest Arkansas and southwest Missouri. By the Battle of Prairie Grove (December 7, 1862), MacDonald had risen to the rank of colonel, commanded a brigade of cavalry, and Governor Jackson had appointed him Provost Marshal General of Missouri. At Hartville, Missouri (January 11, 1863) MacDonald received a fatal wound. His body was returned to St. Louis where he was buried in a private ceremony on February 7, 1863, at the Wesleyan Cemetery.[297]

* * * * * *

Major General John Sappington Marmaduke:

A native Missourian, Marmaduke graduated from the United States Military Academy in 1857, number thirty of thirty-eight. Marmaduke resigned his commission on April 17, 1861, and joined the Missouri State Guard with the rank of colonel, commanding an infantry regiment in the Sixth Division. He resigned from the Guard in June 1861, following his defeat in the Battle of Booneville, Missouri. He entered Confederate service as a first lieutenant and commanded a regiment at Shiloh where he was wounded. Following Shiloh, Marmaduke crossed the Mississippi River and joined the First Corps, Trans-Mississippi Army. On September 30, 1862, General Thomas C. Hindman placed Marmaduke in command of a division composed of Charles A. Carroll's and Joseph O. Shelby's cavalry brigades. He was promoted to brigadier general, effective November 15, 1862. At Prairie Grove Marmaduke commanded a cavalry division of three brigades and scored the Confederates' greatest success of the day, capturing several standards and numerous prisoners.

---

[296] J. L. M. Curry, "Secession and the Civil War", *Confederate Military History*, vol. 1, 673-674; Boatner, *Civil War Dictionary*, 406; Warner, *Generals in Gray*, 141; *O.R.*, vol. 13, 855; *O.R.*, vol. 22, pt. 2, 798, 803; *O.R.*, vol. 34, pt. 1, 3.

[297] *O.R.*, vol, 3, 25, 186, 189; *O.R.*, vol. 8, 310, 319, 324; *O.R.*, vol. 22, pt. 1, 208-210; Special Order letter book, Special Order No. 45, Headquarters Trans-Mississippi District. "Remains of Emmett Macdonald," Civil War Scrapbook No. 5, page 20 of unnumbered pages.

Colonel Emmett MacDonald
(*Banasik*, Prairie Grove, *396, Photo no. 6*)

Major General John Sappington Marmaduke
(*Courtesy of Special Collections, LSU Libraries,*
Hill Memorial Library, Baton Rouge, LA)

Throughout the remainder of the war Marmaduke played an important role west of the Mississippi River, participating in numerous cavalry raids into Missouri and most of the major battles in the region. He was at the Battle of Helena and the Little Rock Campaign. On September 6, 1862, he fought a duel with Lucius M. Walker, his superior officer, near Little Rock and mortally wounded his foe. No action was taken against him because of the on going defense against the Federal forces who were pressing the Arkansas capital. In 1864, he participated in the Battles of Poison Spring, Jenkins' Ferry and Price's 1864 Missouri Raid. Marmaduke was captured during Price's Raid at Mine Creek, Kansas (October 25, 1864) and remained a prisoner of war until the close of the war. He was the last major general in the Confederate Army, appointed by the rebel Congress on March 17, 1865.

Following the war he was elected Governor of Missouri (1885-1887) and died on December 28, 1887 at Jefferson City while still in office.[298]

* * * * * *

Major General Mosby M. Parsons:

Born in Virginia on May 21, 1822, his family moved to Missouri in 1835, where they settled along the Missouri River in Jefferson City. Educated in Missouri, Mosby organized a company which fought in the Mexican War, where he was cited for gallant conduct. Returning to Missouri, he resumed a legal career and then entered politics. Parsons's sympathies rested squarely with the South, being, according to Robert E. Miller, "a zealous, outspoken advocate of slavery and state's rights." In the Presidential Election of 1860, Mosby supported John C. Breckinridge.

When the war began, Parsons moved to the forefront to advocate that Missouri align itself with the rest of the South. Following the Camp Jackson affair, Governor Jackson appointed him commander of the Sixth Division, Missouri State Guard. He participated in the Battle of Boonville in June 1861, the Battle of Wilson's Creek, and the siege of Lexington. Though Parsons's troops were in the Battle of Pea Ridge, he was absent in Richmond, Virginia as part of a delegation of Missourians. Next, Parsons followed General Price to the east side of the Mississippi River as the commander of the Missouri State Guard. After a short stay on the east side of the river Parsons returned to the Trans-Mississippi with a Confederate commission as brigadier general, dated November 5, 1862.

Assigned to command a brigade in General Daniel M. Frost's Second Division, First Corps, Trans-Mississippi Army, Parsons played a major role in

---

[298] Moore, "Missouri", *Confederate Military History*, vol. 9, 215-217; Boatner, *Civil War Dictionary*, 513; Peterson, *Sterling Price's Lieutenants*, 181; Special Order letter book, Special Order No. 9, 79; Warner, *Generals in Gray*, 211-212.

Major General Mosby Monroe Parsons
(*Courtesy of Special Collections, LSU Libraries,*
Hill Memorial Library, Baton Rouge, LA)

the battles fought west of the Mississippi River. At Prairie Grove, Parsons's Missouri Brigade held the Confederate center and left a lasting impression to both sides that his Missourians were one of the finest group of fighting men in the Confederate Army. The brigade sustained their largest casualties during the war in the abortive attempt to take Helena, Arkansas. They lost 764 men out of 1,868 or 40 percent of the entire command. The brigade was present at the capture of Little Rock in September, but did little other than occupy trenches and retreat when General Price ordered the city to be abandoned.

Rising to the rank of major general, Parsons saw active campaigning during the Red River Campaign of 1864 as his units participated in the Battles of Pleasant Hill, Marks Mills, and Jenkins' Ferry. In late 1864, he accompanied Price in his 1864 Missouri Raid, while his division stayed behind.

At the war's end Parsons never surrendered but went to Mexico where he was killed on August 17, 1865, by *Juarista* irregulars.[299]

* * * * * *

Major General Sterling Price:

Price was born on September 20, 1809 in Virginia, immigrated to Missouri in 1831, where he was appointed a brigadier general in the Missouri Militia. At the beginning of the Mexican War, Price resigned from the U.S. Congress, raised a regiment of troops, and successfully led them in the war. Prior to the end of the Mexican War, Price was promoted to brigadier general of volunteers and returned home a hero. He was elected governor of Missouri in 1853, helped in a large measure by his service in Mexico. He left office in 1857.

With the outbreak of civil war, the Governor of Missouri appointed Price a major general and head of the Missouri State Guard. Price proved successful at Wilson's Creek and the siege of Lexington. At Pea Ridge Price's troops fought well but circumstances prevented a Confederate victory.

Price accepted a Confederate commission to major general in March 1862 and led the Missouri troops to the east side of the Mississippi River. After spending about a year east of the Mississippi River, Price returned to the Trans-Mississippi Department where he spent the remainder of the war.

Back in Arkansas, Price participated in the Battle of Helena on July 4, 1863, and commanded the Confederate forces that evacuated Little Rock in September. In October 1864, Price led his last raid into Missouri. Fondly referred to as "Old Pap", Price survived the war and died from cholera in St.

---

[299] *O.R.*, vol. 22, pt. 1, 413, 415, 520; *O.R.*, vol. 34, pt. 1, 601-603, 809-811, 823; *O.R.*, vol. 53, 431-434, 448-450, 458-461; Moore, "Missouri," *Confederate Military History*, vol. 9, 217-218; Robert E. Miller, "General Mosby M. Parsons Missouri Secessionist," *Missouri Historical Review* (October, 1985), vol. 80, no. 1, 33-35, 37, 41, 47; Warner, *Generals in Gray*, 228-229; Boatner, *Civil War Dictionary*, 622.

Major General Sterling Price
*(Courtesy of the Alabama Department of Archives and History,
Montgomery, AL)*

Louis, Missouri on September 29, 1867.[300]

* * * * * *

Brigadier General Joseph O. Shelby:

He was born in Lexington, Kentucky, December 12, 1830, to a wealthy and prominent family. Shelby was educated at Transylvania University and moved to Waverly, Missouri, in 1852, where he became one of the wealthiest landowners in Lafayette County. A staunch believer in the concept of slavery, Shelby participated in the border wars with Kansas during the fifties, and grew to hate abolitionists. He had no formal military education.

Shelby joined the Missouri State Guard in June 1861. He participated in the early engagements of the Civil War, including Wilson's Creek and Pea Ridge, and faithfully followed General Price in his quest to secure Missouri for the Confederate cause. When Price led his Missouri army to Memphis in April 1862, Shelby followed. Later, he returned to Missouri, raised a regiment of cavalry, and became the brigade commander of the "Iron Brigade" of the west. His brigade of Missouri cavalry would have no equal in the Trans-Mississippi.

John N. Edwards, the adjutant of Shelby's brigade, described General Shelby as a "bold, reckless and self-reliant" cavalryman who had the ability to divine the enemy's intentions. He always led his column and never followed. In dress and stature Jo Shelby was a "smart-looking officer...wearing a felt hat over the chestnut hair, its front brim pinned back, cavalry style, with a gold buckle; the collar of his uniform was solid gold...and buttoned tight. It gleamed beneath the russet beard he was wearing." He sported a mustache and a goatee.

Shelby fought in numerous engagements in the Trans-Mississippi including Cane Hill, Prairie Grove, and several cavalry raids into Missouri. He was appointed a brigadier general on December 15, 1863. When the Trans-Mississippi surrendered, he refused to give up, led his command to Mexico, but later returned after the collapse of Maximilian's government. He lived out his remaining years in Missouri.[301]

* * * * * *

---

[300] Moore, "Missouri", *Confederate Military History*, vol. 9, 218-221; Warner, *Generals in Gray*, 246-247; Albert Castel, "Sterling Price," *Confederate General*, vol. 5, 59-63; Boatner, *Civil War Dictionary*, 669.

[301] This biography is a shortened version of the one I presented in my Prairie Grove book. A few small items have been added. Banasik, *Prairie Grove*, 479-480.

Brigadier General Joseph Orville Shelby
(*Courtesy of Jim Joplin Collection*)

General Edmund Kirby Smith:

He was born in St. Augustine, Florida on May 16, 1824. Smith graduated from West Point in 1845, number twenty-five of forty-one. During the Mexican War, Smith received two brevets for gallantry. From 1849 to 1852, he served as a mathematics instructor at West Point, until his assignment to the Texas frontier. Smith resigned his commission in April 1861, following his state's lead, and joined the Confederacy. He was appointed a brigadier general on June 17, 1861, and led a brigade at First Manassas [Bull Run], where he was wounded. In October 1861, Smith was promoted to major general and in March 1862 he assumed the command of the Department of East Tennessee. Following Braxton Bragg's late summer and autumn campaign in Tennessee and Kentucky, Smith was promoted to lieutenant general in October 1862. On March 7, 1863, he assumed command of the Trans-Mississippi Department, a position he held until the end of the war. Smith was promoted to full general in February 1864. During the Red River Campaign, he had a severe disagreement with General Richard Taylor over the conduct of the campaign. Taylor was reassigned to the east side of the Mississippi River. E. Kirby Smith surrendered the Trans-Mississippi Department on May 26, 1865. He died on March 28, 1893, being the last surviving full general who served in the Civil War.[302]

* * * * * *

Major General Frederick Steele:

Steele was born in Delhi, New York, on January 14, 1819. He graduated from West Point, number thirty of thirty-nine, in 1843. Serving with distinction in the Mexican War, Steele earned two brevets for bravery. At the beginning of the Civil War he was stationed at Fort Leavenworth, Kansas. Steele commanded a battalion of regular infantry at Wilson's Creek and was appointed colonel of the Eighth Iowa Infantry in September 1861. Congress appointed him a brigadier general on January 29, 1862. In March 1862 General Halleck appointed Steele to command the troops in Southeast Missouri and directed him to occupy northeast Arkansas. During Samuel Curtis's Little Rock Campaign of 1862, Steele commanded a division. After the capture of Helena, Arkansas, in July 1862, Steele moved to the east side of the Mississippi River, where he served through the capture of Vicksburg, Mississippi. He was promoted to major general on November 29, 1862.

On August 5, 1863, Steele assumed command of the forces in Helena, Arkansas and led them on a successful campaign which captured Little Rock on September 10, 1863. Steele was appointed the commander of the Seventh Corps

---

[302] *O.R.*, vol. 22, pt. 1, 3; Warner, *Generals in Gray*, 279-280; Boatner, *Civil War Dictionary*, 769-770.

General Edmund Kirby Smith
(*Courtesy of the Alabama Department of Archives and History,
Montgomery, AL*)

Major General Frederick Steele
(*Courtesy of the Arkansas History Commission, Little Rock, AR*)

and the Department of Arkansas on January 6, 1864. During the Union spring offensive of 1864, he commanded the northern wing of the Federal columns that advanced on Shreveport, Louisiana. Steele captured Camden, Arkansas on April 15, 1864, but due to Nathaniel Banks's defeats in Louisiana, he was forced to retreat to Little Rock. Steele completed his Civil War service on the Gulf of Mexico coast. He died in a freak accident in 1868 when he fell out of a carriage, while stationed in California.[303]

* * * * * *

Colonel Alexander Steen:

He was a native Missourian and lived in St. Louis. Steen entered military service on April 9, 1847, being appointed a second lieutenant in the Twelfth United States Infantry. His father, Enoch, and father-in-law, P. Morrison, were both colonels in the United States regulars—both fought for the Union. The younger Steen served in the Mexican War. His regiment disbanded in 1848, but he remained in the military. In June 1852 he accepted a commission as second lieutenant in the Third U.S. Infantry, a rank he held until the Camp Jackson affair. Steen was elected lieutenant colonel of the Second Missouri Volunteer Militia and held the position concurrently with a brevet major in the United States Regular Army. He avoided capture at Camp Jackson and promptly resigned his U.S. commission the same day. Governor Jackson appointed Steen brigadier general of the Fifth Division, Missouri State Guard in July 1861. His command fought at Wilson's Creek, the siege of Lexington, and Pea Ridge. Steen was sick during the siege of Lexington and absent in Richmond during the Battle of Pea Ridge, seeking a Confederate commission to brigadier general. General Thomas C. Hindman appointed Steen colonel of a Missouri infantry regiment on November 10, 1862. He died at the Battle of Prairie Grove, while leading a charge, felled by a single shot to the brain.[304]

* * * * * *

[303] *O.R.*, vol. 8, 578-579; *O.R.*, vol. 22, pt. 1, 6; Warner, *Generals in Blue*, 474-475; Boatner, *Civil War Dictionary*, 794.

[304] *O.R.*, vol. 3, 191-192; *O.R.*, vol. 53, 710; Moore, "Missouri," *Confederate Military History*, 51, 110; Banasik, *Prairie Grove*, 449; "Brigadier Gen. Steen," *Missouri Republican*, December 10, 1862; National Archives, Record Group M861, roll no. 36; Records of Confederate Movements, Tenth Missouri Infantry; Peterson, *Sterling Price's Lieutenants*, 154; Donald J. Stanton, Goodwin F. Berquist, and Paul C. Bowers, eds., *The Civil War Reminiscences of General M. Jeff Thompson* (Dayton, Ohio, 1988), 135-136.

Colonel Alexander Steen
(*Banasik*, Prairie Grove, *408*)

Lieutenant General Richard Taylor:

Richard Taylor was born on January 17, 1826, near Louisville, Kentucky. His father was future President Zachary Taylor. Richard studied at Edinburgh in Scotland, before transferring to Harvard and then Yale, where he graduated in 1845. Prior to the Civil War, Taylor had limited experience in military affairs, serving as his father secretary during the Mexican War. In 1850, following his father's death, he inherited the family plantation in Louisiana. In 1855 Taylor was elected to the Louisiana Senate, a position he held until the outbreak of the Civil War. Elected colonel of the Ninth Louisiana Infantry, Taylor led the command in Virginia. Though lacking military experience, he was appointed a brigadier general in October 1861, in part because his former brother-in-law was Jefferson Davis. Taylor proved to be a natural leader, serving successfully during Stonewall Jackson's Valley Campaign of 1862. He was promoted to major general in July 1862. Because of health reasons Taylor was transferred to Louisiana, assuming command of the District of Louisiana in August 1862. He successfully parried Union efforts in Louisiana during 1863, and achieved his greatest success in 1864, by defeating Nathaniel Banks's Red River Campaign. Because of a disagreement with his superior, General E. Kirby Smith, Taylor left the Trans-Mississippi and assumed command of the Department of Alabama, Mississippi, and East Louisiana in July 1864. Taylor was appointed a lieutenant general, to rank from April 8, 1864, making him one of only three non-West Pointers to hold the rank in the Confederacy. Taylor completed his military service east of the Mississippi River. He died unexpectedly in 1879 at age fifty-three, while visiting a friend in New York City.[305]

* * * * * *

Major General Earl Van Dorn:

He was born on September 17, 1820, near Port Gibson, Mississippi, attended West Point, where he graduated number fifty-two of fifty-six in 1842. Van Dorn served in the Mexican War, where he was wounded, and on the Indian frontier. He rose to the rank of major in the regular army while fighting Indians. On January 31, 1861, he resigned from the U.S. military and joined the Mississippi state forces, rising to the rank of brigadier general in the Confederacy on June 5, 1861. In September 1861, he was appointed to major general in the Confederate Army and sent to Virginia. After a short stay in the East, Van Dorn headed West in January 1862 to command the Trans-Mississippi District. In March 1862 he lost the Battle of Pea Ridge and then led his army to the east side of the Mississippi River.

---

[305] Boatner, *Civil War Dictionary*, 827-828; Warner, *Generals in Gray*, 299-300; T. Michael Parrish, "Richard Taylor," *Confederate General*, vol. 6, 29-31; *O.R.*, vol. 13, 877.

Lieutenant General Richard Taylor
(*Courtesy of the Alabama Department of Archives and History,
Montgomery, AL*)

Major General Earl Van Dorn
(*Courtesy of the Alabama Department of Archives and History,
Montgomery, AL*)

As commander of the District of Mississippi Van Dorn again lost in battle—this time at Corinth (October 3 and 4, 1862). In the latter part of 1862 Van Dorn led a successful raid on the Union supply depot at Holly Springs, Mississippi. Van Dorn's career ended suddenly on May 7, 1863, when a disgruntled husband accused Van Dorn of improprieties with his wife and killed him.[306]

---

[306] Charles E. Hooker, "Mississippi," *Confederate Military History*, vol. 12, 273-275; Warner, *Generals in Gray*, 314-315; Boatner, *Civil War Dictionary*, 867.

Appendix C[307]
Units Assembled at Camp Jackson
May 3-10, 1861

First Brigade, Missouri Volunteer Militia (Brigadier General Daniel M. Frost):
   7 officers

First Regiment (Lieutenant Colonel John Knapp):
   6 officers

    Company A (St. Louis Grays)[308]—Captain Martin Burke
       4 officers and 26 men; organized October 1832

    Company B (Sarsfield Guards)—Captain Charles W. Rogers
       2 officers and 44 men

    Company C (Washington Guards)[309]—Captain Robert Tucker
       3 officers and 37 men; organized July 25, 1853

    Company D (Emmett Guards)—Captain Philip Coyne
       3 officers and 39 men

    Company E (Washington Blues)—Captain Joseph Kelly
       2 officers and 39 men

    Company F (Laclede Guards)—Captain W. H. Fraser
       3 officers and 34 men

    Company G (Missouri Guards)[310]—Captain George W. West
       3 officers and 27 men; organized June 28, 1858

    Company H (Grimsley Guards)[311]—Captain B. Newton Hart
       3 officers and 37 men; organized May 2, 1861

---

[307] The strength of the units varied depending on when the value was taken. The numbers presented here were recorded on May 7, 1861. Peckham, *Missouri In 1861*, 132-135; "Military Encampment," *Missouri Republican*, May 7, 1861.

[308] "Military Matters—Military Companies of St. Louis—No. 2—The St. Louis Grays," Missouri Militia scrapbook, page 5 of unnumbered pages.

[309] "The Grand Military Encampment," Missouri Militia scrapbook, page 17 of unnumbered pages.

[310] "Military Companies Of St. Louis—No. 5. Missouri Guard," Missouri Militia scrapbook, pages 6 and 17 of unnumbered pages.

[311] On May 4, 1861 General Frost issued an order which designated companies H, I, and K in lieu of units which had disbanded or to fill vacant positions in the regiment. The Montgomery Guards and City Guards disbanded. "Military," General Order No. 37, *Missouri Republican*, May 5, 1861.

Company I (Jackson Guards)—Captain George W. Fletcher
4 officers and 42 men

Company K (Davis Guard)—Captain Charles Longuemare
4 officers and 44 men

Squadron of Dragoons—Captain Emmett MacDonald

Total First Regiment (excluding dragoons)
37 officers
<u>369</u> enlisted
Grand Total   406

Second Regiment (Colonel John S. Bowen):
8 officers

Engineer Corps (National Guards companies no. 1 and 2)[312]—
Captain William B. Haseltine; 4 officers and 36 men; Company No.1
organized July 16, 1852; Company No. 2 organized July 28, 1858.

Company A (Independent Guards)[313]—Captain Charles H. Frederick
Organized October 19, 1859.

Company B (Missouri Videttes)[314]—Captain O. H. Barrett
45 officers and men

Company C (Minute-men)—Captain Basil W. Duke[315]

Company D (McLaren Guards)—Captain W. W. Sandford
4 officers and 57 men

Company E (Minute-men)—Captain Colton Greene

Company F (Jackson Grays)—Captain Hugh A. Garland
4 officers and 61 men

---

[312] Listed as Company A in the *Missouri Republican*. "Military Encampment," *Missouri Republican*, May 7, 1861; "Military Companies of St. Louis—No. 4. National Guard—2nd Company," and "National Guards—First Company," Missouri Militia scrapbook, pages 6 and 18 of unnumbered pages; Scharf, *History of Saint Louis*, vol. 2, 1858.

[313] Listed as Company B in *Missouri Republican*. "Military Encampment," *Missouri Republican*, May 7, 1861; "Independent Guards," Missouri Militia scrapbook, page 7 of unnumbered pages.

[314] Not listed in the *Missouri Republican*. In accordance with the *Republican* Company B is probably one of the units expected from the Southwest Expedition. "Military Encampment," *Missouri Republican*, May 7, 1861.

[315] The same Duke, who rode with John Hunt Morgan.

Company G (Dixie Guards)—Captain G. Campbell
    4 officers and 44 men

Company H (Southern Guards)—Captain J. H. Shackelford
    4 officers and 41 men

Company I (Carondelet Rangers)—Captain James M. Loughborough
    50 officers and men

Total (incomplete)

Appendix D[316]
Passengers of the *Iatan*—December 2, 1861

Part I:
  List published in *Missouri Republican*.

Anderson, Sam
Bambaugh, W. M. [William A. Bamberg]
Bates, A. V.
Blacke, John
Bull, John T.
Bull, William
Cameron, M. W.
Carrol, Edward
Chappel, Edward F.
Curtis, Frank; First Lieutenant
Dix, Henry
Duvall, Jr., L. C.
Ferber, F. M.; Second Lieutenant
Ferguson, C. D.
Fox, Alexander C.
Gaynes, Ed
George, James; Captain
Grady, M.
Harrington, R. H.; First Lieutenant
Harrison, M. H.
Hefferman, Cornelius
Hennassy, John M.; Lieutenant
Hennesay, John
Holiday, John Duncan
Hopton, A. W.
Horan, Thomas
Hughes, Lake
Jenkins, Henry
Kavanaugh, Daniel [or Kavanagh or Cavanaugh]
Kennedy, Dan
Kennedy, James R.
Langdon, John C.
Martin, James
McBride, E. D.; First Lieutenant
McBride, Stephen; First Lieutenant

---

[316] "The Camp Jackson Prisoners," *Missouri Republican*, December 3, 1861; Frost letter book, Mesker Papers, Box 2, Missouri Historical Society, 11-12.

McFarlan[e], Daniel
McGinnis, A. J.; Captain
Merriman, Frei (?)
Moulton, J. C.
Moylan, Thomas; Second Lieutenant
Mullen, John
Murray, William Q.; Second Lieutenant
Noonan, D.
Paalodius Jr., D. (?)
Perks, William
Polock, M. E.
Reedington, M.; First Lieutenant
Redman, John
Ryan, ——
Ryan, Thomas
Schley, William
Scott, Joseph S.; Doctor
Shelton, C. O.
Shubey, Ed
Slicer, Lawrence
Smith, L. H.; First Sergeant
Spellen, Stephen
Sprague, D. P.; First Lieutenant
Thompson, J. West
Trowley, E.; First Lieutenant
Underwood, J. W.; First Lieutenant
Ward, A. W.
Wood, Edward P.

Part II:
Known to be on the *Iatan* but not listed on the roster published in the *Missouri Republican*.

Frost Daniel, M.; Brigadier General
Keith, Thomas; First Lieutenant
Williams, Henry W.; Major

Appendix E[317]
Dead and Wounded
Surrounding Camp Jackson Affair

Dead:

Bodsen, Charles
Carter, Jacob
Dean, Christopher
*Doane, P.
Dunn, Benjamin
*Eisenhardt, William
English, John
Gerde, Jaques
Glencoe, Casper H.
Hahren, Thomas A.
Jones, J. J.
Juenhower, William
Jungle, Henry
McAuliff, Mrs. Elisa

*Knoblock, Nicholas
Latour, Armand
Leister, Phillip
McDonald, James
McDowell, Walter
Roepe [or Koeper], John
Sheffield, William
Somers, Emma
Somers, William Patton
Sweikhardt, John
Underwood, John
Waters, John
Wheelan, Francis
Wright, Erie

* = From General Frost's command.

Wounded:

Allen, Fred D.
Bradford, ——-
Carroll, W. L.
Downey, Jerome
Mathews, John

Meek, Thomas
Rice, John
Ropke, Dr. ——-
Scherer, John James
Wilson, C.

---

[317] McElroy, *Struggle For Missouri*, 155-156.

Bibliography

Books/Pamphlets/Articles

Banasik, Michael E. *Embattled Arkansas: The Prairie Grove Campaign of 1862.* Wilmington, NC: Broadfoot Publishing Company, 1996.

Bartels, Carolyn O. *The Forgotten Men Missouri State Guard.* Shawnee Mission, KS: Two Trails Publishing, 1995.

_____. *Missouri Confederate Surrender: Shreveport & New Orleans May 1865.* Shawnee Mission, KS: Two Trails Publishing 1991.

Bearss, Edwin C. *Steele's Retreat From Camden & The Battle of Jenkins' Ferry.* Little Rock, AR: Pioneer Press, 1966.

Boatner, Mark. *The Civil War Dictionary.* New York: David McKay Company, Inc., 1959.

Brugioni, Dino A. *The Civil War in Missouri as Seen from the Capital City.* Jefferson City, MO: Summers Publishing, 1987.

Byers, S. H. M. *Iowa In War Times.* Des Moines, IA: W. D. Condit & Co. 1888.

Castel, Albert. *General Sterling Price and the Civil War in the West.* Baton Rouge, LA: Louisiana State University Press, 1968.

Churchill, Winston. Introduction by Joseph Mersand. *The Crisis* Original n.p., 1901. Reprinted New York: Washington Square Press, 1962.

Coggins, Jack. *Arms and Equipment of the Civil War.* Garden City, NY: Doubleday, 1962. Reprinted Wilmington, NC: Broadfoot Publishing Company, 1987.

Commager, Henry Steele. ed. *The Blue and the Gray Two Volumes in One: The Story of the Civil War As Told by Participants.* Indianapolis, 1950. Reprinted New York: Fairfax Press, 1982.

Crowley, William J. *Tennessee Cavalier in the Missouri Cavalry Major Henry Ewing, C.S.A. of the St. Louis Times.* Columbia, MO: Kelly Press, 1978.

Crute, Joseph H. *Units of the Confederate States Army.* Midlothian, VA: Derwent Books, 1987.

Davis, William C., ed. *The Confederate General.* 6 volumes, Harrisburg, PA: National Historical Society, 1991.

Dyer, F. H. *Compendium of the Civil War.* Des Moines, 1908. Reprinted Dayton, OH: The Press of Morningside Bookshop, 1978.

Evans, Clement A., ed. *Confederate Military History.* 13 Vols. Atlanta, 1899. Reprinted Secaucus, NJ: Blue & Gray Press, 1974.

Evans, Clement A. and Bridgers, Robert S., eds. *Confederate Military History Extended Edition.* Atlanta, 1899. Reprinted Wilmington, NC: Broadfoot Publishing Company, 1987.

Frémont, Jessie Benton. *The Story of the Guard A Chronicle of the War.* Boston: Ticknor and Fields, 1863.

Gibson, Tony. *Warships and Naval Battles of the Civil War.* New York, 1989.

Hewett, Janet., ed. *Supplement to the Official Records of the Union and Confederate Armies.* 100 volumes approximate, Wilmington, NC: Broadfoot Publishing Company, 1994-ongoing.

Ingenthron, Elmo *Borderland Rebellion A History of the Civil War on the Missouri-Arkansas Border.* Branson, MO: Ozark Mountaineer, n.d.

Jones, Jr., Charles C. "A Roster of General Officers, Heads of Departments, Senators, Representatives, Military Organizations, etc., etc. in Confederate Service During the War Between the States." *Southern Historical Society Papers.* Richmond, VA, 1876. Reprinted, Wilmington, NC: Broadfoot Publishing Company, 1990.

Livermore, Thomas L. *Numbers and Losses in the Civil War in America: 1861-1865.* Bloomington, 1957. Reprinted, New York: Kraus Reprint Co., 1969.

McElroy, John. *The Struggle For Missouri.* Washington, DC: National Tribune Co., 1909.

McLaughlin, William F. "Artifacts of a Confederate General: Daniel Marsh Frost." *North South Trader's Civil War* 20 (July-August 1993):18-25.

Miller, Robert E. "General Mosby M. Parsons Missouri Secessionist." *Missouri Historical Review* 80(October, 1985):33-57.

Parrish, T. Michael. *Richard Taylor Soldier Prince of Dixie.* Chapel Hill, NC:

University of North Carolina Press, 1992.

Peckham, James. *Gen. Nathaniel Lyon, and Missouri in 1861: A Monograph of the Great Rebellion.* New York: American News Company, 1866.

Peterson, Richard C., and McGhee, James E., and Linbdberg, Kip A., and Daleen, Keith I. *Sterling Price's Lieutenants: A Guide to the Officers and Organization of the Missouri State Guard.* Shawnee Mission, KS: Two Trails Publishing, 1995.

Phillips, Christopher. *Damned Yankee: The Life of General Nathaniel Lyon.* Columbia, MO: University of Missouri Press, 1990.

Primm, James Neal. *Lion of the Valley: St. Louis, Missouri.* Boulder, CO: University of Colorado Press, 1981.

Ruffner, S. T. "Sketch of First Missouri Battery, C.S.A." *Confederate Veteran* 12 (1912):417-420.

Scharf, Thomas J. *History of Saint Louis City and County, From the Earliest Periods to the Present Day; Including Biographical Sketches of Representative Men.* Philadelphia: Lewis H. Everts & Co., 1883.

Shalhope, Robert E. *Sterling Price: Portrait of a Southerner.* Columbia, MO: University of Missouri Press, 1971.

Shea, William L. and Hess, Earl J. *Pea Ridge: Civil War Campaign in the West.* Chapel Hill, NC: University of North Carolina Press, 1992.

Snead, Thomas L. "Conquest of Arkansas." *Battles and Leaders of the Civil War.* Vol. 3, 441-459. New York: The Century Co., 1887-88.

_____. *The Fight For Missouri From the Election of Lincoln to the Death of Lyon.* New York: Charles Scribner's Sons, 1886.

Stanton, Donald J. and Berquist, Goodwin F. and Bowers, Paul C., eds. *The Civil War Reminiscences of General M. Jeff Thompson.* Dayton, OH: The Press of Morningside Bookshop, 1988.

Street, Jr., James. *The Civil War: The Struggle for Tennessee, Tupelo to Stones River.* Alexandria, VA: Time-Life Books, 1985.

Warner, Ezra J. *Generals in Blue: Lives of the Union Commanders.* Baton Rouge, LA: Louisiana State University Press, 1964.

_____. *Generals in Gray, Lives of the Confederate Commanders*. Baton Rouge, LA: Louisiana State University Press, 1959.

Wright, Marcus J. *Arkansas in the War 1861-1865*. Batesville, AR: Guard-Record Company, 1963.

Government Sources

Library of Congress. *Newspapers in Microfilm, United States, 1948-1983, Vol I A-O*. Washington, DC, 1984. Government Printing Office.

National Archives. Record Group 109. Confederate muster rolls for various units. Washington, DC

_____. Record Group M322. Compiled Service Records. Assorted rolls and units.

_____. Record Group M861. Records of Confederate Movements and Activities. Assorted rolls and units.

United States War Department. *The War of the Rebellion: A Compilation of the Official Records of the Union and Confederate Armies*. 70 volumes comprising 128 books. Washington, DC, 1880-1901. Reprinted, Harrisburg, PA: National Historical Society, 1985.

_____. *The War of the Rebellion: Official Record of the Union and Confederate Navies*. 31 volumes. Washington, DC: GPO, 1894-1922.

Manuscripts/Special Collections

Arkansas History Commission:
 Lotspeich, C. B. Manuscript diary 1862-1863.
 Skaggs, W. L. Collection

Columbia University:
 Peter W. Alexander Collection:
  Frost, Daniel M. Letters.
  Letter book, June-Dec. 1862. Hindman's command.
  Letter book, Jan.-Mar. 1863. Hindman's command.
  Marmaduke, John S. Letters.
  Parsons, Mosby M. Letters.
  Report of Troops.
  Special Order letter book, June-Dec. 1862.
   Hindman's command.

Telegrams.

Missouri Historical Society (St. Louis, MO):
   Bull Family Papers:
      Bull, John and William. Letters.
      Bull, William. Manuscript reminiscences and diary.
   Camp Jackson Papers:
      Exchanged prisoner list.
      News clippings.
   Civil War Scrapbook No. 5.
   Fordyce Collection.
   Leighton, George E. Collection.
   Mesker Papers.
   Missouri Volunteer Militia scrapbook.
   Pinnell, Eathan. Manuscript diary.

New York Historical Society:
   Herron, Francis J. War papers:
      Roberts, W. Manuscript report.

Southern Historical Society Collection (University of NC):
   Wallace, James T. Diary.

State Historical Society of Missouri (Western Historical
Manuscript Collection):
   Hoskin, William N. Diary.
   Mitchell, Spencer H. Collection.
   Quesenberry, John P. Manuscript diary, 1862-1865.

University of Arkansas (Little Rock):
   Turnbo, Silas C. Unpublished manuscript.

Newspapers

Missouri Republican (St. Louis)
Washington Telegraph (Washington, Arkansas)

Photo Credits

* Alabama Department of Archives and History, Montgomery, Ala.
* Arkansas History Commission, Little Rock, Ark.
* Banasik, *Prairie Grove*, 396, photo no. 6; 408, photo no. 6
* Orville Banasik, Marion, Iowa
* Jim Joplin Collection, Springfield, Mo.
* Library of Congress
* Missouri Historical Society
* Special Collections, Hill Memorial Library, Louisiana State University Libraries, Baton Rouge, La.

Index